THE
EVERYTHING
HOMESCHOOLING
BOOK

Take charge of your
child's education

Sherri Linsenbach

Adams Media Corporation
Avon, Massachusetts

With appreciation to my son, Devin, who made our homeschooling adventure fun and rewarding; my husband, Don, who provided ideas along the way; and my parents, Robert and Patricia, for their support and encouragement.

An Everything® Series Book.
Everything® is a registered trademark of Adams Media Corporation.

Published by Adams Media Corporation
57 Littlefield Street, Avon, MA 02322 U.S.A.
www.adamsmedia.com

ISBN: 1-58062-868-0
Printed in the United States of America.

J I H G F E D C B A

Library of Congress Cataloging-in-Publication Data
Linsenbach, Sherri.
The everything homeschooling book / Sherri Linsenbach.
p.   cm.   --(An everything series book)
Includes index.
ISBN 1-58062-868-0
1. Home schooling–United States. I. Title: Everything home schooling book. II. Title. III. Series: Everything series.

LC40 .L56 2003
371.04'2–dc21

2002153887

This publication is designed to provide accurate and authoritative information with regard to the subject matter covered. It is sold with the understanding that the publisher is not engaged in rendering legal, accounting, or other professional advice. If legal advice or other expert assistance is required, the services of a competent professional person should be sought.

—From a *Declaration of Principles* jointly adopted by a Committee of the American Bar Association and a Committee of Publishers and Associations

Many of the designations used by manufacturers and sellers to distinguish their products are claimed as trademarks. Where those designations appear in this book and Adams Media was aware of a trademark claim, the designations have been printed with initial capital letters.

This book is available at quantity discounts for bulk purchases.
For information, call 1-800-872-5627.

The
EVERYTHING.
Homeschooling Book

Dear Reader,

This book was written to help make your homeschooling experience happy, successful, and rewarding!

When I first began homeschooling, I didn't know where to begin. I didn't know anyone who educated their children at home. I wasn't even sure if it was legal! After months of research, I finally found that a homeschooling community did indeed exist.

Not only did I find this caring community, but I found a multitude of resources, educational materials, schools, and support designed for those of us who wish to provide an education for our children at home. And now I wish to share all of this with you.

I sincerely hope that your homeschooling adventures will be as exciting and fulfilling as ours have been. I wish you and your family to experience the joy and closeness that home education can provide. I hope that you, too, will witness the educational and social benefits of homeschooling, as you watch your children blossom through a true love of learning that will last them a lifetime.

Feel free to share your homeschooling experiences and ideas by visiting my Web site at ✎ *www.HomeschoolFun.com*. I look forward to hearing from you.

Happy homeschooling!

Sherri Linsenbach

The EVERYTHING® Series

Editorial

Publishing Director	Gary M. Krebs
Managing Editor	Kate McBride
Copy Chief	Laura MacLaughlin
Acquisitions Editor	Bethany Brown
Development Editors	Lesley Bolton
	Michael Paydos
Production Editor	Khrysti Nazzaro

Production

Production Director	Susan Beale
Production Manager	Michelle Roy Kelly
Series Designers	Daria Perreault
	Colleen Cunningham
Cover Design	Paul Beatrice
	Frank Rivera
Layout and Graphics	Colleen Cunningham
	Rachael Eiben
	Michelle Roy Kelly
	Daria Perreault
	Erin Ring
Series Cover Artist	Barry Littmann

Visit the entire Everything® Series at everything.com

Contents

Top Ten Benefits of Homeschooling / x
Introduction / xi

1

Homeschool Orientation / 1
A Brief History Lesson **2** • Meet the Staff **3** • The Student-Teacher Connection **5** • Credit Hours **8** • Scheduling Strategies **9** • Financial Services **12** • Benefits of Homeschooling **15**

2

Learning and Teaching Styles / 19
Educational Theorists **20** • Common Learning Styles **22** • Your Child's Learning Style **25** • Your Child's Strengths and Weaknesses **26** • Individualized Patterns **28** • Finding Your Teaching Style **30** • Your Own Strengths and Weaknesses **32**

3

Getting Started / 33
Legal Requirements **34** • State Homeschool Departments of Education **35** • Homeschool Groups **36** • Withdrawing Your Child from School **38** • Registering for Homeschooling **39** • Determining Educational Philosophies, Goals, and Objectives **40** • School Support for Homeschoolers **42**

4

Types of Homeschooling / 45
Secular Homeschooling **46** • Religion-Based Homeschooling **47** • Umbrella and Satellite Schools **50** • Charter Schools, Vouchers, and Cooperatives **51** • Independent Study Programs **53** • Virtual Learning and Cyber Schools **56** • Eclectic Schooling **57** • Unschooling and Deschooling **58** • Unit or Theme Studies **59** • Year-Round Schooling **60**

Understanding Unschooling and Unit Studies / 63

Unschooling: A Way of Life **64** • Deschooling Each Day **69** • Children As Teachers **70** • Unit Studies Year-Round **72** • Theme Studies and the Core Curriculum **74** • A Combination of Ways: Eclectic Schooling **75**

Answering the Socialization Question / 77

Social Skills and Child Development **78** • Socialization Opportunities for the Homeschooler **81** • Daily Social Situations **84** • Maturity Levels of the Homeschooled Child **85** • Learning Proper Etiquette, Morals, and Values **87** • Preparing for the Future **88**

Choosing a Curriculum / 89

Curriculum Guidelines **90** • Packaged Curricula **90** • Designing Your Own Curriculum **92** • Creating Your Own Lesson Plans **94** • Free Educational Resources **97** • The Student's Input **99** • Handling Advanced Subjects **100** • Educational Excursions **101**

Homeschooling Schedules / 103

A Plan That Works **104** • Flexibility in the Homeschool **106** • Learning Naturally Every Day **107** • Scheduling Suggestions **110** • Time Management Tips **112** • Time for Rest and Relaxation **116**

Homeschooling One or Several / 117

Homeschooling the Only Child **118** • Socialization for the Only Child **120** • Homeschooling Multiple Children **120** • Assistance from Siblings **122** • Keeping the Schedule on Track **123** • Time off for the Teacher **124**

Typical Homeschool Days / 127

What Is a Typical Day? **128** • Recording Your Typical Day **128** • Breaking the Monotony **130** • Attaining a Well-Rounded Education **132** • Examples of Typical Homeschool Days **133** • Keeping Faith Each Day **138**

11 Record Keeping / 139

Planning Ahead 140 • Your Lesson Plan Book 142 • Keeping a Daily Logbook 143 • Maintaining a Homeschool Portfolio 145 • Assessment Alternatives 147 • Recording Grades and Credits Earned 148 • Granting Awards and Certificates 150

12 Organizing Your Homeschool / 151

A Place for Everything 152 • Storing Homeschool Supplies 152 • Creating an Idea File 155 • Activity Centers and Lab Stations 156 • Quiet Corners and Libraries 158 • Keeping Home and School Separate 160

13 Homeschooling and the Single Parent / 161

Single-Parent Homeschools 162 • Educational Options and Alternatives 164 • Special One-on-One Time 166 • Weekend and Evening Homeschooling 167 • Flexible Work Options 168 • Single-Parent Support Groups 170 • Help from Family and Friends 171 • Child-Care Options 172

14 Homeschooling and the Two-Career Family / 173

Balancing Work and Family 174 • Flexible Work Schedules 176 • Homeschooling Dads 177 • Involving Relatives 178 • Dividing and Organizing Responsibilities 179 • Homework by Day, Homeschooling by Night 182 • Weekend Learning Activities 183 • Family Field Trips 183

15 Homeschooling in the Early Years / 185

Toddlers and Preschoolers 186 • Learning Through Play 188 • Creating a Stimulating Environment 189 • Overcoming Stranger Suspicion 190 • Ready for Kindergarten 191 • Daily Educational Activities 194 • Length of School Day 195

16 Homeschooling in the Elementary Years / 197

Teaching a Child to Read **198** • Ready for Math **199** • Living History **201** • Scientific Explorations **202** • Art and Music **204** • Testing and Test Results **205** • Socialization Opportunities **206**

17 Homeschooling in the Middle Years / 207

Moving at Your Child's Pace **208** • Focusing on Weaknesses **208** • Enhancing Comprehension Skills **209** • Exploring and Learning Together **212** • Allowing Time for Educational Interests **212** • Self-Directed Learning **214** • Socialization Skills **215** • Volunteering in the Community **216**

18 Homeschooling in the Teen Years / 217

Living with Teens **218** • Teaching High-School Courses **218** • Subjects Required for College **220** • Driver Education **222** • The Social Life **223** • Volunteering and Apprenticeships **224** • Working Part Time **225** • College Preparations **226** • High-School Graduation **228**

19 Homeschooling Special-Needs Children / 229

Learning Disabilities **230** • Helping Learning-Challenged Children **232** • Support and Resources **235** • ADD and ADHD Information **236** • Dyslexia Support **237** • Autism Assistance **237** • Down Syndrome and Special Needs **238** • Vision-Impaired and Hearing-Impaired Help **238** • Gifted Children **239**

20 Veteran Homeschoolers and Burnout / 241

Encouragement for Your Homeschool Journey **242** • Rekindling the Fire **243** • Staying Motivated and Inspired **245** • Reconsidering Curriculum Choices **246** • New and Refreshing Ideas **248** • Handling Unexpected Challenges **249** • Explaining Goals **251** • Taking Time Off **252** • A Happy and Successful Homeschool **252**

21

College and Beyond / 255

Colleges Welcome Homeschoolers **256** • College Considerations and Preparations **259** • Transcripts and Documentation **260** • Entrance Exams and Interviews **261** • Online and Distance Learning **263** • The Job Hunt **264**

22

Adult Homeschoolers / 267

Life After Homeschool **268** • Options for Homeschooled Graduates **268** • Lifelong Learning **273** • Homeschooled Parents Homeschooling Their Children **274** • Comments from Homeschooled Adults **275** • Life After the Nest Is Empty **279**

Appendix A • Resources / **282**

Educational Materials **282** • Free Educational Materials **283** • Resources and Materials for Special-Needs Children **283** • Resources and Materials for Gifted Children **284** • Faith-Based Supply Resources **284** • Free Lesson Plan Ideas **284** • Correspondence and Online Schools **285** • College Resources **286** • Publications **286** • Driver Education **287** • Virtual Field Trips and Museums **287** • Travel **287**

Appendix B • Curriculum Providers and Programs for Homeschoolers / **288**

Appendix C • National Homeschool Organizations / **290**

Appendix D • State Departments of Education / **292**

Index / 297

Top Ten Benefits of Homeschooling

1. Homeschooled children score at or above the national average on standardized tests.
2. Colleges and universities now welcome homeschooled children.
3. A relaxed learning atmosphere that reduces stress is a natural by-product of homeschooling.
4. Teaching your child at home brings the whole family closer.
5. Homeschooling promotes "real world" learning experiences.
6. You can tailor your child's curriculum to match their learning style and abilities.
7. Homeschooling encourages creativity and critical thinking.
8. You can incorporate one-on-one interaction with more hands-on learning approaches.
9. Homeschooling is growing in popularity and there are numerous resources and support systems available today.
10. Your child will be able to socialize with people of varied age groups.

Introduction

▶TODAY, NEARLY EVERYONE KNOWS SOMEONE who home-schools their children. This isn't surprising, considering that an estimated one million children are now home educated in America. This number continues to rise by approximately 15 percent each year. Some predictions indicate that over 3 million children will be homeschooled by the year 2010.

As homeschooled children reach adulthood, news of their success reaches the world. Not only have these children attained a well-rounded education, they are also upstanding citizens.

Colleges and universities welcome homeschooled students. Scholarships are available to them, and professors find them an asset to the classroom. Employers are impressed by their ability to work on their own or as team members and by their desire to continue learning and enhancing their skills and knowledge.

The vast majority of adults who were homeschooled have also acquired something even more valuable—happiness in their lives and in their work. Having had the ability to play a large role in their own education, they have been able to self-direct their learning and develop a fuller sense of self-reliance and responsibility.

With the flexibility inherent to home education, students had the time they needed to pursue topics and hobbies that interested them. Those things they were passionate about took precedence in their lives. The very things they enjoyed as youngsters, they now enjoy in their life's work.

Home education is also the nucleus that the family revolves

around. It's been said that the family that schools together, stays together. Family members take an active interest in home education, sharing their daily experiences, brainstorming together on new ideas and topics to study, and communicating openly and frequently.

Homeschooling, however, is not "school at home." Rather, it is a lifestyle, a learning style, that is a natural part of each day. It doesn't revolve around the ringing of bells; it needn't take place at a desk or in a classroom.

In this book, you'll see how homeschooling can become a part of your family's lifestyle, leading to a quality education for your children. You'll see how to determine your children's unique learning styles and how to use materials that best suit their styles. And you'll see how your children gain joy in learning when they realize that homeschooling isn't just "school at home."

If you are new to homeschooling, you'll find everything you need to make the homeschool experience easy, affordable, and fun. If you are a veteran homeschooler, you'll find new ideas and techniques that help keep home education interesting and challenging. If homeschooling is proving to be more of a challenge than you had anticipated, you'll find ways to eliminate stress and make learning at home more enjoyable for everyone.

Whether you are a single parent, working parent, or stay-at-home parent, you can homeschool your children. This book provides the tips and guidance that will help you succeed. If your children have already entered a conventional school, you still have time to change direction and homeschool them, whether they are in first grade or tenth grade. As you will see, homeschooling requires much less time and money than one might imagine.

Each child deserves a quality education, one-on-one attention, and guidance in finding the road that leads to his or her happiness and success in life and in work. Every child benefits from learning in a safe, caring, stimulating environment surrounded by those who truly love and value him. Never doubt that you are the best teacher your child could have.

Come along on the journey that will help you provide an excellent education for your children, along with unique advantages and opportunities. It's sure to be one of the most treasured and rewarding experiences of your life. Enjoy the adventure! Ⓔ

Chapter 1

Homeschool Orientation

You don't need to be a professional teacher to homeschool your child; children are natural learners, and parents are natural teachers. However, homeschooling has its own set of challenges (and rewards!) to be prepared for. This chapter will show you what to expect from homeschooling your child and will also lay down some basic requirements for a successful homeschooling endeavor.

A Brief History Lesson

From the earliest days, a child's education took place inside the home. Children learned from parents, from a large extended family, and from everyday life. They learned to read books on their own or from older siblings. They practiced their alphabet, penmanship, and doing math sums on slate with a slate pencil. Families made sure their children learned important life skills; reading, writing, and math skills; and socialization skills. They taught their children morals and values, proper manners and etiquette, how to get along with others, and how to respect their elders.

Public Schooling

In 1642, the Massachusetts Bay Colony passed a law that required parents to make sure their children could read. Just five years later, they passed another law that required towns with fifty families or households to establish an elementary school, and towns with at least 100 households to establish a grammar school. The first public school, the Boston Latin School, opened in 1635. By the mid-1600s, schools began to crop up in other New England towns. Many of these were plain, one-room schoolhouses.

Public school did not become mandatory in the United States until individual states began to enact compulsory attendance laws in the mid- to late 1800s. Even then, it was difficult for every child to attend school, especially children of farm families during the spring planting and fall harvesting seasons. Some children were kept at home by inclement weather, snowstorms, thunderstorms, or floods. Not every child could walk the distance to and from school, and mass transportation was not yet an option. These children continued to be educated at home by parents or taught by a tutor, while others received instruction in a nearby church.

Modern Homeschooling

As the Industrial Revolution swept the country, school transportation improved and so did attendance at public schools. However, in the 1960s and 1970s, some families, disappointed with the public school system, began teaching their children at home. Early homeschool pioneers and advocates broke new ground in the homeschool territory.

Many of the families that began homeschooling didn't know anyone else who homeschooled at that time. They had no homeschool support groups, and they could find little information on homeschool resources or curriculum. However, as the number of homeschoolers grew, and as the media began to run news stories on this growing phenomena, more families learned that they could do it, too.

By the mid-1980s, the successes and benefits of homeschooling had become more apparent. Research was documented, books were printed, dedicated magazines took hold, and word spread like wildfire. It's estimated that approximately 150,000 to 200,000 children were home-schooled in the mid-1980s. By the mid-1990s, the number had grown to approximately 500,000 to 600,000.

In 1999, the Parent Survey of the National Household Education Surveys Program (Parent-NHES) reported approximately 850,000 children being homeschooled. Recent estimates place the number of home-schoolers at about 1.5 million, with a growth rate averaging 15 to 20 percent each year. Because not every family registers with its school district, estimates are based upon surveys and through information provided by the states.

FACT

The number of homeschooled children continues to increase rapidly. More parents are homeschooling because they feel they are best able to pass morals and value systems on to their children, and because they believe they have more time for their child, as well as a better understanding of their child's educational needs.

Meet the Staff

If you're considering homeschooling, you might find yourself questioning your capabilities as a "teacher" or fear that you won't be able to "teach." Parents often say, "Homeschool my children? I wish I could, but I don't know how to teach." The truth is that as a parent, you are the best teacher your children could have. No one knows your children better than you. No one knows their strengths and weaknesses as well as you do. No one has seen their successes and failures, their ups and downs, their joys and despair, as you have.

You have already been and continue to be your child's teacher. You are the one who cared for your child as a baby, and you are the one who taught your baby to walk, to talk, to eat the right foods, to cross a street safely, to treat others kindly, and so on. Those first few years of your child's life are some of the most precious and the most delicate. Yet, you were that child's teacher, hardly ever daring to think "But I don't know how to parent my child; I don't know how to teach my child."

FACT

Former U.S. Secretary of Education Richard W. Riley declared in his first "State of American Education" address: "I believe that all parents, indeed any adult, regardless of his or her station in life or even their level of education, has the capacity and obligation to teach their children a love of learning."

You'll be pleased to know that the key to a sound education for homeschoolers doesn't rely on the formal educational background of the parent or on the parent's being a state-certified teacher. Rather, it relies on the parents' natural ability to nurture and raise their children and to instill a love of learning within the child.

Research has shown that the keys to a sound homeschool education rely upon the ability to do the following:

- Interact one-on-one with each child.
- Tutor and mentor each child.
- Design a curriculum best suited to each child's learning style.
- Take advantage of learning opportunities whenever they arise.
- Learn together and seek answers together.
- Learn through hands-on approaches.
- Pinpoint a child's weaknesses and spend time right then to help improve those areas.
- Exhibit patience and good humor.

- Share moral beliefs and values with each child.
- Share deep love and close bonds with each child.

Most of these points come naturally to parents, and they no doubt come naturally to teachers in traditional schools, as well. Unfortunately, in traditional schools, teachers aren't always awarded the luxury of having only two, four, or six children in their classrooms. Consequently, they can't always provide individualized instruction one-on-one with each child or design different curricula to best suit each child in the class.

The Student-Teacher Connection

Many homeschool families actually dislike the term *homeschooling*. They view what they do as a natural part of living, not as something separate or distinct as "school at home." Some families prefer to use "home learning," "life learning," or a "learning journey" to describe what they do. Regardless of the term used, it involves understanding and connecting with your child.

For starters, think about the terms *teach* and *instruct*. These can take on harsh implications within the home and seem out of place there. Rather than teaching or instructing a child, consider homeschooling as guiding a child.

ALERT!

Although the terms *teaching, schooling,* and *education* are used in this book, remember that *teaching* should be *guiding*, and *homeschooling* or the *educational process* should be a *learning journey*, rather than forced instruction.

Reconnecting with Your Child

Parents who have recently withdrawn children from a traditional school often need to reconnect with their children. Former U.S. Secretary of Education Richard W. Riley, concerned over the gap widening between parent and child, stressed that there is a need today for parents and children to reconnect. He stated, "There is a disconnection here that demands our attention . . . a disconnection so pervasive between adult America and child America that we are all losing touch with one another." He encouraged all adults to take a special interest in young people and to "guide that child's education."

You can reconnect with your children by simply sitting down with them each day and talking or by going on walks together or for a ride around town or through the country. Many homeschool parents who have withdrawn their children from school suddenly wonder what they will talk about with their children all day. They may sit down together and find that the gap between them has grown wider than they had anticipated. Other than the basic "How was your day today?" or "What would you like to do this week?", they're not sure what to say or even where to start. By suggesting a walk to the corner store or a drive to the lake, you and your child can find room to breathe, share a different environment for awhile, and encounter new experiences together.

After an outing with your child, you'll find yourself talking about many little things on the drive home or later that day. You may remind him of the osprey you saw at the lake, or the funny conversation you overheard between an elderly couple at the café. At the dinner table, you may talk about the biography you read together on Albert Einstein, the surprising facts you both learned about the ancient civilization of Mesopotamia, or the spectacular erupting volcano your son created that day. By sharing daily experiences, you and your child quickly reconnect with one another, bringing the entire family closer together.

Children are natural learners. Learning is an integral part of their lives, woven throughout the hours that make up each day. As they go about their normal lives, they encounter, gather, process, and grow from the information they naturally absorb. This is learning.

Learning and Bonding

By being a part of your child's education, you naturally connect. By learning together, reading together, playing games together, and going on simple, relaxing outings together, you build experiences that bring you and your children closer. When your children are in school each day, the opportunities to connect are diminished. But when your children are in the home, opportunities present themselves throughout the day. The learning experiences that are woven into each day are like threads of yarn connecting you and your children, forming a strong bond that unites the whole family.

You can enhance your child's learning by applying the following tips in your homeschool:

- Provide a creative, stimulating, hands-on environment.
- Encourage experimentation, explorations, and problem solving.
- Engage in lively conversations and discussions.
- Play a variety of strategy or "what-if" games each day.
- Contribute new ideas and experiences on a regular basis.
- Demonstrate ways to seek answers to questions.
- Explore neighborhoods, businesses, and cultural centers together.
- Read together every day.

Listening Instead of Instructing

It's been said that the fool talks, while the wise man listens. The parent who listens to his child is a wise parent, indeed. Keep in mind that "listening" does not mean "taking orders from," however. When you truly listen to your child, you hear what's on her mind, where her thoughts lie, where her interests lie, what she would like in her life today, and what she would like out of life tomorrow.

Children experience thousands of thoughts and feelings each day. Some are more important than others, yet none is inconsequential. It's these types of daily thoughts and feelings that lead to further discussions, questions, explorations, and, ultimately, to greater learning.

When children are able to speak about their thoughts and feelings—and know that parents are listening—they feel that their thoughts are valued. When they can discuss their thoughts and ideas, they also gain a better understanding and a deeper learning.

Your child feels valued when you listen to her. Here are some ways to truly hear what your child has to say:

- Stop what you're doing and look at your child while asking her to explain what she thinks or how she feels about something.
- Keep your hands still and retain eye contact with your child while she explains her thoughts and feelings.
- Avoid busying yourself with other things or becoming distracted while she is talking. Give her your undivided attention.
- Avoid the temptation to interrupt, fill in her sentences, place your ideas over top of hers, or hurry her along. Remain silent, and allow her to speak and think through her feelings.
- Respond with short sentences, such as "I see" or "That's interesting," to show that you follow and understand what she's saying.
- Encourage your child to elaborate by suggesting that she share more about her experience or ideas, and how they make her feel and think.
- Ask questions appropriate for your child's age, such as "What do you think?" or "How do you feel about it?" Questions for older children could include, "What do you feel you've learned from that?" or "What do you think could happen as a result of this?"

ALERT!

Don't worry about not being "qualified" to teach. As a parent, you are the most qualified person to help your child learn. It's more important that you have the right attitude and understanding so that you can encourage and enable your child's learning abilities. It's your child that is important, not a specific qualification.

Credit Hours

Even though most traditional school days are approximately six hours long, you and your child won't need to sit at a desk in your home for five or six hours each day. Some states may require you to keep a daily schedule and attendance record, showing that you homeschool a certain number of hours a day, 180 days a year, but the hours and days can be flexible. Chapter 8 talks more about daily schedules and record keeping.

On average, the time required to focus on core skills (reading, math, language arts, social studies, and science) can be broken down per age group as follows:

- **Preschool and kindergarten:** 30 to 60 minutes
- **Elementary ages:** 60 to 90 minutes
- **Middle-school ages:** 1½ to 3 hours
- **High-school ages:** 2 to 4 hours

This time includes one-on-one time with the parent, focusing on required skills for a particular age group. While younger children may require more of your time, older children are usually more in charge of their study time. For most homeschoolers, the rest of the day is spent on other educational activities, such as reading, art, music, hobbies, strategy games, educational videos, and researching and exploring special areas of interest. For many parents, these activities provide additional opportunities for individualized one-on-one time with their children as they learn, explore, and share activities together.

As the parent and teacher, you have more control over the type of education your child receives. You decide what, when, and how your child learns. If you're not sure what your child should learn, guidelines are easy to obtain. From these guidelines, you can steer the direction you want your homeschool to take, based upon your own morals and values and upon what you want for your child now and in the years ahead.

Scheduling Strategies

Flexibility in the homeschool schedule is one of the most important keys to success. You should understand that there will be days when things won't go according to schedule. You may even find that several weeks go by in which things simply are not going according to the plan you had initially formulated. Don't worry or allow yourself to panic or become stressed. This is merely an indication that you need to look at your child's learning style and your family's lifestyle and try a different approach.

Every family has its own homeschool style, and you'll find the one that works best for your family, too. In Chapter 4, several styles of homeschooling are discussed. You may find one there that works for you, or the information may provide ideas or inspiration for developing a unique style just for your family.

Free Time

Some families cover the core skills and busywork in the mornings. That leaves the afternoons open for "free time," during which the kids explore their own areas of interest. For some, the earlier part of the day is free time, then the family gathers together in the evenings to spend time studying the core skills. This schedule works well especially for two-career families or single-parent families.

When unexpected situations cause the family to miss out on their normal study times, many make up for this by spending a few hours catching up during the weekend. Sometimes, events arise to upset the normal homeschool schedule by several days or weeks. Remember that flexibility is your friend! You can decide to take spring break a little earlier than planned, or you can take a midwinter break and then spend a couple weeks in the summer to catch up if necessary.

ALERT!

Children learn more—and retain more—through play than through instruction. This is an innate quality of all animals, providing everything from basic survival skills to an all-encompassing education. Provide plenty of games, books, creative activities, and a stimulating environment to encourage play and learning throughout each day.

Have a backup plan in mind for unexpected situations. Pick up an armload of books from the library that you know your children would enjoy reading. Keep a few puzzles, games, or models stacked in the corner of a closet. Your kids will be thrilled to get new "toys," and they'll stay busy, having fun and exercising their minds during this unexpected free time.

Decompression Time

If your child has been in school for some time and you remove him, he will need some decompression time, or time to adjust to his new lifestyle. Take Nathan, for instance. He has been accustomed to moving through his school day in time to the ringing bells. He was conditioned to focus on one subject for forty minutes, then put that topic aside, and immediately switch to studying another subject for forty minutes. Then he had to backburner that topic, and switch to another subject for forty minutes, on and on, throughout the day. For Nathan, education has been a fast-food compendium of information quickly ingested to the tune of ringing bells, with little time left for him to think in between, let alone absorb.

At home, the day stretches before him, undivided by forty-minute classes marked by ringing bells. At first, he feels somewhat at a loss. He's not sure how to "go to class" without the warning bells. He's not sure when to "stop studying" without the sounding of the bells. Even though he's been eager to homeschool, he's suddenly not sure how to make the transition from school to homeschool.

To him, being at home during the school year has meant vacation time, holidays, summer break, and freedom. There were even a few times when he played hooky—not really sick, but not really up to going to school. And as the day wore on, he felt a little guilty about not being at school. Now that he's home all the time, he still feels a little guilty, even though he's legally a homeschool student. Somehow, doing schoolwork at home feels a little strange to Nathan.

This is a normal reaction for children who have spent time in school. This is why they need to decompress and be provided with free time for them to adjust and become comfortable in their homes on a daily basis. You can help them by letting them know it's okay to do nothing for a few days. Let them get used to the idea of being at home and doing some of the things they've been wanting to do but haven't had the time. If they begin to feel bored, you can suggest some things to do, such as a field trip, a nature walk, a trip to the library, or going through some old toys they haven't played with for a while.

QUESTION?

How do I know what to teach?
A Typical Course of Study for Kindergarten through Grade 12,
from World Book Educational Products, is available on the Web at
✎ *www.worldbook.com*. Just click on "Parents," then "Typical
Course of Study," and the guidelines are at your fingertips.

Soon they'll be learning new things on their own, just by getting back
in touch with themselves and with their surroundings. Then, gradually, you
can begin incorporating your homeschool plans into their lifestyle as you
both work out a schedule they are comfortable with.

Financial Services

The cost of homeschooling is as flexible as the homeschool schedule.
Some parents spend $200 to $300 per school year. Others spend more;
others may spend less. Some spend more when they first begin
homeschooling as they collect supplies to last several years, while others
wait until the microscope or chemistry set is needed. The average amount
spent per child per year, according to research conducted by the National
Home Education Research Institute (NHERI), is about $450. The money
you would spend on back-to-school clothes, book bags, special binders,
special gym sneakers, and other "must-haves" could easily cover your first
year of homeschooling.

It's tempting to overspend in the beginning. You might think you need
to purchase a curriculum package or enroll your child in a
correspondence school, yet you aren't sure which would be the best for
your child. Take time to observe your child's learning style first, before
committing to a particular program. You might also check the type of
curriculum packages other families use. (Chapter 7 includes more
information on curriculum packages and correspondence schools.)

In lieu of a packaged curriculum, you might feel that you need lots of
textbooks, workbooks, science equipment, and so forth. In reality, you
don't need to spend anything before you start homeschooling. Consider
using free or low-cost ideas before you begin spending.

Free Resources

The library is the perfect resource for reference books. A world of information is literally contained within its walls. In fact, nearly any book you will ever need to use in your homeschool, from the preschool years through college preparation, is available free of charge at your local library. From library books, you can create your own lesson plans and design worksheets, if you plan to use them, rather than purchasing workbooks.

Public libraries also have a wide selection of educational videos on history, nature, science, math, and travels to foreign lands. They have audiotapes of music, literary works, biographies, and foreign languages. Kids can spend hours at the library with educational magazines, puzzles, chess games, and software. Most libraries today have a dedicated computer room and educational CD-ROMs for children to use.

Programs offered by libraries include story time, sing-alongs, kids' clubs, reading and artwork contests, game nights, and special holiday events. If necessary, you can even enlist the help of tutors provided by the library. Book sales are usually held at least a couple times a year, and you can pick up some great finds for only a few cents each.

Find free educational materials on the Internet by using search engines such as Google or Yahoo! Or check out the free worksheets, games, software, and activities at *www.school express.com*. Try *www.edhelper.com* for free lesson plans, worksheets, and puzzles, or *www.abcteach.com* for free printable games and activities, unit studies, research projects, and more.

Low-Cost Resources

To keep homeschool expenses to a minimum, set a budget and stick with it. Put off purchasing items until you absolutely need them. By acquiring free resources first, you limit your costs before you even begin. Although some purchases are unavoidable, such as paper, pencils, and crayons, you can usually find great deals on these items in July and August, during the back-to-school sales.

Teacher supply stores usually offer discounts or special deals to teachers, and they often extend these specials to homeschool families. You can take your children along, and together you can see what books, games, science projects, or construction sets catch their interest. When visiting the store, present a copy of your homeschool registration paperwork and find out the type of discounts they offer to homeschool families or groups.

A good source for used educational items is the local consignment shop. You can find microscope sets, planetarium sets, telescopes, globes, games, puzzles, books, and more, all at affordable prices. And it's a place where you can put your used homeschool items up for sale when you no longer need them.

Buying in Bulk

Some local homeschool groups purchase educational supplies in bulk at reduced prices. If you have enough members in your group, this can be an affordable way to stock up on notebook paper, construction paper, folders, rulers, pens, pencils, and other items.

FACT

Abraham Lincoln, one of the greatest statesmen and presidents of all time, received most of his education from his stepmother, Sarah, in a southern Indiana cabin. With less than a year of formal schooling, Lincoln stated, "Still, somehow, I could read, write, and cipher to the Rule of Three."

Check with your homeschool support group to see if they offer a book loan program for members. This is a good way to acquire textbooks, which can be expensive. Borrowers will be able to use the books for several weeks or even a semester. And loaners will be able to clear their bookshelves of used textbooks and make room for more immediate needs.

Homeschool groups and state organizations often hold curriculum fairs once or twice a year. These are great for purchasing used books, software, and supplies, as well as used curricula other families have outgrown. At these fairs, you are able to look over the books and curricula firsthand and ask the sellers questions about the products. (Chapter 7 includes more information on different types of curricula, the costs, and sources for discounted curricula packages.)

Benefits of Homeschooling

The benefits of homeschooling are many. Not only do homeschooled children receive a broad and well-rounded education, but the entire family is brought closer together through the homeschool experience. Parents and children get to know each other better, they share experiences they otherwise would have missed, and their homeschool years provide a myriad of memories that will last a lifetime.

Reduced Stress

The stress and chaos of morning rushes to catch the school bus, to send children off in the early hours of the day without a nutritious breakfast, and to realize that the children will spend the day with a crowd of strangers is unsettling, to say the least. And the evenings are not much better—pages of homework to do, tears over not understanding the assignment, extracurricular activities to attend (after an already long school day), basic chores to do, and, if you're lucky, squeezing a quick dinner into the schedule.

When children receive their education at home, the morning ritual is far more relaxing. There is time for preparing and eating a nutritious breakfast together, chores are done together and completed early in the day, and children are calm and relaxed in their own homes as their learning day begins. And all the while, parents and children are talking, interacting, laughing, playing, learning, and generally sharing their days and their lives.

By evening, "homework" has already been completed during study times earlier in the day, and there were no misunderstandings regarding assignments on either the children's or parent's part. Extracurricular activities are a part of the regular school day, and chores are completed before the homeschool day begins. That leaves the evenings open for family time together, a relaxing dinner, and free time for reading, game playing, and other enjoyable activities.

FACT

A relaxed child learns more easily than a stressed child. Some studies show that stress actually inhibits the formation of new neurons in the brain. Dr. Carla Hannaford, biologist, educational consultant, and author, states, "Chronic exposure to stress inhibits full brain development." This, in turn, can result in learning problems, such as ADD (attention deficit disorder), ADHD (attention deficit/hyperactivity disorder), or behavioral problems.

Above-Average Test Scores

Studies on the academic achievement of homeschoolers continue to demonstrate that they consistently score at or above average on standardized tests. In a 1997 study of standardized academic achievement tests (conducted by Brian Ray, Ph.D., with the National Home Education Research Institute), homeschooled children averaged at or above the eightieth percentile. The national average for traditionally schooled children on standardized tests is the fiftieth percentile.

A 1999 study by Dr. Lawrence Rudner, director of the Educational Resources Information Center Clearinghouse (ERIC), found that test scores of homeschooled students ranged in the seventy-fifth to eighty-fifth percentiles. Although test scores vary from state to state, recent studies clearly indicate that homeschooled children are testing at least as well as, or better than, the national average in many cases.

Homeschoolers also tend to score higher on SATs and ACTs, especially in the areas of English, reading, and vocabulary. In math and science reasoning, they scored at or above national averages. A 1997 study conducted by Dr. Rhonda Galloway and Dr. Joseph Sutton, *College Success of Students from Three High School Settings,* showed that homeschooled college students ranked higher than other students in the following areas: academic, affective-social, cognitive, and spiritual.

The College Experience

Aside from test results (which is a controversial subject in itself for many people), homeschoolers are welcomed—and in some cases, actively sought—by colleges and universities today. And many now offer scholarships to homeschoolers. More and more college professors are speaking out on their experiences with homeschoolers in their classes. In many cases, they have found homeschoolers to be more mature (emotionally and socially), better prepared academically, strong in class participation and leadership skills, and high achievers.

As Jay W. Wile, a university professor with a Ph.D. in nuclear chemistry, says, "I experienced thousands of students. By far the best students that I had were the homeschooled ones. They were serious about learning, they could teach themselves, and they were far more likely to be able to think critically than any of their counterparts."

FACT

Jane Austen, author of classics such as *Pride and Prejudice* and *Sense and Sensibility,* was educated mostly by her father. Even without formal schooling, she loved reading and writing. She dedicated her life to observing the role of family in society, and she conveyed her views and observations through the skillful writing of six novels.

Social Skills

With more opportunities to socialize with a wider group of people on a more regular basis than traditionally schooled children, homeschoolers develop better social skills for the real world. Since their learning takes place in the real world, away from the confines of a classroom or institution, they develop social skills that are applicable in everyday situations.

On the whole, they socialize more often with varied age groups, as well as with people from all walks of life, rather than the same age group in a classroom, day after day. They have more opportunities to interact with businesspeople, community workers, group leaders, volunteers, neighbors, and friends. More information and studies on socialization and child development are included in Chapter 6.

The benefits of homeschooling continue to make themselves well known. When studies on homeschooled students—as well as the firsthand knowledge most people now have of homeschoolers—clearly demonstrate the students' academic abilities, social adeptness, leadership skills, concern for family and community, and well-adjusted attitude toward life and learning, the results speak for themselves. (E)

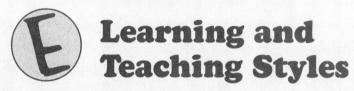

Chapter 2

Learning and Teaching Styles

When you understand the ways in which your child naturally learns, your job will be easier, your child will be happier, and homeschooling will be a joy for the both of you. This chapter will help you to enhance your child's learning experiences by incorporating the information-processing methods that come naturally to him or her.

Educational Theorists

The brain is a complex organ, composed of billions of neurons, or nerve cells. By age three, a child's brain has approximately 1,000 trillion synapses (learning connections or pathways), which is twice as many as an adult. The synapses connect the neurons in the brain, enabling the advancement of thought processes and learning.

As a child seeks and acquires new experiences, new synapses will grow and strengthen in the brain. If the number of stimulating, new experiences drops off, the number of synapses will diminish and be lost, breaking some of the learning connections. Those synapses that are not used regularly are "pruned off" in the second decade of life and lost forever.

ALERT!

To strengthen synapses, the brain requires frequent new stimuli. This is why bonding, nurturing, positive interactions, creative stimulation, explorations, and new experiences are encouraged in the learning environment from birth. They will provide crucial reinforcement and strengthening of neural pathways that will be important for acquiring, processing, and applying knowledge later in the child's life.

Though much about the brain remains a mystery, scientists, psychologists, and behaviorists continue to learn more about the way it functions and processes information and intelligence. The following sections review the findings of a few educational theorists.

Jean Piaget on Children's Intellect

In his studies of human intelligence, Swiss educational theorist Jean Piaget found that quality learning took place when children were actively involved in their own learning process. Through exploration and discovery, children turned their experiences into learning patterns that provided foundations for further explorations and subsequent learning. Piaget found that children's cognitive skills, or the way they process information, were enhanced through physical experiences and perceptions. He believed in active learning environments in which children could discover, absorb, and build on new experiences and information. Much of his research focused on the developmental stages of children's intellect and learning readiness.

Maria Montessori on Children Learning

Maria Montessori was the first woman in Italy to receive a medical degree. After working in the psychiatric clinic at the University of Rome, she opened her own schools for children, incorporating methods she had used at the clinic. She believed that the child's learning environment should be endowed with simple manipulatives, or tactile materials, that hold the child's interest and promote exploration and learning. Teachers were to be "guides" who encourage children to freely explore the learning materials in their surroundings. Her style eventually became known as the Montessori Method, a self-motivated learning style that is intended to enhance a child's self-confidence and self-discipline.

FACT

Dr. Maria Montessori believed that education was not something "the teacher does," but, rather, a naturally occurring process in humans. "The teacher's task is not to talk," explained Dr. Montessori, "but to prepare and arrange a series of motives for cultural activity in a special environment made for the child."

Howard Gardner on Learning Styles

Educational psychologist Howard Gardner, proponent of the theory of multiple intelligences, believes children develop their own learning and thinking patterns between birth and age five (intuitive learning). When entering the school system, a different educational style is introduced (academic learning), which is not necessarily in line with the child's style. This can result in contradictory messages, making the learning process even more difficult for children. His suggestions include the development of more varied learning methods and environments that allow children to further use, and benefit from, their individual learning styles.

Common Learning Styles

Although learning styles and multiple intelligences are based upon in-depth research and scientific studies (incorporating theories and principles that exceed the boundaries of this book), you should be aware of three general styles of learners. Observe your children to see if they exhibit any of these learning styles:

1. **Visual learners.** These children prefer to spend time poring over pictures and graphics, and they respond to bright colors and visual stimulation. They tend to learn best through visual presentations.
2. **Auditory learners.** These children enjoy listening to music, audio-tapes, and people reading aloud or talking. They can learn best through discussions and verbal information.
3. **Tactile-kinesthetic learners.** These children like to move around, touch things, and talk; plus they have a difficult time sitting still. They learn best through an active, hands-on approach.

Even though a child may appear to be a visual learner or kinesthetic learner, it doesn't exclude him from possessing qualities of the other learning styles, as well. And it doesn't mean that approaches used for another style of learning cannot be incorporated into his lifestyle. The key, however, is to help your child learn in the way that makes the most sense to him (that is, his specific learning style) while still providing a well-balanced learning environment that includes visual stimulation, discussion times, and physical activities.

Some studies have shown that people remember 10 percent of what they read, 20 percent of what they hear, 30 percent of what they see, 50 percent of what they see and hear, 70 percent of what they say, and 90 percent of what they say and do. Even when you've determined your child's best learning style, it's important to provide a variety of learning styles to help children process and retain what they've learned.

Visual Learners

Visual learners learn through seeing and visualizing images. Whether it's words on a page, the person who is speaking, or a presentation mounted on the wall, they need to see it in order to fully absorb it. When thinking and processing information, they see pictures in their minds. Even if it is a word, they see, in their mind's eye, an image of that word.

Visual learners also like to take notes, even if they already have written material in front of them. By writing down bits of information, they are able to see it on their notepaper and inscribe their notes in their mind's eye.

Here are some tips to help your visual learner make the most of his learning style.

- Hang educational charts, displays, illustrations, maps, and mobiles.
- Read colorfully illustrated reference books.
- Create graphics, posters, or colorful pictorials to accompany lessons.
- Use attractively designed flashcards for various subjects.
- Design colorful cards for spelling, vocabulary, and English concepts.
- Use flow charts, pie charts, and diagrams to illustrate math and scientific concepts.
- Make eye contact while explaining lessons or concepts.
- Encourage note-taking, illustrating, or diagramming of topics.
- Allow educational videos on topics studied.
- Suggest writing and illustrating stories on topics studied.
- Provide a quiet area of the home for studies, free of distractions.

Auditory Learners

Auditory learners learn through hearing. They may read information or texts, but they don't fully grasp what they've read until they hear someone read it aloud or summarize it in their own words. The tone, rhythm, and inflection of the voice are important to the learner's comprehension. When recalling oral instructions or information, auditory learners hear the speaker in their mind, as they replay the tone and rhythm of the voice as it stresses this point or that. The way in which a speaker conveys her message helps the auditory learner glean the important facts and details from the information.

Here are some tips to help your auditory learner make the most of his learning style.

- Read material aloud to auditory learners.
- Present material in an interesting storytelling format.
- Use rhythm and voice inflection when reading and talking.
- Tape-record lessons for playing and replaying.
- Encourage the reading of books or information aloud.
- Engage in lively discussions and debates on various subjects.
- Allow audiotapes or books-on-tape relating to topics studied.
- Create musical presentations of topics studied.
- Include and encourage speeches and verbal presentations.
- Turn off the television and radio, and limit distractions.

Tactile-Kinesthetic Learners

Tactile and kinesthetic learners learn through touching and moving. This learning group is sometimes broken into two separate categories: tactile and tactile-kinesthetic. Both groups are similar, with the tactile-kinesthetics enjoying hands-on experiences as well as lots of movement in their learning styles. They process information through physical sensations, and they learn best when participating in activities and actively applying fine-motor and gross-motor skills. Where the visual learner is distracted from learning by noise or commotion, the tactile-kinesthetic learner is negatively distracted when remaining quiet or sitting still for too long. In order to learn, the tactile-kinesthetic learner must keep moving, exploring, and experimenting.

Here are some tips to help your tactile-kinesthetic learner make the most of his learning style:

- Understand that movement and touch is imperative for learning.
- Provide numerous manipulatives for hands-on learning.
- Incorporate games, construction sets, Geo-Boards, and/or Cuisenaire rods into lessons.

- Invest in lab equipment for reinforcing science and math concepts.
- Put on dramatic plays that bring social studies and literature to life.
- Create colorful, textured cards for spelling, vocabulary, and English concepts.
- Read or study while swaying to and fro or in time to tapping feet.
- Create lesson plans choreographed to dance music.
- Encourage the use of computers and electronics.
- Devise brief time slots for sit-down study times.
- Allow classical music during study times.
- Take frequent field trips related to topics studied.

Tactile-kinesthetic learners—indeed, many learners—can relate to this wise Chinese proverb: "I hear and I forget; I see and I remember; I do and I understand." Hands-on learning often results in better comprehension. This proverb is a good motto for families to adopt in their homeschools.

Your Child's Learning Style

By now, you've probably recognized your child in some of the learning processes described in this chapter. Even though she may practice some learning styles from each of the three groups, as you observe the results of her learning, you may realize that she comprehends concepts better as a visual learner, auditory learner, or tactile-kinesthetic learner.

When you've made this determination, you can help your child by incorporating the tips outlined above. In addition, you will want to provide the basic materials and create the type of environment that will keep her motivated and learning. Inspire her to use pictures, graphics, artwork, and color if she has visual learner tendencies. If she has auditory learner inclinations, encourage her to read aloud, make speeches and presentations, and discuss things that are on her mind. If she's a tactile-kinesthetic learner, allow her more freedom to move, dance, touch, and explore as she learns about her world and her place in it.

Whatever your child's preferred manner of learning, avoid focusing *only* on that style of learning. You give your child an advantage when you adapt learning and lesson plans to suit her natural style of processing information. However, your child benefits even more when she's aware of other ways of assimilating information, too.

As the years pass and your child grows and changes, her learning style may shift as well. She may encounter situations where familiarity with different learning styles will be helpful to her, perhaps in sports, music, college, or career changes. By staying in tune to your child, you'll be able to provide the basis and variables that will result in optimal lifelong learning.

FACT

In *Discover Your Child's Learning Style,* by Mariaemma Willis and Victoria Kindle Hodson, the authors give the following advice: "When you help your child identify and respect his own learning strengths, interests, talents, and needs, you give him roots in the gifts he was born with. When you help your child discover his dreams, passions, and goals, you give him the wings of motivation and purpose for becoming an eager, self-directed learner."

Your Child's Strengths and Weaknesses

In observing your child's learning styles, you'll also gain insight to his strengths and weaknesses. When you're in tune to your child and the work he is doing, you will be able to see how quickly your child grasps some skills, as well as determine where difficulties lie in other areas.

Studying Kyle

Kyle was a bright, quick, and witty eleven-year-old. Math came naturally to him, and in many instances, he was able to explain math concepts to his mother in a logical way that amazed her. He had a knack for creating gadgets out of electronic parts and small motors. He was always telling jokes and riddles, and he could focus on a 1,000-piece puzzle for hours. But when it came to writing a two- or three-paragraph paper, you'd think his mother had requested a 10,000-word dissertation!

Rather than insisting on writing the paper, Kyle's mother observed him carefully when he was absorbed in close work. Although he enjoyed drawing and artwork, his was a free-flowing, abstract style, taking up a large expanse of paper with few intricate details. She also realized that assignments he completed were printed in short sentences or phrases, usually with the letters large and touching each other. His math papers also contained letters and numerals that were printed large but close together, one against the other.

As she watched Kyle work, she noticed his cramped style of printing and the way he often laid down his pencil and stretched his fingers before picking up the pencil again. She also noticed that he labored over the writing of his name at the top of his pages when she asked him to spell it in cursive writing.

She soon understood that doing paperwork with pen or pencil was not the most comfortable thing for Kyle. The three-paragraph paper she had requested in cursive writing would be an even more difficult feat to accomplish. After further investigating, she found that boys are often later than girls in developing fine-motor skills, such as gripping a pencil, making it move in the proper directions, and creating fancy letters or intricate artwork.

When Kyle's mother allowed him to write his three-paragraph paper on the computer and print it out, it turned into a four-page story. Since then, she has allowed him to use the computer more often for writing assignments. In the meantime, she helps him improve his fine-motor skills by continuing to work puzzles, build gadgets, thread berries and popcorn onto strings for the birds, and to use a slanted easel or board while drawing or printing.

Observing Children Closely

By homeschooling your children—and observing their learning styles and work habits—you will be able to pick up on weaknesses before they become a larger problem. You can also ask your children if there are things they do each day that are somewhat difficult for them. Ask if they find a particular lesson or activity difficult, and follow up on why it might feel that way for them.

In Kyle's case, he might have said that his hand started cramping after writing four or five words in cursive. His mother might have thought it was a convenient excuse to get out of writing the paper. Or she might have paid closer attention, as she did in Kyle's case, and found that it was indeed something more.

FACT

Once you have determined your child's learning styles and where his strengths and weaknesses lie, you will have a good idea of the educational focus for your home learning environment. From there, you can add the tools and resources to help your child build upon his strengths and skills.

Individualized Patterns

When homeschooling your child, you are in tune to his rhythms, his sleeping and eating patterns, and his biological makeup, which has been a part of who he is since he was a baby. You can see when he is widest awake, when he is most alert, and when he is better able to focus and to learn. You can also provide him with more nutritious meals and snacks throughout the day to keep his blood sugar normal, eliminating the highs and lows that can result from improper eating habits. And you can ensure that he gets a good night's sleep to fit his homeschooling patterns, as well as rest and relaxation time when needed throughout the course of the day.

You will be better able to work with his weaknesses, take advantage of his strengths, and provide a more balanced day of educational activities. As a result, he will respond and react more positively to his natural peak learning times, which are in tune to his particular lifestyle and learning patterns.

Peak Learning Times

Some people are morning larks. Others are night owls. Some prefer to get right to work first thing in the morning, then enjoy their afternoons with a clear conscience of a good day's work already done. Some savor the relaxation of quiet morning hours, then rev up for excitement and activity in the late afternoon and evening hours.

Children also experience peak hours throughout their day. Some are still groggy and sleepy-eyed at 10:00 in the morning. Others are bouncing on the beds and throwing balls around the room at 5:00 A.M. Some can't seem to focus well until late afternoon, while others are ready for lessons at 7:00 A.M.

You can see what a difficult time these children would have focusing and learning if they were in school between 8:00 A.M. and 3:00 P.M.! Peak learning times are also influenced by sleep habits and by food that is consumed.

Sleep Patterns and Learning

Your child's particular sleeping patterns can affect learning and the ability to focus. Some children simply will not fall asleep before 11:00 P.M., no matter how hard you've tried. Some fall asleep before 8:00 P.M., even though you'd rather they stayed up later (because you know they'll be up at the crack of dawn!).

Some children never took naps when they were young, others took morning and afternoon naps. This is all a part of who they are. Changing children's sleep habits can be done over time, but it can also go against their natural biological makeup, never quite setting well with them.

ALERT!

Research has shown that a good night's sleep is critical for alertness, learning, and retaining information. When sleep is limited or interrupted, the mind's ability to focus or to recall information is limited. Some researchers have recently found connections between sleep problems and ADD or ADHD.

Nutrition and Learning

When children go off to school without a nutritious breakfast, their blood sugar generally falls around midmorning. This creates the midmorning slump, resulting in tiredness and a reduced ability to focus. If math class was held in school at 10:00 or 10:30 each morning, and your child was not doing well in math, the midmorning slump could be part of the problem.

The same effect occurs around 2:00 or 2:30 in the afternoons. Depending on what the school lunch consisted of (hot dogs? pasta? pizza?), your child may experience a mid-afternoon slump. He would be especially affected if he were an early riser, had been awake since 6:00 A.M. had missed out on a good breakfast, had a less-than-nutritious lunch, and was awarded no time to relax between classes. With his body running low on fuel and rest by the 2:00 class, his level of alertness and learning receptiveness has dramatically diminished.

ALERT!

Studies on nutrition and brain function have shown that poor nutrition or meal skipping can impair a child's mental and physical performance. As you prepare nutritious meals for your family, educate children on the importance of a well-balanced diet and healthy snacks—lessons that will ensure a long and healthy life.

Finding Your Teaching Style

As noted in Chapter 1, homeschooling is not "school at home," and you do not need to be a professional, certified teacher. As a parent, you are already qualified to teach your children. You don't need to take on the persona of a traditional classroom teacher in your home, or stand at a blackboard and jot down instructions, or sit behind a desk and grade papers.

Blackboards can be fun and desks can be handy, but when homeschooling your child, take advantage of the *home* and don't worry so much about *school.* Relax on the couch, and pull your children close to you as you read to them, work on math problems, or discuss the Revolutionary War and recite "Paul Revere's Ride" together. The warmth, love, and closeness of a mother or father is a powerful learning conveyance in itself.

Your teaching style should not be something separate from who you are. Your teaching style is a part of your innate parenting style. It's the part of you that is concerned about your children, cares for your children, and wants the best for your children.

Keep a Positive Attitude

Remind yourself each day that your duty is to *guide* your child, not force instruction upon him. Your role is to help her learn *how* to learn and to encourage her to seek answers to questions, find materials and information that will help her learn, explore the things that interest her, and find new and challenging ways to learn. You will want to have patience and a positive attitude as "guider" in the homeschool. Adopting a relaxed, easygoing, humor-filled frame of mind is also helpful.

Teaching Tips

First and foremost, homeschool in a manner that you and your child are comfortable with. Try some of the following tips to see how they work in your homeschool.

- Stress the values and qualities you feel are important in life and learning.
- Use resources around the home to help children learn basic skills.
- Take advantage of every hands-on learning opportunity.
- Make connections from one subject matter to another.
- Ask questions, and encourage the use of reasoning and thinking skills.
- Brainstorm together on new or better ways to learn.
- Provide positive feedback on daily activities.
- Read, read, read, and discuss, discuss, discuss.

When a child learns about a subject in several different ways, he learns it better and retains the information longer. Therefore, incorporate aspects from various learning styles into your lesson plans to widen your child's experiences and sensations.

Your Own Strengths and Weaknesses

Just as each child has his own strengths and weaknesses, so do all parents. You may have a great grasp of the English language, but you may be slipping a bit in the math department. Fearfully, you wonder how you will ever be able to teach math to your child. Don't worry. Some homeschooled kids grasp concepts quicker than parents do, and soon they'll be explaining it to you. But what if they don't?

No one said you have to be an expert in every subject in order to homeschool your child. When *you* don't have the ability or resources to teach a subject or two, there is always someone else who does. There are tutors at the library, college kids down the street, or retired teachers in the community.

Another helpful resource is your local homeschool group. There you can find moms and dads who have a special knack for math, science, art, or music. While they help your child in areas you are weak in, you can help their child in an area you are strong in.

Older homeschooled children are especially eager to help younger ones learn, so don't overlook them for helping with math or reading skills. Sometimes, a child finds it difficult to learn something from mom or dad, but put him with a "study buddy" and he picks it up in a flash.

Together, you and your children will be able to pinpoint and improve weak areas as well as build upon strong areas, culminating in a solid learning environment that works for the whole family.

Chapter 3

Getting Started

As little as ten or fifteen years ago, homeschoolers had difficulty finding information on home education. Today, nearly everyone knows someone who has homeschooled, and information is readily available. But to make things easier on you, this chapter presents the information and resources that you need to get started.

Legal Requirements

Homeschooling is legal in every state, but each state has its own set of requirements. The laws and regulations can vary widely from state to state, so you will need to read the laws pertaining to your specific locale.

Some states require homeschools to operate similar to private schools. Some ask to see an outline of your educational goals, and others require that a form be filled out and submitted to your superintendent's office. Some states require that a certified teacher observe your child's progress periodically, some require you to keep a portfolio of schoolwork and projects, and others require standardized testing.

Most states offer one or two options, so that you can abide by the law that will work best in your family. In some states, for instance, you may have the option of establishing a home school, operating as a private school, or using a private tutor. You may opt to have your child's progress evaluated by a certified teacher, have your child take a national standardized test, or participate in testing on a local level. Some states are more lenient and do not require testing, evaluating, or record keeping, while others are more stringent in varying degrees.

If state regulations seem too confusing or unfathomable, don't be intimidated. If there's something you don't understand, such as "operate a home school as a public school," "be supervised by a certified teacher," or "file a notarized affidavit," don't let the legalese deter you! The wording of the laws is usually more confusing than the actual regulation.

Your State's Homeschool Laws

To find homeschool laws and regulations for your state, visit the Home School Legal Defense Association's Web site, *www.hslda.org*. Click the "Legal" tab, then "Home School Laws," then select any state. You'll find the legal options, attendance requirements, subjects that may be required, necessary qualifications, notices, record keeping, and testing. If your state does not specify what subjects to cover or does not require testing or other criteria, "None" will be noted in that category.

The Home School Legal Defense Association

If you have any concerns, questions, or problems regarding legal aspects of home education, contact the Home School Legal Defense Association (HSLDA). This nonprofit organization defends parental rights to homeschool, represents families who may experience legal conflicts over homeschooling, lobbies Congress on homeschool issues, and monitors laws and conducts research on home education.

The Web site for the Home School Legal Defense Association, *www.hslda.org,* includes the latest information on homeschool laws, parental rights, legislation, and legal news affecting homeschoolers. You can sign up for their free electronic newsletter, which covers national and international issues, proposed bills, or changes in state homeschool laws.

The HSLDA also encourages homeschoolers and homeschool groups to work together to better educate the public and legislators on the benefits of home education, to participate in homeschool legislative issues at local and state levels, and to involve state representatives and senators in homeschool organizations and conferences. Through sharing personal successes with legislators and the public, families can continue to communicate the educational benefits and moral outcomes of home education. This, in turn, helps to promote public awareness of every family's right to educational freedom and the right to a quality education for their children.

State Homeschool Departments of Education

Each state's department of education can assist you with homeschool requirements. Simply make a phone call to the homeschool division of your state department of education or to your local school district. Most have a homeschool division or an alternative education department, or, at the least, they'll be able to put you in touch with the proper person. If you have Internet access, you can visit your state's department of education Web site and determine what you need to know.

To find your state's education agency via the Internet, you can access the map at ✍ *www.ccsso.org/seamenu.html* and click on your state. For instance, clicking on Florida will bring up the Web site for the Florida Department of Education. You can then scroll down the menu until you reach Home Education, and click "Go." Everything you need to know about homeschooling in Florida is presented to you, including the phone number and e-mail address for the contact person, regulations on homeschooling, how to file a notice of intent to homeschool, curriculum resources, the state's homeschool organization, Florida Parent-Educators Association (FPEA), and even a link to Florida's Virtual School.

FACT

Homeschool events and conferences can be found on the Home School Legal Defense Association's Web site at ✍ *www.hslda.org.* Click the "Home Schooling" tab, then "Events Calendar." Check with your local homeschool group for events in your area, too, such as curriculum fairs, science fairs, field trips, and other educational or recreational activities.

Whichever state you're in, you will be able to find the necessary information for homeschooling in your area. Or, if you're planning a move to a new state, you can check that state's requirements ahead of time and begin making arrangements. If you're unable to find homeschool information on the Web site you've selected, call the state department of education directly and ask them to send their homeschool information packet to you.

Homeschool Groups

Homeschool groups have played a major role in clarifying homeschool laws, bringing homeschools and traditional schools closer together and also helping to educate the public and the media on homeschooling philosophies and principles. Not only do the groups monitor laws and legislation at local, state, and national levels, they also provide the contact that homeschool families need with each other.

Even parents who have supportive friends and families often find that they need time with others who are in their shoes, who understand what homeschool days are like, and who share similar concerns and goals for their families. This is the role of the local homeschool groups.

If your community does not currently have a local homeschool support group, you can always start one yourself. Place notices in community centers, public libraries, parks and recreation departments, educational supply stores, and children's consignment shops. Advise the homeschool division of your local school district of your intent and ask the administrator to direct interested parties your way.

Local Homeschool Groups

Nearly every town, county, or community has at least one homeschool group. Many have several, with each group serving different needs within the community. Yet all local groups share the same goals: to provide information, support, and a gathering place for homeschoolers.

Some groups have specific religious affiliations, while others are open to all, regardless of faith or philosophies. Many groups produce monthly newsletters, convey information to the local media, set up an information hotline, arrange field trips and educational activities, establish book loan programs, share curriculum ideas, and otherwise help families with homeschool and socialization needs. They may also hold curriculum fairs, co-op classes, sports events, skating parties, musicals or theatrical presentations, and much more.

State Homeschool Organizations

State organizations provide information on state laws, are aware of proposed changes regarding home education in their state, and work with legislative bodies. They may produce homeschool guides that answer questions on homeschooling within their state, as well as newsletters that are distributed to local homeschool groups around the state. They also arrange state conferences, curriculum fairs, and workshops. In addition, they may participate in state and national surveys on homeschooling, provide statistical information on homeschoolers within their state, and keep databases of state certified teachers, testers, psychologists, or special-needs therapists who enjoy working with homeschool families.

National Homeschool Associations

National associations tend to focus on specific areas or concerns, such as the Home School Legal Defense Association, National Challenged Homeschoolers, African-American Homeschoolers, Native American Homeschool Association, National Association of Hispanic-American Homeschoolers, or the American Homeschool Association. Others may have religious affiliations.

In general, these national groups provide a contact point for state groups. They gather and report on homeschool news across the nation, and they also maintain Web sites or databases with links to resources concerning their special interest groups.

Listings for local, state, and national homeschool organizations are available on the Web. Use search engines such as Google or Yahoo! to find the group of your choice. If you're unable to find a group in your area, call the homeschool division of your local school district, the public library, or an educational supply store. They often keep lists of homeschool groups or contacts.

Withdrawing Your Child from School

Some states may allow you to remove your child from school at any time during the year, as long as you file a notice of intent to homeschool within thirty days of establishing your homeschool. Others require you to file a notice of intent fourteen days *prior* to withdrawing your child from school. Still others do not require a notice of intent to be filed at all, but they may have other regulations you'll need to follow.

FACT

You can reinstate your child in school at any time. If your child wants to return to public school, visit the school, talk with teachers and administrators, and fill out the paperwork. Set up a meeting with teachers to discuss your child's homeschool background and share any recent test results, schoolwork, or the homeschool portfolio. This provides the teacher with a better understanding of your child's current academic achievements.

Some parents prefer to let the child finish the current school year; others make the transition during semester breaks. Some can begin homeschooling their children in the middle of October if they'd like, or the latter part of February. Just be sure to check with your state's requirements before beginning. As a parent, you don't want to be the one who is uninformed when homeschooling laws are concerned. Determine what your obligations are in advance, and plan accordingly.

Registering for Homeschooling

After you've determined your state's homeschool requirements, you can take the necessary steps to register your child. If you prefer to establish a homeschool environment based on creating your own curriculum, you may find that registering with your school district is the way to go. Depending on your state, you may need to file a notice of intent to homeschool with your superintendent's office. You may also need to keep a portfolio of your child's projects and school achievements and to have your child's progress evaluated or tested at the end of each school year.

Along with the notice of intent, some states require that you include a letter listing your reasons for wanting to homeschool and why you feel qualified to teach your children. They may also require a description of your goals and objectives for the coming school year, the type of curriculum you plan to use, or a list of subjects you plan to teach.

File a notice of intent to homeschool by requesting the proper form from your local school district. The form is simple to fill out, generally requiring your child's name, date of birth, and grade level, and your signature. After submitting the form, you should receive an acknowledgment of enrollment from the school district, verifying that you are in compliance with your state's home education laws.

If you plan to operate your homeschool under an umbrella or satellite school, or through a private school or via distance learning, you won't need to register with your school district. (See Chapter 4 for the types of homeschooling.) However, you will want to have the pertinent documentation on hand if any questions should arise.

Determining Educational Philosophies, Goals, and Objectives

When registering your intent to homeschool, you may need to submit a letter listing your reasons for wanting to homeschool, as well as your qualifications. This letter need not be difficult to write. Simply look inside yourself and jot down all the reasons that come to mind. You won't need to include all your reasons in your letter, but this free-thinking, free-writing method will help you get your reasons down on paper.

Your Reasons for Homeschooling

Think about your own children and why you feel homeschooling is better for them than traditional schooling, then create your own list. Here is a list of ideas:

- Your children learn better in quiet surroundings.
- Your children learn better when they can move and explore.

- Your children need more creative-thinking activities.
- Your children need more opportunities to direct their own learning.
- Your family enjoys learning and discovering together.
- Your family enjoys taking educational field trips together.
- Your family enjoys reading books and discussing events together.
- Your family prefers to take an active role in the education process.

Educational Philosophies and Goals

Educational philosophies focus on what you feel your children should learn to prepare them for their lives today and for a happy, successful adulthood. Since you are the child's parent and you understand your child better than anyone, you might feel that you are the most qualified to pass these philosophies on to your children. Your educational philosophies and goals for your children may include any of the following:

- Learn how to get along with others.
- Learn proper manners and respect for others.
- Care about family and your place within the family.
- Have a sense of duty within the home and family.
- Care about the community and your place in it.
- Have a sense of duty within the community.
- Appreciate the environment and beauty of nature.
- Live healthfully, happily, and responsibly.
- Understand and reflect family values, morals, and religious beliefs.

Educational Objectives

Your educational philosophies may remain fairly constant throughout your family's homeschooling years; however, your goals may change and expand as your child grows and matures. Your educational objectives should go hand in hand with your goals, supporting your overall philosophy of what you believe your children should learn in preparation for life. You should review your goals and objectives at the beginning of each new school year. The following are some basic educational objectives.

- Develop a good sense of self-worth and self-confidence.
- Improve self-discipline and self-control.
- Acquire proper social skills for real-world interactions.
- Learn how to access and apply information.
- Read quality literature and classics.
- Improve speaking and writing skills.
- Improve mathematical and scientific abilities.
- Enhance musical, artistic, and creative skills.
- Understand world and national history and politics.
- Function responsibly as a citizen and respect cultural differences.
- Strengthen understanding of right and wrong.
- Learn and apply good decision-making skills.
- Develop life skills and skills critical to career goals.
- Practice healthy habits, emotionally and physically.
- Have time to explore and enjoy surroundings each day.

You can create your own curriculum for your child based upon your educational philosophies, goals, and objectives. Apply your family's mission and goals to each subject area (such as reading, writing, math, science, and social studies) and weave your objectives into the daily lessons. You'll quickly see how well your child is learning according to your family's philosophies and desires.

School Support for Homeschoolers

Although there have been stories and cases of cantankerous school officials creating anguish for homeschool families, the number of incidences have declined in recent years. This is due, in large part, to a better understanding of home education, more media coverage of homeschool families, and the opportunity to view a broader cross-section of the homeschool population.

This all leads to better acceptance on the part of school officials, and, in many cases, to their genuine interest in working with homeschool families. Consequently, some public schools are now more open to homeschooled children attending part time or enrolling in individual courses such as science, chemistry, home economics, or shop classes. Some schools may even allow homeschoolers to participate in band, drama, or school sports.

Sports and School

Sports can be a sticky subject, since maintaining passing grades is imperative for sports participants, particularly at the high-school level. Homeschoolers who are allowed to take part in sports programs may be required to provide proof of their grades and follow the same rules that apply to all students enrolled in school sports. At the high-school level, some schools must abide by the rules of their state athletic association. Check with your school, and ascertain what rules would apply to your child in relation to its sports program.

QUESTION?

How can my child participate in team sports?
Start your own homeschool sports team! Get other homeschool families involved, arrange to use local ballparks or basketball courts, and designate practice and game times. Allow kids to take turns being cheerleaders, team assistants, and to operate refreshment booths or sell homeschool bumper stickers to benefit the team and your homeschool group.

Sports are also offered in a variety of ways within the community. Check with your parks and recreation department or community colleges. They often hold organized sports events or have volleyball and softball teams, tennis, golf, bowling, skiing, martial arts, gymnastics, choreographed swimming, and other recreational activities for all ages.

Materials Made Available

In 1999, the U.S. Department of Education's National Household Education Survey (NHES) released information on a number of homeschool families receiving support from public schools or local school districts. Approximately 10 percent of the parents surveyed reported that they used books or materials provided by their district, 8 percent used the curriculum that was available, 7 percent used meeting places provided by the district for homeschooled children, and less than 3 percent enrolled their homeschooled children in part-time school classes.

However, over 27 percent of the parents surveyed did not know books or materials were available through their districts, 30 percent were unaware that there was a curriculum available, 19 percent were unaware of meeting places for homeschooled children in the school district, and 31 percent were unaware that their children could attend part-time classes in those states.

Even if your school district does not provide the support you would like to have, remember that homeschool groups and associations are there to support your homeschool endeavors. They can help you find the type of homeschooling or curriculum you need, help you comply with state laws or explain the laws to you, and demonstrate how easily and successfully homeschooling is working for their families and children. You need never feel as if you are in this alone. Hundreds of thousands of other families are homeschooling, too!

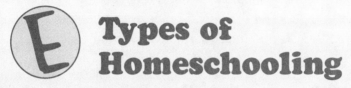

Chapter 4

Types of Homeschooling

The type of homeschooling your family engages in will largely depend upon your child's learning style and your personal teaching style. Some families prefer to establish themselves as umbrella or satellite schools. Some will register with a correspondence school, while others like a more flexible, eclectic approach. This chapter will explain these and other types of homeschooling.

Secular Homeschooling

Many homeschool curricula and materials are Christian-based, such as Abeka, Alpha Omega, and Bob Jones University Press, to name just a few. While these are popular curricula, some families prefer to use secular materials, which are not specifically religious in content. With this style of homeschooling, you can supplement the curriculum where you deem it necessary, decide the order in which topics are studied, or skip parts of the curriculum that do not meet your family's educational goals.

Secular materials can be similar to the curriculum used in public schools. However, in the homeschool, you can choose which materials to purchase, and you'll have more control over the lessons. You can purchase a complete curriculum for a specific grade level, or only the materials you currently need.

It's also not necessary to purchase all the materials from one company. You can purchase materials from various publishers or suppliers. For instance, you may choose to use math books from a publisher who specializes in math materials, grammar books from a publisher specializing in language arts books, etc.

Secular Materials

Many public school systems offer textbooks and educational materials to homeschool families, so check with your local school district. Local teacher or school supply stores also carry a wide variety of resource books, activity books, workbooks, software, and educational games, covering most subject areas.

Mail-order catalogs usually carry a wide variety of educational books and materials. Here, you can often find popular books and manipulatives, such as *Miquon Math,* Cuisenaire Rods, "Backyard Scientist" series, and Adventure in Science kits. There are Usborne's history-theme cut-out Models, *A History of Us,* Smart Cubes word games, *Learning Language Arts Through Literature,* and many other secular books and games.

If your child enjoys reading textbooks and answering the questions at the end of the chapters, you might want to invest in a few good textbooks. These can be found at book sales; through publishers, such as Addison Wesley, Holt, Houghton Mifflin, Prentice Hall, Scott Foresman, and other textbook publishing companies; or through used homeschool suppliers, such as The Back Pack (✐ *www.thebackpack.com*), The Educator's Exchange (✐ *www.edexbooks.com*), or Laurelwood Books (✐ *www.laurelwoodbooks.com*).

Secular Curriculum Providers

If you find that trying to choose among the variety of materials is getting too confusing, secular curriculum suppliers, such as Core Curriculum of America (✐ *www.core-curriculum.com*) or Curriculum Services (✐ *www.curriculumservices.com*), might be the way to go. These types of services can provide a complete curriculum for an entire year, or you can create a curriculum specifically tailored to your child's interests and needs.

Homeschool support groups often dedicate one or two meetings a year to displaying and discussing the curriculum or resources they use with their families, and they welcome other interested families to attend.

Before making a decision, always try to talk with other homeschool families about the materials or services they use. They can provide wonderful insight into the products, format, scope and sequence, and the way the curriculum or materials suit their child's learning style. In Chapter 7, we'll look at curriculum choices in more detail, as well as how you can create your own curriculum.

Religion-Based Homeschooling

Many families believe that a spiritual foundation is key to a moral education. If this describes your family's philosophy, a multitude of curricula and materials are available for your faith-based homeschool. You may use a traditional curriculum similar to the one taught in public schools, such as the suggestions noted above, and add a study unit based on your family's religious beliefs. Or you may prefer that each subject area of the curriculum incorporates your family's spiritual beliefs.

A science curriculum, for example, may be secular and focus more on an evolutionary theory, while a faith-based science curriculum may incorporate a creationist point of view. These can be important points for families to consider when purchasing curriculum and supplemental books.

Homeschool curriculums and books are available for nearly every religious belief and culture. From Catholic to Islamic, Jewish, Latter-Day Saints, or Native American, you'll be able to find resources to suit your family's homeschool style.

Christian Homeschool Choices

If you plan to incorporate Christian doctrines into your homeschool, you'll have a multitude of curricula and materials to choose from. Many of the Christian correspondence schools and curriculum companies offer testing services, evaluations, grading, record keeping, and diplomas. You often have the choice of teacher assistance to help guide you through the school year or of being in charge of the program yourself, allowing for more flexibility.

FACT

If your community is interested in starting its own Christian school, meet with interested parties and include parents and the community. Research, discuss, and finalize your mission; develop a curriculum; determine how the school will be operated; settle on a budget and tuition; and seek teachers who share your visions for the school. Alpha Omega Publications (*www.aop.com*) also offers a guide called *How to Start a Christian School.*

Abeka (*www.abeka.org*) provides a curriculum package with or without teacher assistance, as well as educational programs available via video or DVD and numerous textbooks to choose from. With Alpha Omega (✐*www.aop.com*), you can choose the LIFEPAC curriculum, the Switched-On Schoolhouse curriculum on a CD, or their new online curriculum, ✐*www.Classes2You.com.* Bob Jones University Press (✐*www.bjup.com*) offers a complete curriculum or you can choose from textbooks, videos, satellite programs, and other resources. The Christian Liberty Academy School System, called CLASS (✐*www.homeschools.org*), provides a curriculum based upon each child's needs and abilities, plus a full-service plan or a family-service plan, which allows you to control the workload.

Catholic Homeschool Choices

The Catholic Home School Network of America (✐*www.chsna.org*) and the National Association of Catholic Home Educators (✐*www. nache.org*) provide extensive information on Catholic home education programs. Seton School (✐*www.setonhome.org*) and Kolbe Academy (✐*www.kolbe.org*) both offer a full curriculum for kinder-garten through the twelfth grade. Catholic books, games, and other supplemental materials are available through Heritage Catholic Curricula (✐*www.chcweb.com*).

Additional Faith-Based Homeschool Choices

Islamic homeschoolers can look to ArabesQ (✐*www.arabesq.com*) for homeschool curriculum for kindergarten through the twelfth grade, or they can visit Islamic School's site (✐*www.islamicschool.net*). Families can also turn to the Muslim Homeschool Web site (✐*www.muslimhomeschool.com*) for homeschool resources.

Jewish families have the Jewish Home Educators Network (✐*www. snj.com/jhen*) and the Bnos Henya Project (✐*www.bnoshenya.org*), both providing information on curriculum resources. You can also find Jewish homeschool supplies at A.R.E. Publishing, Inc. (✐*www.arepublish.com*), Behrman House Publishers and Booksellers (✐*www.behrmanhouse.com*), and Torah Aura Productions (✐*www.torahaura.com*).

Latter-Day Saints can contact the LDS Homeschooling Organization at ✐*www.ldshomeschooling.org* or the Latter-Day Saints Home Educators

Association at ✍ *www.ldshea.org* for homeschooling information, curriculum, and books.

Native American families can find support in the Native American Homeschool Association at ✍ *www.expage.com/page/nahomeschool.* The organization provides educational resources, lists of support groups, and a homeschooling newsletter.

Whatever your religious beliefs, there are books, curriculum, and supplemental materials designed just for you and your family.

Umbrella and Satellite Schools

You can establish your homeschool under an umbrella or satellite school. These schools are set up to provide cover, or an "umbrella," for families who were unable to homeschool on their own or who would just rather not go it alone. The umbrella schools are often private or alternative schools.

ALERT!

Some people believe that umbrella schools are solely religion-based. Although some are, many are not. Don't be afraid to ask when contacting the school. Better yet, speak with families who are enrolled with the schools, and always ask the school to send their complete information packet to you.

The umbrella or satellite schools can provide curriculum guidance, materials, testing services, record keeping, high-school transcripts, accredited diplomas, and other areas of assistance. Yet the education still takes place in the home; it isn't necessary to travel to a specific school or facility each day. A fee is charged for the services that umbrella or satellite schools provide, depending on the range of services offered.

To find umbrella or satellite schools in your area, contact your local school district and ask if they keep a list of such schools. Your homeschool support group is another good source of information on umbrella schools in your area. If you're unable to locate a school through these resources, try calling local private schools or church-based schools to see if they offer home education programs through their facilities.

Charter Schools, Vouchers, and Cooperatives

Charter schools were initially set up by a group of interested parents and teachers who drew up a "charter," or written document, outlining the purpose and goals for their school. These schools were usually funded by private individuals or institutions. Today, many charter schools and the voucher system have become a project of the state, and the schools may be publicly funded at the state or local levels. Additionally, when conventional public schools receive "failing grades" within a certain time frame, such as two years out of four, students can choose to use vouchers in a specific dollar amount and leave that school to enroll in a private school or other school of choice.

In some states, a charter school may still be funded by private institutions or grants. School boards are formed; members invest in the school; and parents, teachers, and staff operate the school. Even though the charter school may be similar to a traditional school, the teachers and staff have more input regarding the curriculum and teaching methods than they would have in a public school.

FACT

Over 2,400 charter schools opened within ten years of the time the first charter school law was passed in 1991. To learn more about charter schools, or to find those in your area, visit *www.edreform.com/charter_schools/websites.* Click on the state, then select the charter school nearest you and visit their Web site.

Cooperatives As Alternatives

Today, when parents wish to create a place where homeschoolers can come together for learning activities, it's usually called a cooperative, rather than a charter school. If your group is interested in forming a homeschool co-op, spend some time discussing your reasons and establish a format that is agreeable to all. If possible, talk with others who have had experience in setting up a co-op. You may want to elect a few people or a committee to be in charge of overseeing the activities, to set up meetings or arrange field trips, and to schedule volunteers. Each parent whose child participates in the co-op should be willing to volunteer services or assistance when his or her time comes around.

Teaching in a Cooperative

Parents who have stronger skills in a certain subject area will often be in charge of teaching or guiding that topic. If several parents are interested in the same subject area—for instance, arts and crafts or science experiments—they can contribute on a rotation basis: this parent this week, that parent next week, and so on. If no one is stepping forward with an interest in math or history, perhaps a couple of parents could work together to create projects in those areas.

Co-ops may require fees to help offset the cost of materials, craft supplies, or books. Some may charge a small monthly fee, while others may ask participating families to chip in when planning a specific project, based on the number of children taking part and the cost of materials.

If no one in your cooperative possesses mathematical or scientific skills, don't worry. Contact your local college or association of retired business professionals and see if they know of anyone who might be interested in guiding the children through some related concepts or experiments. The same is true if your group appears to have no one with artistic or musical talents. Your community's parks and recreation department often offers art and music classes, so contact them about your co-op's needs. The fee to bring in an outsider might be more than your co-op had planned on, but the dividends could pay off quite well in your children's education and hands-on experiences.

Hosting a Cooperative

In some cooperatives, parents take turns hosting the classes in their homes—perhaps in a family room, basement, dining room, or kitchen. In other co-ops, one or two families offer to host the classes, understanding that some families simply don't have the extra space or that their schedule doesn't allow for hosting regular classes. Some co-ops have found that they can meet at a local church, and, for some projects and climates, they find that using the shelter in a nearby park works out well.

As you discuss and refine plans for your homeschool cooperative, you may come up with ideas that will work beautifully for everyone involved. As you progress through the months ahead, parts of the co-op may even shift and change.

Independent Study Programs

Independent study programs, such as Clonlara School (*www.clonlara.org*) or Home Study International (*www.hsi.edu*), sometimes called ISPs, are a form of correspondence or distance-learning schools. The concept is that a student is sent a curriculum package via mail. He then studies, completes the lessons, and returns the lessons to the school to be assessed and graded. Tests are sometimes administered, graded, and returned to the student, or evaluations of the student's capabilities may be conducted.

Most of these schools take care of the record-keeping process (and can provide verification of such to your school district, if need be) and they take care of the lesson planning, both of which free up a parent's time. As a result, you will have more time to spend with your children, providing the interaction and one-on-one guidance that is important in a homeschool setting.

Not every child is suited to the independent study procedure, though. In many cases, families supplement the ISP with additional hands-on activities, field trips and learning excursions, and more participation in community events to help add variety to the program. In fact, most distance-learning programs encourage students to become involved in the community and in a variety of extracurricular classes and projects.

The majority of independent study programs developed for homeschoolers are geared toward providing a well-rounded education in the best way they can. Many offer options, such as designing a curriculum individually tailored to your child's needs or assigning a specific teacher to your child. These services may require a separate fee in addition to the enrollment or course fees. Check with each school to determine what their services and fees cover.

Many of these schools are well respected and accredited, keeping transcripts of your child's high-school years and granting diplomas upon graduation. Some even go to the next level, holding formal graduation ceremonies and encouraging all graduating seniors to attend. They may even hold yearbook signings and proms for students who live nearby or who are able to travel the distance to attend.

Remember that you don't have to remain with a program that's simply not working for your children or your family. Rather than giving up on homeschooling, look into the many other options that are out there. You can use a combination of curricula, create an eclectic blend of your own, or follow the unschooling route.

Enrolling in an Independent Study Program

Before contacting a school, have a list of questions ready, and obtain as much information as possible over the phone. When you receive their information packet, be sure it answers all your questions. If not, call the school for further information.

Before enrolling your child in an ISP, you will want to consider several points:

1. Be cognizant of your child's learning style and study habits. If your child is not one who can learn well while sitting still or who requires more physical activity while learning (a kinesthetic-tactile learner), some ISPs may not be for her.
2. Discuss with your child her ability to study on her own and to stay on a task with limited reminders from others, as well as her ability to

be fairly responsible for her studies.

3. Determine how much structure, or flexibility, your child seems to need in his studies.

4. Request the school's information packet and samples of their typical lessons or assignments, then go over these with your child.

5. Talk with other families enrolled in the ISP and have them share their experiences with you and your child.

6. Find out from the ISP exactly how much busywork, reading, worksheets, or "homework" is required, so that you and your child will know what is required from the beginning.

7. Ask the ISP if they accept artwork, construction projects, hands-on activities, or extracurricular classes to meet some of the requirements for the program.

8. Determine exactly what each fee covers, and find out if the school offers a refund policy if you decide to cancel within a specific time frame.

FACT

Some independent study programs offer a choice of textbook-based studies, video-based studies, or lessons on CD-ROM. Some may even offer online courses or satellite programs in lieu of the traditional correspondence program. Be sure to ask which formats the programs offer when requesting their information packet.

Costs of an ISP

Tuition fees can range from $300 to $700 per school year, depending on the school. Fees at some schools are all inclusive, while others may have extra fees for additional services. In some cases, costs may be broken down by enrollment or registration fee, tuition fee, and materials or supplies fees. Keep in mind that a kindergarten or first-grade curriculum is usually priced lower than a fourth-grade or sixth-grade curriculum. The costs for high-school programs are often based on a per-course fee. Most schools have installment payment plans available.

You can check with the following correspondence schools for information on their services.

- American School: ✍ *www.americanschoolofcorr.com*
- Cambridge Academy: ✍ *www.cambridgeacademy.com*
- Chrysalis School: ✍ *www.chrysalis-school.com*
- Citizen High School: ✍ *www.citizenschool.com*
- Clonlara School: ✍ *www.clonlara.org*
- Home Study International: ✍ *www.hsi.edu*
- Laurel Springs: ✍ *www.laurelsprings.com*
- Moore Academy: ✍ *www.moorefoundation.com*
- Oak Meadow: ✍ *www.oakmeadow.com*
- SeaScape Educational Center: ✍ *www.seascapecenter.com*

If your teenager is interested in a high-school independent study program, check to be sure it's fully accredited. The Distance Education and Training Council keeps track of accredited high schools, colleges, and business and training schools that provide correspondence studies. Visit their Web site at ✍ *www.detc.org* to view their list of accredited schools.

Virtual Learning and Cyber Schools

A virtual school or cyber school is an educational program available through the Internet. Education provided on the Web continues to attract interest and gain acceptance. Today, many school systems have developed a Web presence that provides courses via the Internet. Several of the traditional correspondence schools and curriculum providers also offer programs over the Internet. Students can study online and correspond with instructors and classmates via e-mail, thus reducing the turnaround time of lessons, grades, and feedback.

On the downside, online courses can eventually become as tedious as workbook pages. Supplementing the virtual learning with hands-on learning will enliven the child's environment, helping to keep learning fun. By monitoring the coursework and topics being studied, you and your child can develop experiments, activities, and field trips that can complement and reinforce the online courses.

The online K12 homeschool program (✍*www.k12.com*), directed by former education secretary William Bennett, currently includes a complete curriculum online for kindergarten through the fifth grade. Students can enroll in the complete program or choose individual courses. Alpha Omega's Classes2You (✍*www.classes2you.com*) curriculum is now offered for grades three through twelve. You have the choice of purchasing the full year's online program or buying only one study unit at a time.

Cyber high schools are also gaining popularity. There's Babbage Net School (✍*www.babbagenetschool.com*), CompuHigh online (✍*www.compuhigh.com*), Francis Virtual School (✍*www.francisvirtualschool.org*), or the International High School (✍*www.internationalhigh.org*). Several states also offer online courses, such as Florida Virtual School (✍*www.flvs.net*) and Texas Virtual School (✍*www.texasvirtualschool.org*). A comprehensive list of cyber schools is available at the Distance Learning Resource Network's Web site, ✍*www.dlrn.org/virtual.html.*

Eclectic Schooling

Families who use an eclectic format may use parts of a packaged curriculum along with activity books from the local school supply store, educational games on the Internet, and a few textbooks from local book sales. They may pick and choose individual courses from a curriculum provider, enlist in a course or two through a virtual school, select a variety of hands-on experiments for science, some geography and history games for social studies, and Saxon textbooks and Cuisenaire Rods for math concepts.

An eclectic style does not tie a family to one type of curriculum or teaching method. In an eclectic homeschool, you can channel the curriculum more toward your child's individual learning style and interests. You'll have endless opportunities to creatively supplement the curriculum, and your child will be less likely to become bored.

An eclectic style could combine a good mix of stimulating activities with quiet learning activities. For instance, you can offset the time spent on a virtual school's history course, an educational computer game, and a grammar workbook with your own chemistry set, 3-D logic puzzles, and a robotic construction set. You can spend family time together, reading through interesting books from the library; playing a few rounds of challenging board games, such as Life, Monopoly, or chess; and engaging in recreational games outdoors for your physical education class.

Unschooling and Deschooling

Unschooling can be similar to an eclectic style of homeschooling but with even less daily structure. Rather, it's the belief that learning is a natural part of each day. As we live, so do we learn; the experiences encountered each day contribute to one's education. Unschooling usually follows the child's interests and learning style, and often the child is largely responsible for his weekly activities, with some guidance and input from mom or dad. Chapter 5 covers unschooling in more detail.

Deschooling is similar to unschooling, in that it further distances itself from conventional schooling. Deschooling may be considered a part of the decompression period when a child leaves a traditional school environment and adjusts to the homeschool environment. The parent helps to "deschool" the child—separating him from a rigid school structure—by allowing the freedom to simply sit and think, to read books for pleasure, to function within his day without the sound of bells or moving through lines, and to spend time outdoors. During this time, the child can unwind and decompress, as he moves further away from the confines of a school environment.

Preschoolers

Depending on the age of the child, their self-directed education can encompass a wide range of activities. When observing preschoolers, you'll quickly see how much they learn in a fairly short period of time. They love to imitate and play make-believe, day in and day out. Through this play and imitation of siblings or grownups they naturally learn, grow, and fine-tune their skills.

Elementary-Aged Children

By the time they are elementary-aged, most children are eager to "play school." Again, their learning comes through play. By allowing them to play school, you are allowing them to learn. Sometimes, they want to be the student in their play schools, and sometimes they want to be the teacher. As teachers, these new, young students can teach us a lot! We need only sit back and watch in order to be amazed by their fresh knowledge and abilities.

Teenagers

By the time they are teenagers, children have so many interests, thoughts, and ideas they want to pursue that there is hardly enough time to embrace them all. When they are allowed to follow their interests and self-direct their learning, they are better able to experience—and learn from—the many elements of life that have captivated and inspired them.

ALERT!

The key to a successful "unschooled homeschool" is to ensure that your child's environment contains stimulating activities, concepts, and discussions; creative ideas and projects for encouraging learning; opportunities to interact with others and to interact with nature; and resources for new ideas and experiences to explore.

Unit or Theme Studies

Unit studies focus on a specific theme or topic while incorporating the core subject areas into the study. The topic or theme is usually one that interests a child at a certain time in his or her life—for instance, animals, dinosaurs, vehicles, sports, popular book series, or holidays. There are no limits to the topics, themes, and areas of interest a unit study can cover.

A unit study can last as little as one week or as long as a semester. A unit study focusing on Thanksgiving may only last for a week prior to the holiday. It could run longer or shorter, but after Thanksgiving has passed, interest in the holiday tends to wane. A unit study revolving around animals, sports, or comic books could last for several weeks.

ALERT!

Although unit studies are a wonderful way to cover several subject areas in an interesting and relevant manner, you won't want to neglect certain math skills, grammar rules, and important historical events or scientific studies. A flexible and varied homeschool format helps to promote knowledge, thinking skills, and interest in learning, which together lead to a well-rounded education.

Heart of Wisdom (*www.homeschoolunitstudies.com*) offers Bible-based unit studies focusing on history and science. These units can run the length of a typical school year, with five to seven lessons covered in one week. With these units, you'll want to add math and language arts to complete the curriculum.

Amanda Bennett's unit study series (*www.unitstudy.com*), another popular program, has weekly learning objectives and daily lesson plans and activities, and are adaptable to elementary students and middle- to upper-level students. A few of these unit studies are also available online.

Some families prefer to create their own unit studies. In Chapter 5, you'll get more information on how this can be done.

Year-Round Schooling

Your state may require that you homeschool 180 days a year, but they may place no restrictions on when those days fall. You may want to homeschool from September through May, so that your children are off in the summer when the neighbor kids are on their summer break. Or, instead of homeschooling five days a week, four weeks a month, which is twenty days per month, your homeschool days may include each day of the month, covering approximately thirty days per month and reaching the 180-day quota in just six months, rather than nine months. Therefore, you might homeschool from the first of January until the end of June.

Following a structured schedule for thirty days in a row, month after month, can become stressful, though—even if you do "get done" three months early! For some families, following a structured schedule for twenty days each month can also be a bit much. That's why some like the concept of a year-round homeschool. You can cover the same amount of ground, but you get to take breaks more frequently.

A Flexible Schedule

With year-round schooling, you may choose to start in September, then take a week off each month. Your schedule will then include fifteen homeschooled days each month (five days a week, three weeks a month). Following this schedule, you'll reach the 180-day quota within twelve months, resulting in year-round schooling, but with a week off each month.

Before making the decision to purchase a curriculum or enroll in a school, try to visit curriculum fairs and homeschool conventions so that you can personally look over the products or services. Have a list of questions ready to ask the representatives at the conventions. Also, talk with homeschool families about the type of educational format they've chosen to use in their homes.

Another option is to follow the traditional twenty-day month, but take a month off between Thanksgiving and Christmas, a month off in the spring, and a month off in the summer, rather than taking the entire summer off. You'll still end up with twelve weeks off.

Sometimes grandparents or friends may plan to spend a month with your family. You'll want to juggle the homeschool year to accommodate their visit and not be tied to a specific schedule while they are in town. Or your family may be expecting a new arrival, and you may want to set aside three months in a row to welcome the new bundle of joy into your family. You can always reschedule the homeschool year accordingly.

Benefits and Drawbacks

Other benefits of year-round schooling include spending less time on review at the beginning of the school year and less time getting the children back into a more formal schedule. When lessons and learning are spread throughout the year, the skills and the schedule come more easily.

If more breaks occur more regularly throughout the year, children and parents are better able to disconnect from the schedule and recharge their batteries more often. Less frequent, but longer, breaks can make it difficult for both parents and children to get back into the school habit when the free days of summer come to an end.

One of the most common drawbacks of year-round schooling is that children feel cheated out of their summer break, which "all the other kids have." A good way to handle this is to allow your children to take off the first week or two that corresponds with the public school's first weeks of summer vacation. After a couple weeks of being with their friends again on a daily basis, summer boredom can begin to set in. Then you can start drawing your children back into the homeschool by following a less structured "summer school" format, with more activities, field trips, and explorations, and fewer workbooks and assignment sheets. By inviting some of the neighbor kids to participate, too, everyone may spend more time at your house, enjoying the fun and novelty of "summer homeschool."

Chapter 5

Understanding Unschooling and Unit Studies

Children are born with a natural curiosity. When their curiosity is suppressed, their learning is dimmed. When their curiosity is encouraged with nurturing guidance, their learning accelerates. Unschooling is a form of nurturing guidance that can help enhance your child's natural curiosity and education.

Unschooling: A Way of Life

As parents, we're all intensely aware of how curious children can be. From their first "Why?" questions as toddlers to their "But *why* can't we have the car keys?", we know they can't help but ask "why" of their surroundings and their lives. It's the way of children; it's an innate part of the way they learn. In order to learn, children must be able to ask why. They must be encouraged to ask why, and they must be able to find answers to the reasons why. Unschooling is one of the most natural ways for children to seek the answers to their "why" questions, and one of the most natural ways for children to learn.

Children gain a huge amount of knowledge and skills between birth and age five, without formal schooling. They learn by experimenting, doing, trying and failing, then trying again. Rarely are they deterred, and rarely do they give up. On the contrary, young children enjoy experimenting—they enjoy trying one way, and if it doesn't work, trying another. Just as curiosity is an innate quality in children, so is the desire to learn new things.

FACT

When children are allowed to remain curious about the world around them, they remain eager to learn. As British author Samuel Johnson stated, "A generous and elevated mind is distinguished by nothing more certainly than an eminent degree of curiosity."

An Unschooling Family

Sara and Michael had each attended public school, then spent a year schooling at home, following a packaged curriculum. For the past three years, they have been involved in an unschooling format. Now, at the ages of nine and eleven, Sara and Michael both read at the eighth-grade level and have middle-school math skills, without following traditional school methods.

Their mother, Karen, explains. "When we first decided to home-school, I don't believe I trusted myself or my children enough. I faithfully followed the curriculum I had purchased, but the kids grew more and more resistant to it. After less than a year of homeschooling, we were all disappointed. And we'd had such high hopes in the beginning!

"A friend suggested that I let the kids follow their own interests more, and allow them more input on what they learn. Even though I had a hard time doing that, I could see how well it worked for my friend's family. I thought I'd try it for a year, before I'd give up and enroll them in school again.

"It was hard at first, to let go of school-like lessons. After all, I had spent over twelve years in school, and it was the only model I had to follow. I was scared that the kids would spend months learning nothing, stagnating. But the strangest thing happened! They were delightedly happy, they kept themselves busy, and they were soon teaching *me* new things. Did I know that Fibonacci numbers could be found in pinecones and sunflowers? Did I know how to create a volcanic eruption out of baking soda and vinegar? They'd then proceed to show me how.

"I could rest assured that each day Sara and Michael would have new bits of knowledge to share with me. Not only could they share their newfound knowledge, but they could explain it, draw diagrams of it, or demonstrate it. Within the first few months of unschooling, I was sold on it. Now, after three years of unschooling, I am amazed at all they have learned and experienced. I couldn't imagine homeschooling any other way."

Examples of Unschooling

Karen's children, Sara and Michael, go about their days in a relaxed style, yet it's not completely without structure. Karen believes, as many unschoolers do, that having some structure each day is important, particularly where chores and responsibilities are concerned. For instance, the children wake up at a decent hour each morning, have breakfast with the family, clean off their plates, make their beds, take their showers, and straighten up any rooms they have used. They feed the cat, take out the trash, sweep off the sidewalk, and complete any other chores required of them.

Once their morning chores are out of the way, they know that their "school day" begins. Since Karen's family discussed the importance of getting a good education at home, and the kids know that their skills will be evaluated at the end of each year, both Sara and Michael understood the importance of unschooling and of learning each day. Compared to their former curriculum, they enjoyed the idea of unschooling so much that they jumped right into it.

A Typical Unschooled Day

On a typical day, the kids find science experiments in library books that they want to do. They conduct the experiments in the kitchen under Karen's supervision, using measuring and math skills, then record the results and their conclusions after the experiments. Michael prefers recording his findings on the computer, while Sara prefers writing in cursive. Michael currently enjoys reading biographies of scientists, and he and Sara often re-enact the scientists' discoveries in the backyard. Even though it's make-believe, they are instinctively reinforcing what Michael has read and shared with Sara.

FACT

When children take an active part in their education, their desire to learn and excel is a joy to behold. Their self-confidence soars and their quest for knowledge knows no bounds. As Sir Walter Scott pointed out, "All men who have turned out worth anything have had the chief hand in their own education."

Sara is reading *Meet Kirsten,* from the American Girl Collection series, and her playtime ventures off from Michael's scientific re-enactments to historic re-enactments of the era surrounding Kirsten's life during the mid-1850s. Sometimes Michael plays along, or he may turn to the cardboard model of Gettysburg that he's been working on in his bedroom. Meanwhile, Sara's interest may move on to feeding the birds in the backyard and taking pictures of them for her "bird and butterfly" photo album. She's trying to include pictures of as many different types of birds and butterflies as possible. She also loves painting with watercolors, and she often paints pictures of the birds and butterflies that she has photographed.

Later in the day, the kids sprawl on the floor to play the Take-Off

Geography game, keeping the globe and a map of the world nearby. They often consult the encyclopedia on different areas of the world and read about the people in those regions. This soon leads to reading various other entries in the encyclopedia on whatever topic captures their interest at that moment.

A Typical Unschooled Evening

As Sara and Michael help with afternoon chores and dinner preparation, they talk with Karen about the things they did or read that day. Over dinner, the entire family discusses their day, as the kids share their daily experiences with their father. This further reinforces the discoveries they made that day and the knowledge they gained.

The evenings are spent similarly to the way they spent their day— working on activities, reading, playing games, doing artwork, spending time outdoors, playing the keyboard, and finishing chores. Karen has asked both children to keep a journal of their daily activities, and most evenings Michael is at the computer, typing about his day of learning, while Sara sits at the dining table, writing about her day in a pink and purple notebook.

Each night, Karen reads aloud from a library book, often a classic or a current bestseller. On this night, it's *Treasure Island*. The television is turned off, the kids are curled up on the sofa on either side of Karen, and Michael doodles on a notepad, sketching pirates, treasure chests, and maps marked with an *X*, as he listens to the story. Dad looks through the day's newspaper, but the kids know he's also enjoying the story being read aloud.

Karen admits that each day is somewhat different, yet each tends to follow a pattern of sorts—the kids do their chores; work on projects and science experiments; play outdoors and re-enact events they've read or learned about; spend time on artwork and music; play games together; read books, magazines, and even encyclopedias; and write each day. A few times a week, they work on math skills and refresh their memories about adverbs and adjectives, building upon knowledge learned in previous weeks. And several times a week they visit the library, attend music classes and gymnastics, run errands, and spend time with family and friends.

Unschool Activities

When children go about their unschooled days, they spend much of their time on topics that interest them the most. Researchers have found that to successfully learn and retain information, children must understand how lessons apply to their interests and goals. These findings appear to support the "unschooled homeschool" method. Here are some activities that you can use in your homeschool to help inspire your child. Ideas like the following can be tailored to your own child's interests and goals:

- Build a birdhouse, dollhouse, robot, radio, model plane, or model city.
- Research the history of dollhouses, robots, radios, planes, or cities.
- Research the scientific background of birdhouses, robots, radios, or planes.
- Encourage the questioning of how these things work, why they work, how they could be improved.
- Write a short book about a dollhouse, a robot, or a model city that comes to life.
- Design the book, type the book, print and bind the book, and distribute it to friends.
- Create artwork for the book, draw diagrams of the project, and take pictures throughout the process.
- Branch off from current interests and activities to explore new projects and ideas.

The Ripple Effect

When it comes to unschooling topics, there is no limit to the ideas and activities that can extend outward from an area of interest. One thing often leads to another, and then to another, until you're amazed at the significant amount of information your child is exploring and absorbing, all on his or her own.

It's similar to the pebble that is dropped into a body of water—the ripples created by that one small pebble extend outward from the pebble, ever-widening and ever-moving, expanding into a much larger area, and finally touching shores never imagined when that pebble first touched the water. Without restrictions or barriers, the ripple effect of unschooling can reach places that one never expected or dreamed possible.

FACT

When involved in unschooling, children learn by experiencing real life on a daily basis, by living, functioning, and interacting in their environment and in society. When confined to a desk in a classroom, the child is removed from the real world, making it difficult for him to connect what is being taught in the classroom to what transpires in the world each day.

Deschooling Each Day

Deschooling is a way to further distance oneself from what one feels is the institutionalized style of educating children. Ivan Illich shared his thoughts on this in his book, *Deschooling Society*. Like many of his time who believed that conventional schools lacked the ability to teach to each child's needs, he felt that schools taught children only what they needed to know to pass tests and to meet the school's grading system. Meanwhile, children weren't learning how to think or how to further their education.

A curriculum can take on the same qualities of a school—uniformity instead of individuality, mass production instead of singular creativity. Thus, a "deschooled" curriculum—in other words, an individualized and customized education—should be the goal in the "unschooled homeschool." The educational format should be geared toward your child's learning style and your child's areas of interest. It should be flexible and stimulating enough to be fun, yet challenging. Rather than learning for the purpose of passing a test or achieving a specific grade, deschooling encourages learning for the purpose of gaining knowledge, learning how to think on one's own, and learning how to learn, with the ultimate goal of remaining competent and capable throughout one's lifetime.

For your family, deschooling and unschooling could mean using no formal curriculum. Or it could mean using a curriculum as a guideline, but doing hands-on activities and taking educational field trips, rather than hammering out worksheets. You may prefer to design your own lessons based on your children's interests to help them grasp concepts, or you may prefer to let your children learn through following, researching, and exploring their interests on their own. Your child may prefer to learn through reading voraciously, or she may prefer to learn by spending hours conducting experiments. Whatever her individual learning style, she can actively pursue knowledge in a way that makes real connections with her life and with her world, in a style that makes the most sense to her.

Always encourage children to follow through on their thoughts, questions, interests, and ideas. As unschooling advocate John Holt puts it: "The learner, child or adult, his experiences, his concerns, his wonders, his hopes and fears, his likes and dislikes, the things he is good at, must always be at the center of his learning."

Children As Teachers

Young children love to play school, and they enjoy taking on the role of a teacher in their make-believe schools. But the learning that occurs is not make-believe as they slip into their teaching roles. The learning is quite real. Nor is it only the young child who enjoys playing teacher. When a teenager can convey new ideas, concepts, or knowledge to an adult, they, too, have acted in the role of teacher. And as Roman philosopher Lucius Seneca insightfully stated, "Even while they teach, men learn."

When children of any age have the opportunity to teach by sharing information and knowledge with others, they automatically and indelibly inscribe that information upon their minds. By listening to your children and showing your appreciation and respect for their abilities and ideas, you encourage them to continue in their pursuit of new information and knowledge. They can see that someone cares enough to listen to them and that someone truly values their opinions and even learns from them. They realize that not only are they able to teach themselves, but they are able to teach others—one of the most rewarding and satisfying achievements in life.

Discussing Ideas

Allow children plenty of opportunities to share their findings with you. Listen attentively to their ideas and opinions, and avoid the urge to say you've "heard that before" or to "correct" their views. When a young child plays school and shows you how to print A, B, and C, you wouldn't walk away in a huff, saying you already know how to do that. You would most likely print A, B, C on a piece of paper and let her look over your printing skills. Similarly, you would want your older child to feel free to share thoughts, ideas, and information with you, because through sharing, doing, and discussing together, you both will learn.

Finding Answers

When youngsters have ideas, questions often follow. When they have the time to pursue those ideas, they can often formulate their own hypotheses based on the information they've gathered. They have the time to analyze their questions and the time to seek answers. By allowing them to come up with their own ideas, you set the stage for them to think, question, seek, and learn, all on their own. You're not getting in the way of that natural process by insisting that they read a specific passage to find the answer, or that they complete a lesson to arrive at what *you* feel is the correct answer. The investigation was *their* idea, and it should be through *their* method of analysis that they come up with the answer that best answers their theories.

ALERT!

Children don't necessarily want quick answers to their questions. Rather, they want to stretch their mind, broaden their conceptual-thinking abilities, and consider the "what-ifs" and "how-to's" of a thought or idea. Refrain from giving quick answers to their questions; instead, help them find resources that will assist them in exploring their questions and ideas.

If, however, youngsters *want* your help and guidance, if they're unsure of how to pursue a thought or idea, or if they don't know where to look for possible answers, by all means offer your assistance. When voicing their thoughts and ideas, children need to know that there is someone who will seriously listen to them without dismissing their notions as inconsequential. They need to know that there is someone who has the time and the patience to provide feedback, suggestions, and discussions of their ideas.

Unit Studies Year-Round

As noted in Chapter 4, unit studies are a grand way to cover a lot of subject areas while focusing on a special area of interest. For the family that is not as comfortable following an unschooled style of home education, the unit study may be the next best thing. And for families who would like their children to keep learning all year long, the unit study is a fairly painless way to attain this goal. Indeed, a summer unit study can capture the interest of the neighborhood children as well as your own.

Introducing a Unit Study

Let's say you are considering the addition of a new pet into your household over the summer, leading to an excellent opportunity to conduct a unit study on the subject of pets or animals. A field trip to nearby pet stores provides a real-life opportunity to interact with different types of animals: hamsters, mice, guinea pigs, rabbits, birds, fish, turtles, snakes, kittens, dogs, even chimpanzees. As children interact with each kind of pet, they'll learn about its needs, diet, habitat, behavior, and other pertinent information.

As they go about gathering information on the pet you'd possibly want to welcome into your home, your children can further research the animal or reptile, its ancestry, how it came to be in this country, where its native habitat is located, and other facts regarding its initial place of origin or its natural habitat. These areas of research will lead to historical, geographical, and natural science data.

Your children will also need to consider how they will care for and feed the new pet. This requires additional field trips to the pet store or grocery store to research the price of dog food, cat food, bird seed, turtle, fish, or rabbit food. If the pet consumes X amount of food per day, as the pet store clerk indicated, how long will a bag or box of food last? If a bag or box of food costs X amount of dollars, and lasts X amount of days, how many bags or boxes will need to be purchased each month? And how much will it cost to feed the pet over the course of a month or a year? What about its habitat? How much will it cost for litter, cedar shavings, toys or decorative elements, or aquarium or cage maintenance?

The Learning Never Stops

After doing the math, and after researching the pet, its history, habitat, and geographical location, your children can activate their language arts and fine arts skills. Again, this is a great opportunity for neighbor kids to become involved, too. Children can record information gathered about the animals, write brief reports on them, draw pictures of them, sketch the animal's native habitat, and come up with ideas for constructing a cage or area for the pet to live. They can mimic the sounds of the various animals they've studied and create a song of their own based upon the sounds of the animals.

QUESTION?

What are some good unit study topics?
Insects, animals, dinosaurs, marine life, weather, seasons, holidays, cooking, construction, gardening, rock collections, sports, artists, musicians, famous people, explorers, the U.S. presidents, inventions, transportation, travel, your state, the rain forest, the environment, ancient civilizations, cultures and traditions, the solar system, space travel, favorite books, and favorite hobbies are some good unit study topics, just to name a few.

You can embark upon a nature walk to see if you can locate some of these animals in the wild: birds, fish, turtles, mice, snakes, or rabbits. What about wolves and panthers, which are related to dogs and cats; are there any in your area, and can you find their tracks? How fast does a panther run, a rabbit, a mouse? How do snakes, turtles, and fish move? Children can act out the animals' movements for their physical activities: running, hopping, slithering, crawling, and swimming. Highlight the unit study with a trip to a nearby zoo to learn even more about animals and their furry or slithering relatives.

Theme Studies and the Core Curriculum

When integrating ideas into a theme or unit study, children will use and enhance their knowledge of core subject areas—reading, writing, history, geography, science, and math, as well as art, music, and physical education—all interwoven with a topic that interests them at a certain point in their lives. Each area of the curriculum connects in a cohesive manner, helping children to understand the reason that different skills are important and how they relate to a single purpose. Besides putting their reading, writing, and arithmetic skills to use, they can hone their research, thinking, and problem-solving skills in a way that is fun and almost effortless. And because the subject matter is one that especially interests them at this time in their life, the chances of growing bored and resisting the "lessons" are quite diminished.

To make your unit study preparations even easier, use the Internet to get ideas. Some homeschooling and educational Web sites include outlines and ideas for theme studies that you can put right to use. Libraries, bookstores, educational supply stores, and hobby shops are other great resources for pulling together a unit study.

It's helpful to plan unit or theme studies in advance, so that you can help guide children when they have questions, need to acquire special supplies for projects, or seek additional research methods. If you know, for instance, that you'll be doing a unit study on gardening, you'll want to have gardening tools on hand, vegetable and flower seeds, and a good idea of where you'd like the garden to be planted—*before* the children head into the yard with shovels and hoes. You may want to make notes or create an outline of what you plan to accomplish in each phase of the unit study, and you'll want to have an idea of how long you expect each phase to last.

A Combination of Ways: Eclectic Schooling

The eclectic method of homeschooling draws upon an assortment of elements from various educational resources, as explained in Chapter 4. It can also incorporate elements from different styles of homeschooling. If you would like to try unschooling, but you are hesitant about drifting too far from your current curriculum, use a combination of ideas presented in this chapter as you "test the waters."

Exploring Interests

You can begin by allowing more "free learning" time and encouraging children to explore their own areas of interest. This could be so foreign to them that they may not even know how to begin. They may even believe that *nothing* interests them if their opportunities for exploration and free thinking have been shut down for too long. It could take some family brainstorming sessions to get your child in touch with things that truly interest her, or hobbies or topics that she might want to pursue and explore.

Using Unit Studies

Introduce a couple of short unit studies, and help your child become comfortable with that educational experience, which can be quite different from conventional school or a traditional curriculum. Start with the new interest that she recently found, and create the unit study around that topic. When she realizes that schooling can revolve around her own interests, it will open up a whole new view for her.

Adding Unschooling Days

Let her take the unit study or theme-centered learning style even farther by allowing for some "unschooling" days. On those days, she's free to work on the unit study, work on her original curriculum, or simply be involved in some project, whether it's reading, writing, cooking, sewing, painting, playing music, or working on a totally new idea that interests her.

The Result

Within a few weeks of experiencing this new, eclectic style of homeschooling, composed of a variety of styles—her original curriculum, unit studies, unschooling, and exploring new interests—your child will no doubt surprise you with her enthusiasm; her creative, innovative side; and her ability to demonstrate how much she is learning—and is teaching to you! Ⓔ

Chapter 6

Answering the Socialization Question

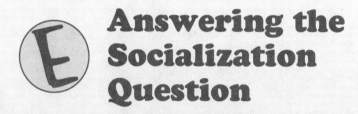

One of the most frequent questions asked of homeschool families is this: "What about socialization?" While many consider this a legitimate concern, several educators and homeschoolers have long understood that socialization and recreation naturally occur outside of the school environment, just as learning does. This chapter intends to help you answer those questions you may have about the socialization of homeschooled children.

Social Skills and Child Development

Concerns over socialization of homeschooled children tend to center on how they will "learn" to interact with, and get along with, others. The ability to socialize well with others is based upon learning and implementing proper social skills. Social skills include taking turns, sharing, praising and thanking others, treating others with respect and kindness, listening to others, conversing with others, showing interest in others, following directions, exercising patience and tolerance, resolving conflicts, and resisting negative peer pressure.

A child can achieve these social skills in the home by learning basic manners and proper conduct, interacting with family members, developing quality friendships, engaging in conversations with others, and through role-playing to further hone their social skills for a variety of situations they may eventually encounter. When a child has practiced and achieved good social skills and proper manners, and understands right from wrong, these qualities will see him through nearly any social gathering.

A study conducted in 1993 by Dr. Gary Knowles, assistant professor of education at the University of Michigan, centered on adults who had previously been homeschooled. His study further supported the concept that homeschooled children do not suffer from a lack of social interactions. Of those interviewed, 94 percent believed that homeschooling had prepared them to function as healthy, independent adults, and 79 percent said that their homeschool experiences led to interactions with others from different levels of society.

It's important to note that there is a difference between "socialization," which means to participate in a social group setting, and "social skills," which are closely related to good, old-fashioned manners. It's not necessary to attend a formal school in order to learn proper manners or sound social skills.

Parental Influence

Today, the "socialization question" initially posed to homeschoolers has begun to focus in another direction. The question asked more often today is, "Why aren't schooled children as socially well-adjusted as homeschooled children?"

Dr. Larry Shyers, a psychotherapist and chairman of the Florida Board of Clinical Social Work, Marriage and Family Therapy, and Mental Health Counseling, conducted a study on the adjustment and social skills of conventionally schooled children and homeschooled children. In his 1992 study, Dr. Shyers found that, when involved in free play and group activities, traditionally schooled children displayed more behavior problems than homeschooled children.

Dr. Shyers went on to deduce that homeschooled children were better behaved because they had adults as more consistent role models, while the school children tended to model their behavior after each other. He also found that schoolchildren were generally louder and more aggressive than the homeschooled children. Dr. Shyers stated, "The results seem to show that a child's social development depends more on adult contact and less on contact with other children as previously thought."

FACT

In a study conducted by Dr. John W. Taylor of Andrews University, homeschooled children were found to have a higher degree of self-concept and self-esteem than their conventionally schooled counterparts. Research shows that children with higher self-esteem normally perform better academically than those with low self-esteem.

Family Ties

It's no surprise that the early years of a child's life between birth and age five are important for developing familial bonds and emotional ties. Many child development experts believe that children build their social skills upon these close family ties. By age five, most children have learned basic concepts of right and wrong. For instance, it's okay to play in the yard, but it's not okay to play in the street. It's okay to hit a ball with a bat, but it's not okay to hit a car with a bat. If they step out of the bounds of right and wrong, they risk damaging something (themselves in the street, the family car with a bat). They also risk losing the pride and trust of their parents. The disappointment reflected in their parent's eyes or demeanor, because of their misbehavior, can be crushing.

As children continue to mature, learn more complex rules of right and wrong, and develop stronger bonds with their families, the desire to jeopardize their parent's respect and trust further diminishes. This closely describes the relationship homeschooled children have with the family unit. They are less likely to be left on their own for hours each day, interacting with and developing relationships with others outside the family unit who may not be as concerned about right and wrong or disappointing those who love them. Rather, they continue to develop close relationships with the very ones who love them and care about their well-being.

Parental Involvement

According to Child and Adolescent Health and Development (CAHD), a department of the World Health Organization, the importance of parental involvement in the *overall development* of children is critical. CAHD refers to child development as "maturity in terms of physical, cognitive, language, social-emotional, temperament, or fine and gross motor skills development."

FACT

The investment of time that parents put into teaching their children, whether the children are homeschooled or conventionally schooled, pays great dividends in the long run. When a child has a solid foundation beneath her, a good concept of right and wrong, has practiced and achieved good social skills, and understands how to display proper social behavior in public, she will have few socialization problems as she grows toward adulthood.

In research conducted over the past several decades, CAHD has found more substantial proof that "the relationships among health, physical growth, psychological development and parental caregiving have become clearer. Combined growth and development interventions that help families practice 'responsive parenting' have the potential to promote better psychological development, as well as physical growth."

The U.S. Department of Education has found that parental involvement in the education of their children has positive influences on the overall success of their children as youths and adults. Recent studies have found that "parental involvement in education is associated with higher grades and test scores, better attendance, more homework completion, more positive attitudes and behaviors, and higher graduation and college attendance rates." They've determined that successful student outcomes are based on parents serving as good role models and on "involving the entire family" in the child's education.

It's not surprising that homeschooled children—whose families are closely involved in all areas of their education—are achieving high levels of success academically and socially.

Socialization Opportunities for the Homeschooler

It's one thing to practice social skills at home while role-playing, and it's another to put them to use at social gatherings. Having started your child on good manners and social skills when she was young, she naturally employs them when she's socializing with others. This could be with family members and relatives during the holidays or reunions or when she's with friends during birthday parties and sleepovers. The homeschooled child may not attend a traditional school for her education, but she still participates in get-togethers with others, just as conventionally schooled children do. In fact, she sometimes has more opportunities to socialize with a wider range of people than conventionally schooled children, who must remain in the classroom for the majority of each day.

Homeschooled children have ample opportunities to run errands with parents and interact with a variety of people, young and old, from varying backgrounds. Your child may be able to go to work with you, become involved in community activities, take part in church and youth groups, or join scouting groups, clubs like 4-H, or the YMCA. They can participate in activities such as music, art, gymnastics, or sports. And, of course, there are neighbor children and your child's friends, who they'll want to spend time with.

Teen and preteen children have time during the day to volunteer in nursing homes, hospitals, libraries, businesses, nature centers, museums, and other community centers. In fact, homeschoolers usually have more time available for community involvement than do traditionally schooled children. By volunteering and taking part in community classes or events, homeschoolers can interact with various age groups in different situations, allowing plenty of opportunities to exercise their social skills in their daily lives.

Extracurricular Activities

If you fear that your child will have limited opportunities to interact with others, rest assured that it's nearly impossible to *not* have social activities available to you and your child. Nearly every city or town, no matter how large or small, has a parks and recreation department, and they offer a multitude of classes and activities. If your nearest town does not have a parks and recreation department, chances are the next largest city has one.

Here are some activities generally offered by parks and recreation departments:

- Preschool programs focusing on social skills, listening skills, motor skills, kindergarten-readiness skills, and creative play.
- Tumbling, dancing, ballet, and gymnastics.
- Ceramics and jewelry-making.
- Drawing, painting, or cartooning classes.
- Tennis lessons and golf lessons.
- Martial arts and swimming lessons.
- Foreign language classes.
- Babysitting courses.
- Rent-a-teen programs.
- Summer break programs.

School-Sponsored Events

Some school districts may allow homeschoolers to take part in the school band or drama club. However, school sports may be governed by the state's athletic association, and certain regulations apply. This doesn't rule out the possibility of your child playing on a baseball, football, or basketball team, though. Many communities have Little League teams or Pop Warner football teams that your child can join.

Community-Sponsored Events

Check with your parks and recreation department or YMCA about basketball teams, soccer, hockey, and Motocross. Your church may have sports teams, too. Or there may be community bowling leagues, tennis teams, swim teams, or golf matches for youngsters to participate in.

Many areas also have community bands, drama clubs, or choirs that are open to anyone, regardless of age. They hold concerts or put on performances throughout the year, to which the public is invited.

Homeschool-Sponsored Events

If there are no sports teams in your area for kids to join, start a team in conjunction with your local homeschool group. Your group's team could play teams from other homeschool groups. Or if there's only one group in your area, your team could divide up and play each other.

FACT

There are no limits to the number of social events, fun events, sporting events, field trips, and community involvement projects for homeschoolers. In fact, some families find that they have to cut back on social outings and get-togethers. Many become involved in too many activities because they were overly concerned about the socialization issue—only to find that it's not really an issue at all.

In addition to sports, homeschool groups often arrange art or music classes, nature study classes, science fairs, and physical education classes. There may be spelling bees, quilting bees, reading and writing groups, or singing groups. Many go on educational field trips or engage in activities such as horseback riding, swimming, skating, or bowling. And they often get to do these things during weekdays when the facilities are not overrun by noisy weekend crowds.

Homeschool groups may also host special-event nights. These can include theatrical performances, musical performances, talent shows, magic shows, or cultural events highlighting a certain culture or region of the world. They may hold dances throughout the year, graduation ceremonies, yearbook signings, and may arrange for "class" rings.

Daily Social Situations

When homeschooled children are out in the real world each day, they have opportunities that are not always afforded to their school-bound classmates. They may spend time at work with Mom or Dad, help Grandfather in the woodshop, or cook alongside Grandmother. They may help with the grocery shopping, bill paying, plumbing repairs, or car repairs. They may go along when the dog is taken to the veterinarian, groomer's, or obedience class. They can take advantage of spur-of-the-moment tours at the vet, groomer's, bank, bakery, or copy shop, especially if it's a slow day. While participating in these activities, they often have the opportunity to meet new people, hold conversations with friends on the street or business professionals in offices, and interact with people of all ages and backgrounds.

Socializing Only with Peers

When children are able to move away from socializing only with peers each day, they gain a better understanding of society and its citizens. When a thirteen-year-old spends the majority of his time walking the school halls with other thirteen-year-olds, eating lunch with other thirteen-year-olds, working on projects with thirteen-year-olds, walking to and from school with thirteen-year-olds, talking on the phone with them each evening, and hanging out at their homes on weekends, he begins to lose touch with other aspects of society. And it becomes more difficult to break the pattern and "spoil the fun" of his lifestyle by going grocery shopping with Mom, helping Dad around the house, or spending time with Grandmother or Aunt Mabel. It's difficult for him to step out of his "comfort zone."

Interacting with Young and Old Alike

But when a child has had more opportunities to interact with various ages, old and young, in homeschool gatherings, classes and workshops, and community events and errands, he is more sociable and adaptable. He is accustomed to spending time with a wider age group, helping in the community and at home, and encountering new situations on a more regular basis. So, when it's time to help out around the house or go to Grandmother's house or to visit with Aunt Mabel, it's more likely to be a natural part of her life. Rather than viewing the visit as "taking her away" from her "24/7" friends and spoiling her fun, she accepts it as part of everyday living.

ALERT!

Peers can't take the place of one's family, and peers can provide neither the proper guidance a child needs nor the proper advice. A child's peers usually aren't any more mature than the child himself, and they can't always display good judgment or proper decision-making skills.

There's certainly nothing wrong with children having friends their own age or with their getting together from time to time to have fun and be kids. But exclusive companionship with one's peers, while shutting out all others, is not healthy and can lead to dangerous ground.

Maturity Levels of the Homeschooled Child

"What a nice young man!" the clerk commented to a friend's son. "I bet you're homeschooled, aren't you?"

My friend was amazed. How could the clerk have guessed that her son was homeschooled after less than twenty minutes around him? Perhaps it was a lucky guess, or perhaps the clerk could simply *tell*. More and more homeschool families are being surprised by others' observations of them. Maybe it's because homeschooling is more common today, and people have had more interaction with homeschooled children. Maybe it's the social skills of the homeschooled children that give them away, or their level of maturity.

Reflecting Parents' Behavior

Kids tend to mimic those with whom they spend the most time. And when kids are homeschooled, they naturally spend more time with their parents. Consequently, the parent becomes a major role model in their lives. Children listen to their parents, learn from their parents, and observe their parents talking to neighbors, handling situations in stores and restaurants, banks and post offices, and generally interacting with others in society on a day-to-day basis. Children absorb this information, learn from their parents' actions, and reflect their parents' behavior.

FACT

Roland Meighan, a professor at the University of Nottingham School of Education, studied homeschoolers while writing an article, "Home-based Education Effectiveness Research and Some of Its Implications," for *Educational Review*. He found that research "demonstrates that children are usually superior to their school-attending peers in social skills, social maturity, emotional stability, academic achievement, personal confidence, communication skills and other aspects."

Studies Show . . .

The ERIC Clearinghouse on Disabilities and Gifted Education notes that several studies have concluded that homeschooling is helpful to a child's social skills and maturity. They cite the research of Dr. Linda Montgomery, which found that "Homeschooled students tend to have a broader age-range of friends than their schooled peers, which may encourage maturity and leadership skills." They further cite studies by Dr. Larry Shyers and Dr. John W. Taylor, indicating that homeschooled children are "likely to be socially and psychologically healthy," based on studies of the homeschoolers' social adjustment and self-esteem.

Learning Proper Etiquette, Morals, and Values

Proper etiquette and good manners go hand in hand with the sound social skills you teach your child. Proper etiquette is an important key to a child's social success, and it's the parent's responsibility to teach good manners early on. These manners, as well as the family's values and moral principles, must be exercised within the home on a daily basis in order to instill them in children. In this way, they become healthy, everyday habits.

Family values and morals are not easily learned at school or in textbooks. Rather, they are a part of life that must be witnessed, felt, and practiced. You can talk to your children about the values that are important to you, your family, and society. You can discuss moral behavior and immoral behavior in ways that are appropriate to your child's age and understanding.

Reporting Teen Behavior

In a 1999 report on teen behavior, over 70 percent of adults surveyed believed that teenagers lacked values, character, and civility. Less than 15 percent of the adults surveyed felt that teens were friendly or helpful to neighbors within the community. Educators across the country also reported a lack of civility and respect from students, as well as an increase in verbal abuse and physical assaults in the schools.

Character Education

Clearly, there's a need for parents to focus on teaching good manners and proper etiquette, social skills, family values, moral behavior, and overall character education. In many homeschools across the nation, these principles are as important in the children's education as the core subjects laid out by curriculum guidelines. Many popular homeschool curricula or correspondence schools include character education as part of the overall package. If they do not, families can find other ways to incorporate character education into their days with unit studies, discussions, and role-playing that accentuate citizenship, responsibility, respect, caring and kindness for others, fairness, trustworthiness, honesty, good sportsmanship, and other important factors of good and civil behavior.

ALERT!

Stephen Carter, author of *Civility: Manners, Morals, and the Etiquette of Democracy,* advises parents to closely observe their children's activities so they can determine where conflicting messages regarding moral and civil behavior come from. He names school, peers, television, music, and the Internet as areas that can compete with a parent's teachings on values, morals, and civil behavior.

Preparing for the Future

Homeschool families want their children's learning experiences to be enjoyable and fruitful and to lead to a lifelong love of learning. If this means that they need to more closely observe their child's social interactions, then they accept it as part of the duties of responsible parenting. If socialization is a determining factor in their child's happiness and success in life, then they'll ensure that their child has plenty of opportunities to socialize in ways that are positive and uplifting for the child.

Families who choose to homeschool feel that they are more aware of their children's friends and the type of peer pressure their children may be subjected to. In addition, they feel that the character education they incorporate into their homeschools, along with strong family values and morals, help their children make good decisions when associating with friends. (E)

Chapter 7

Choosing a Curriculum

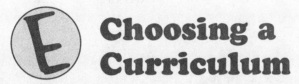

Some families desire a full curriculum, complete with pencils and paper, while others prefer to design their own curriculum. Some have budgeted a few hundred dollars for a year's curriculum, and others have very little to spend on materials. Whatever your desires or budget, this chapter will help you find a homeschool curriculum to fulfill your family's needs.

Curriculum Guidelines

Whether you decide to use a packaged curriculum in your homeschool or to go the unschooling route, the day may come when you wonder if your child is "on track" or is covering everything he or she would cover in a traditional school. One way to do this is to request the "Typical Course of Study" from World Book, Inc. They put together their guidelines based on several national curriculum guides and courses of study, and then the material is reviewed by curriculum experts.

Even if you're not overly concerned about the point where your children are in their education, you might pick up some homeschool ideas from the guidelines. If you have Internet access, visit World Book's Web site at ✑ www.worldbook.com. Click on "Parents," then "Typical Course of Study." You'll see the curriculum guidelines for preschool through the twelfth-grade level, with topics listed under each subject area. You'll also see special activities to reinforce skills in social studies, science, language arts, health and safety, and mathematics at each grade level, which you can incorporate into your own homeschool lessons.

If you're unable to connect to World Book's Web site via the Internet, you can request their "Typical Course of Study" by writing to World Book, Inc., 233 North Michigan Avenue, Suite 2000, Chicago, IL 60601.

Packaged Curricula

In Chapter 4, while looking over the types of homeschool options that are available, we touched on the subject of curriculum providers and programs. As noted, there are the secular curriculum suppliers, biblically based curriculum providers, and specific faith-based programs, such as Christian, Catholic, Islamic, and Jewish.

With many of these packages, you have the option of purchasing a standardized curriculum for the entire school year, or you can have a curriculum tailored more closely to your child's interests and needs. Many of the companies provide testing services, evaluations, grading, and

record keeping, or you can choose to handle these your~
yourself the additional fee that most require for the ser~

A packaged curriculum can be beneficial when y
homeschooling, if you have a career and a family to
are uncertain about creating your own lesson plans, or ii
on unschooling. If your children especially enjoy reading textb
worksheets, and following a regular daily schedule similar to that
traditional school, a packaged curriculum may be just the thing.

Structure and Method

Packaged curricula often follow the scope-and-sequence teaching
method of public schools. This means that the curriculum has a specific
outline of topics to cover in a predetermined amount of time (scope),
and children will need to master the lessons in the order they are
presented so they can move on to the next level (sequence). This
method may be suited to your child's learning style, or it may be too
constrictive. Check with the curriculum provider to see if their materials
follow the scope-and-sequence method, or if their programs allow for
flexibility, and, if so, how much.

ALERT!

Remember: With any homeschool method, you'll want to add
variety to the daily schedule. Otherwise, homeschooling will
quickly grow stale. The kids won't be as enthusiastic as they once
were, and their learning will suffer. Spice up the curriculum with
activities, explorations, and games. Let the kids contribute their
own learning ideas, too.

Cost Considerations

Price is also a consideration when purchasing a curriculum package.
Curriculum packages can range from $400 to $1,000 for one grade level.
The lower grades are less expensive, while the middle- to upper-grade
curricula run more. Prices usually include the basic package, which
includes nearly everything you need. In some cases, it may even include

pencils, papers, rulers, and compasses. If you'd like to have additional products, such as certain readers or math books, there can be an extra charge for those.

Designing Your Own Curriculum

As parents, you'll want to consider your children's wishes and input for the homeschool curriculum during the decision-making process. Children will often surprise you with the wonderful ideas and learning suggestions they come up with! Together, you and your children can create a curriculum that is fun, interesting, and challenging to ensure a well-rounded education, year after year.

QUESTION?

What is the difference between a curriculum and a lesson plan?
A curriculum focuses on the knowledge, skills, and abilities your child should achieve. The lesson plan is comprised of the activities or studies that complement and carry out the intent of the curriculum.

Components of a Curriculum

A curriculum is based upon your educational philosophies, educational aims or ambitions for your child, and the learning goals or objectives necessary to achieve those aims. We'll describe each a little more fully.

- Educational philosophies, as noted in Chapter 3, center on what you feel your children should learn in order to achieve happiness and success in their lives. This can include morals and values, respect and responsibility, manners and kindness toward others, faith and spirituality, a love for learning, a love for life.
- Educational aims or ambitions for your children could include solid life skills and self-reliance, critical thinking and reasoning skills, creative thinking abilities, the ability to work well with others, to enjoy

one's work and career, to show love and respect for one's family, to be a responsible and upstanding citizen, and/or to contribute to the community.

- Learning goals and objectives should support your educational philosophies and aims for your child. For instance, learning self-discipline and self-control is critical to a happy family life and career. Proper manners, social skills, and speaking skills are important when working with others or when contributing to the community. Good reading, math, and science skills are imperative to all areas of one's life, from daily living to getting ahead in one's career. Artistic and creative skills can add joy and meaning to one's life. Learning and maintaining healthy habits can contribute to a long, productive life.

Writing a Curriculum

Once you've determined your family's philosophies, your aims and ambitions for your child's education, and the goals or objectives to support those aims, you can begin designing the curriculum. But don't forget to consider your child's interests and learning styles! (You may want to review the different learning styles mentioned in Chapter 2 to determine what method works best with your child.)

To write your curriculum, you'll want to record your educational philosophies, aims, and objectives, and keep it in a special folder, entitled "Curriculum." On those days when you forget where you are headed with your child's education, this written curriculum will be a great reminder.

As you consider the subject areas your child will study (math, science, social studies, language arts, fine arts, health, and life skills), you'll want to slant them toward the goals and aims that you have for your child's education. For instance, a goal for your child might be to have a healthy, productive life. In studying the human body in science, you might want to emphasize the lessons on health and nutrition. Therefore, the objectives of the science lessons could focus on the way the body functions, how the bones and muscles work in tandem, how blood carries nutrients and oxygen to all parts of the body, how the respiratory and digestive systems work, and how proper nutrition, exercise, and healthful habits help the body function as it was designed to function.

As you can see, once you have your aims and goals established for your child (for example, a healthy, productive individual), you'll be able to focus on the objectives that you want the lessons to convey (in this case, how to achieve and maintain a healthy, productive body).

FACT

Educators know that a "typical course of study" is not a one-size-fits-all curriculum. Children master skills at varying rates. One child may grasp the relation between decimals and fractions at age eight, while another may not grasp the concept until age ten. One child might write well in cursive at age nine; another may not display attractive penmanship until age twelve. Consider your child's unique skills and abilities when setting educational goals and objectives.

Following a Less Formal Curriculum

Designing a curriculum similar to the one above may seem like a lot of work. Yet most parents already have an idea of the educational goals for their children, even if they haven't written it down in a formal outline. Many parents are already in tune with their children's interests and learning styles, so it may not be necessary to document the objectives of each lesson or the manner in which the studies will complement the child's interests and the parent's goals.

In an unschooling environment, the curriculum tends to accommodate the children's curiosity and their interest-led activities. If you need to present evidence of the curriculum you use for your unschooled homeschool, illustrate how your children's interests and activities (such as their hobbies, games, experiments, talents, research, discussions, educational travels, creative projects, or books read) accomplish the goals and philosophies your family believes in.

Creating Your Own Lesson Plans

Lesson plans are the activities or studies that complement and carry out the intent of the curriculum and educational goals for your children. For instance, one of your goals may be for your child to play an active part in your community as a caring and responsible individual. Therefore, you may want to create a lesson plan for social studies, that has the objective of interacting with others for the good of the community.

Lesson plans for this objective could include researching the history of volunteerism in communities (with examples including Benjamin Franklin, who helped to establish the first volunteer fire department, or Clara Barton, who founded the American Red Cross through volunteering her services). Your child could read a book on ways to volunteer in the community, then write or share his thoughts on how he could help others in the community. Other aspects of the lesson plan could include drawing posters of volunteers, visiting the headquarters of local volunteer associations, and taking an active part in community volunteer programs, such as canned food drives, clothing or toy collections, animal shelter assistance, or visiting with the elderly in nursing homes.

Lesson Plan Basics

Creating lesson plans is not difficult. They are simply a way to convey information about a subject and make connections. Being able to present lesson plans in an informative, stimulating way that connects with your child is more important than using worksheets from activity books or generic lesson plans.

Formal, written lesson plans usually cover the following points:

- **Subject:** The subject area the lesson relates to.
- **Grade level:** The grade or age level the lesson is suited for.
- **Description:** A brief overview of the lesson and its intent.
- **Objective:** What you want the child to learn from the lesson.
- **Procedures or plan:** The details of how you'll present or handle the lesson.
- **Materials:** The books, artwork, and/or supplies you'll need to carry out the lesson.
- **Evaluation or assessment:** A determination of what the child learned from the lesson.

You won't need to write such elaborate plans, unless you like the idea of doing so. But you might want to keep the above points in mind when creating your lessons.

FACT

Building upon previous knowledge and skills is the sequential or cumulative way of presenting and mastering lessons. Some feel that testing is one way to determine the child's mastery of knowledge. Others believe that observing the child's overall capabilities is a better way of judging the child's knowledge and skills.

Sample Lesson Plans

Some lesson plans are geared more toward active participation, while others may encourage writing, speaking, calculating, evaluating, or artistic skills. Most are expected to build upon previous skills. For instance, no one would be expected to read Tolstoy's *War and Peace* until he or she had mastered the ability to read a short story. Similarly, a child isn't expected to add or subtract decimals and fractions until he has grasped the concept of parts and wholes.

When children are allowed to learn at their own pace, the family can spend the time that is necessary to help the children comprehend and eventually master skills and subject areas. As you monitor your child's comprehension, acquisition of knowledge, and maturation of skills and abilities, you'll know what topics he is ready for as he sequentially builds upon his knowledge base and interests.

To view some sample lesson plans or obtain ideas for creating your own plans, visit these lesson plan Web sites on the Internet.

- Ask Eric Lesson Plans: *http://askeric.org/Virtual/Lessons*
- DiscoverySchool.com: *www.school.discovery.com/lessonplans*
- Education World: *www.education-world.com*
- Lesson Plan Search: *www.lessonplansearch.com*
- Lesson Plans Page: *www.lessonplanspage.com*
- LessonPlanZ.com: *www.lessonplanz.com*
- Teachers.net: *www.teachers.net/lessons*

Free Educational Resources

As difficult as it may be to comprehend, a homeschool education can truly cost nothing. Some may argue that you have to at least purchase pencils and paper, yet rare is the home that does not already contain a pencil and some paper. And most homes with children at least have crayons and paper of some sort for coloring or drawing. Several families use the public library almost exclusively for their home-school needs.

Using High-Quality Lab Equipment

Sometimes it's difficult to ignore the desire to see and use an astronomer-quality telescope or scientific lab equipment, and that's what field trips are for. Visit the children's science museum often, and make use of all the hands-on equipment. Locate the specialized museums, such as the planetarium, imaginarium, laboratorium, holographic museum, and even the wax museum. Nearly all these facilities offer the opportunity to partake in some hands-on experimentation.

Families in your homeschool group may be interested in sharing or renting out lab equipment they already own. Or families could chip in to purchase equipment for the homeschool cooperative. This could be a nice investment not only for your group's children but for all the homeschool children yet to join your group.

Learning on the Internet

If you have Internet access, a world of information is literally at your fingertips. You can find free curriculum guidelines, free lesson plans, free educational games, and free worksheets. You can visit virtual museums and participate in virtual experiments and virtual classrooms. To find these resources, you need only type a relevant word or phrase into a search engine such as Yahoo!, Google, AltaVista, or America Online, then share the virtual learning experiences with your children.

Free Educational Games

The Internet offers some learning games that kids can play for free. Remember: Always monitor your children's activities when they are on the Internet. Here are just a few of the many resources available:

- Education for Kids: *www.edu4kids.com*
- Education Place: *www.eduplace.com/edugames.html*
- FunBrain: *www.funbrain.com*
- Gamequarium.com: *www.gamequarium.com*
- Kids Games: *www.kidsgames.org*
- Owl and Mouse: *www.yourchildlearns.com/owlmouse.htm*
- Puzzle Depot: *www.puzzledepot.com*

Free Worksheets

Here are some Web sites on the Internet that have free worksheets, most of which are printable:

- ABC Teach Network: *www.abcteach.com*
- EdHelper.com: *www.edhelper.com*
- Learning Page: *www.learningpage.com*
- Math Builder: *www.mathbuilder.com*
- School Express: *www.schoolexpress.com*
- Tampa Reads: *www.tampareads.com*
- Teach-nology: *http://worksheets.teach-nology.com*

Free Teacher Education Courses

These courses are for you, rather than your children. The "Free Education on the Internet" Web site, *www.free-ed.net/catalog*, offers free courses in early childhood education and educational methods. Click on "College of Education," then "Department of Early Childhood Education" or "Department of Educational Methods." You'll be directed to the following courses:

- *About Learning* covers theories on how people learn, such as Piaget's theory, multiple intelligences, right-brain and left-brain thinking, learning styles, and more.

- *Curriculum: What Should Be Learned* covers different curriculum theories, with explanations on core curricula, whole language teaching, outcome-based education, character education, and others.
- *Instruction: How Learning Should Be Designed* contains information on instruction theories, such as mastery learning, thematic instruction, whole brain teaching, cognitive learning, instructional technology, apprenticeships, and more.
- *Assessment: Knowing When Learning Occurs* covers methods to assess a student's capabilities, such as authentic assessment, portfolio assessment, and the methods used in classroom assessment.

If you'd like to brush up on your own math skills, the *www.free-ed.net/catalog* site offers free courses on basic math skills, algebra, geometry, trigonometry, or calculus in their "College of Mathematics." You can also refresh your memory through the free courses offered in the areas of science, social studies, grammar, and literature. These courses might even provide some ideas for your homeschool lesson plans.

The Student's Input

When you sit down to create lesson plans and activities for your children, ask for ideas on what they'd like to learn. They may currently have an intense interest in snakes, castles, basket-making, or a movie that's popular at the theater this year. Let them talk about their hobbies and interests, and encourage them to come up with ideas related to those. For instance, an interest in snakes could branch off to lizards, frogs, and other reptiles. Your son might mention that he'd like to know where the poison dart frog or Komodo dragon lives and to learn more about them and their predators. This is something you could incorporate into your lesson plans for the science curriculum.

Your daughter might wonder what materials basket weavers used centuries ago when making baskets that were necessary for hauling firewood, gathering berries, perhaps even carrying water from a stream. Was there a way to make the basket waterproof? Or did families need to mold pottery from clay in order to transport water? This is a lesson plan idea for history.

Have children brainstorm ideas, too. They may have grown tired of a hobby and now have no new interests on the horizon. Look through age-appropriate magazines, read about others' hobbies, browse through course catalogs and even toy catalogs, and see what sparks their interest.

If they were able to do anything they wanted, ask them what that might be. You may get answers like travel to Mars, fly to Hawaii and go surfing, or visit the Arctic Circle. These thoughts and interests can be worked into lesson plans on space travel for science or geographical travels for social studies. Never take your children's ideas lightly; rather, put them to good use in your lesson plans.

ALERT!

You don't need to be totally responsible for developing all of the educational ideas in your homeschool. Let the ones who are receiving an education—your children—provide some input on what they'd like to learn.

Handling Advanced Subjects

You may have little difficulty in guiding your elementary-aged child through the first years of homeschooling. But when she expresses an interest in learning French, learning to play the violin, or learning computer programming, you might be at a loss. Never fear; your child's ambitions won't need to be nipped in the bud.

Local libraries usually have audiotapes or even videotapes on conversational French and other foreign languages. There might be accomplished violinists in your area who are eager to teach the violin to your child. Contact local music stores or nearby colleges for recommendations of instructors. If your child is eager to learn computer programming, once more you can turn to your local college. They may have programming students who could start your son or daughter on the road to writing code.

When subjects become too difficult for you to confidently handle, then a tutor, mentor, or, in some cases, a well-put-together videotape, may be the answer. Tutors can be found in the Yellow Pages of your telephone book. If this search is not fruitful, call your local school district—they often keep lists of tutors—or contact the public library or college.

If your child balks at the idea of a personal tutor, you might try a tutor in the form of an educational videotape. Teacher's Video (✍*www.teachersvideo.com*) has videotapes on topics such as music appreciation and violin for beginners, art appreciation and artistic techniques, health, physical education, and sports, as well as other topics and subject areas. Library Video (✍*www.libraryvideo.com*) has over 14,000 educational videos, DVDs, and CD-ROMs on a multitude of topics. They also offer teacher guides to accompany some of their videos. For math videos, you may want to check Educational Video Resources' (✍*www.evrmath.com/instructors.html*) assortment of over 3,000 videos, ranging from preschool math through college calculus.

QUESTION?

Retired professionals, especially retired teachers, are often interested in tutoring or being a mentor to a child. Contact your local association of retired professionals, and arrange a meeting between interested parties and your family.

Educational Excursions

Most homeschool support groups work diligently to arrange educational field trips for families to enjoy together on a monthly basis. It's a wonderful way for children to socialize, not only with other homeschoolers but with the many people they meet on the trip.

If you're unable to attend many of the local field trips, you can take "virtual field trips" on the Internet. Though not as exciting or informative as the real experience, children might enjoy the novelty of such a "trip." Search the Web for virtual field trips or virtual tours; new Web sites with such tours are continually being added.

As you go about your errands in your town, make a mental note of places your homeschool group—or family—could visit on their next educational excursion. Don't forget short "field trips" to the library, beach, lake, park, or sporting event, where you'll nearly always have new and interesting experiences. Children can also write a summary of their trips for English class.

Here are some field trip ideas you may want to consider in your community:

- Fire stations, police departments, and city hall.
- Television and radio stations.
- Bakeries and fast-food restaurants.
- Soda-bottling and manufacturing companies.
- Publishing companies and printing presses.
- Post offices, courier services, and banks.
- Farms, ranches, and orchards.
- Airports and shipyards.
- Museums and zoos.
- Performing arts halls, concert halls, and sports stadiums.
- Traveling exhibits (dinosaur exhibits, Vietnam Moving Wall).
- Schools or preschools (some children have never been inside one).
- Your place of business or a friend's place of business.

Chapter 8

Homeschooling Schedules

There are several different ways to schedule your homeschool days. For instance, your family's homeschool day might be paced similar to a conventional school day, or it might revolve around "un-schooled" days instead. Whatever style of homeschool you've chosen, this chapter will help you develop a schedule or format that will work well for your family.

A Plan That Works

The type of schedule your family follows will largely depend upon the type of homeschool your children are involved with. If they are enrolled in a correspondence school, their schedule may need to accommodate the school's time requirements for completing assignments and courses. If they are enrolled in a self-paced independent study program, they're encouraged to complete certain portions of the program within a suggested time frame. If you're using unit studies, you may allot one week or several months for a unit, and you'll have topics you'll want to cover within a period of days or weeks. If your family is following an unschooled or eclectic style, your schedule may be somewhat more relaxed than others.

Getting off to a Good Start

When you first begin homeschooling, ease into it gently. If homeschooling has been a way of life at your house since your first child was born, the transition into homeschooling comes naturally. If, however, you decide it's "time for school" when your child turns five or six, or you've just removed your eight-year-old, twelve-year-old, or fifteen-year-old from a traditional school, the transition requires some tender handling.

For the child removed from school, allow for the much-needed decompression time before implementing a homeschool schedule. She will need time to unwind from the hectic schedule she's been following. She will also need to learn how to move through her day without the prompting of bells. She'll need to get in tune with the natural ebb and flow of daily life in her own home.

For the five- or six-year-old who is "ready for school," ease into a homeschool schedule that fits her abilities, skills, attention span, and level of maturity. Some kindergarten-aged children can sit still for thirty minutes at a time, while others simply can't. Some have well-developed fine motor skills, enabling them to handle crayons and pencils well. Others still have difficulty getting the pencil to move exactly where they'd like. For these children, spending thirty minutes printing A-B-Cs is nearly torturous, sometimes leading to painful cramping in the fingers and hand. Other children, however, might enjoy printing their A-B-Cs and "writing" letters or stories for an hour at a time. Know your child, his learning style, and his abilities before implementing a homeschool style.

ALERT!

Avoid the temptation to structure homeschool days based on your memories of school schedules. School schedules were developed to handle hundreds of students each day and move them through the system as quickly and efficiently as possible. Since you won't have nearly as many children in your home, a school-based schedule is neither appropriate nor necessary.

Easing into a Schedule

Schedules shouldn't be too binding or restrictive. Basically, schedules provide structure to our days, and structure helps to delineate our daily lives. For children, structure can provide feelings of security and stability. It helps to establish a foundation with everyday routines and a way of life that children can depend on and feel comfortable with.

As you create a schedule for your child's homeschool day, stick close to the routines they are already familiar with. If your children are accustomed to waking at 7:30 and having breakfast at 8:00, there's no need to change that schedule when you begin homeschooling. After breakfast, the children can help clean up the kitchen, make their beds, and get ready for their day. You can plan to have lunch and dinner at your usual times, playtime and bedtime as before, and weave the educational activities into the daily routine.

Start gently, perhaps by reading aloud from a favorite book in the mornings and doing artwork or crafts before lunch. Following lunch, the children can play quietly with puzzles or games, then go outside or into the garage for recreation time or take a walk to the park. Upon returning to the house, you may want to do a lesson that focuses on history or science. The next day, perhaps you'll want to include a math lesson or a spelling game. Most important, avoid trying to do too much in one day, especially as you are starting out.

Flexibility in the Homeschool

Flexibility is the key to a smooth-running homeschool, and it is also a stress-reliever. When you expect too much of yourself—or too much of your children—you'll burden yourself with a schedule that's difficult to keep. And you'll set your family up for a less-than-enjoyable homeschool experience.

Taking on the education of your child is an immense responsibility. So it's understandable that you'll want to do everything "right" or by the book. But, as you've already found as a parent, some things don't go exactly as planned. There are times when you need to try some trial-and-error tactics as you raise your child. The same is true when homeschooling him.

A Harried Homeschool Schedule

Shannon had spent a year collecting and researching homeschool information before she began the home education program for nine-year-old Jonah. She had the schedule all worked out and posted on the refrigerator door. There were timeslots for each subject, chore, and breakfast, lunch, snacks, and dinner. After the morning chores were done, English was scheduled from 9:00 until 9:30, math from 9:30 until 10:00, science from 10:00 until 10:45, and social studies from 10:45 until 11:15. From 11:15 until lunch, which was scheduled for 11:30, Jonah could have some "free time."

At first, Shannon felt like they were accomplishing a lot. She felt satisfied and on top of things, having covered so much territory from breakfast until lunch. After a few weeks, however, she began to worry. Although she had allowed extra time for science (forty-five minutes, rather than the thirty minutes she'd scheduled for the other subjects), some days their experiments ran longer than she had anticipated. This cut into the time she had scheduled for social studies, which took away Jonah's "free time" before lunch, and even pushed lunch back on some days.

She tried rushing through the science experiments, which upset Jonah, since that was the part he liked the most about each day.

He started complaining about social studies to the point that he wouldn't listen or apply himself to the history lessons. At about the same time, the math lessons became a bit more complex, requiring extra time during the 9:30 to 10:00 time frame, which threw off the entire morning schedule. Shannon grew increasingly worried and frustrated with each passing day.

A Kinder, Gentler Homeschool

Shannon's husband, Mike, made a suggestion, as he removed the schedule that was posted on their refrigerator door. "Try doing lessons without a timetable," he said.

Shannon could barely fathom that, but she knew something had to give or she would drive herself—and probably her family—insane. She and Jonah began taking each lesson as it came, spending the time they felt was necessary on the lesson, whether it was twenty minutes or two hours. Soon, both felt more relaxed and began to enjoy their lessons more.

At first, Shannon had panicked when they didn't cover history one day (because they had spent two hours on science experiments). But she soon saw that they could cover the history lesson the next day, when they had a shorter science lesson. She also saw that Jonah was much happier, and she was less frazzled. She had found the key to an enjoyable homeschool experience: flexibility.

FACT

When your children have time to learn and explore on their own, you'll soon see how they can learn quite effectively—without being tied to a tight schedule each day. Allow them time to find their own niche and learning style. If you feel they're straying too far from some topics, gently help to guide them back. At the end of each month, you'll be surprised at how much ground they have covered by themselves.

Learning Naturally Every Day

Once you're able to look back on a few weeks and see how much your child has learned on his own, you'll understand that adhering to a strict schedule is not a requirement in the homeschool. Children *will* learn; you need not worry about that. As long as you set a good example, show interest in reading and learning new things, show interest in your children and in *their* interests, provide some guidance and be available to help answer their questions, children will learn.

Now, they may not always learn exactly what you want them to learn at the exact time you want them to learn it, but that's the beauty of built-in flexibility. If they don't learn algebra this year, they can learn it next year. If they can't grasp genetic engineering this year, they can try again next year.

As you've found, not every child walks or talks or learns to tie his shoes or ride a bike, at the same age. Similarly, not every child can grasp algebra at age fourteen or genetic engineering at age fifteen.

QUESTION?

My seventeen-year-old still doesn't understand algebra; what can I do?
Certain topics may be especially important for your child to learn, due to college plans or a particular career. Enlist the aid of a reputable tutor. He or she can help your child grasp concepts and be well prepared for college or an important career.

The Unschool Schedule

The schedule an unschooler follows may not include English class from 9:00 to 9:30, math from 9:30 until 10:00, and so on. However, the unschooler usually finds himself reading and writing each day, mainly because he enjoys it. And, as a result, his English and composition skills improve through practicing something that he enjoys. The unschooler often uses math skills, logical thinking skills, and computational skills as he designs, measures, and builds a birdhouse or helps reconcile the family's checkbook and learns how to live within a budget.

The unschooler understands that part of his responsibility as a youngster in his household is to get a good education. He has usually been encouraged to read anything that interests him, to pursue any hobbies that interest him, and to research any subjects that interest him.

As a result, the unschooler naturally establishes a routine of sorts that works for him and his areas of interest. Although it may not be the type of homeschool schedule some families follow, it's a familiar direction that his days take, one that he's comfortable with.

Although an unschooler's day may not be as cut and dried as a more stringent homeschool day, you can still keep daily records. Write down the activities your child is involved with each day. Document the books read, the progress of projects, research conducted, and experiments performed, or have your child write them in a journal.

Trusting Natural Learning

Since many children have never experienced unschooling or natural learning, they could feel confused by the concept of it. To see how they respond, try opening up your homeschool schedule by allowing more free time between studies for pursuing things that interest your child. For instance, if you have English from 9:00 to 9:30, let your child work on a hobby between 9:30 and 10:00, then go on to a math lesson for half an hour, then allow a couple hours for scientific explorations that interest him.

After lunch, you could read a biography or history book together, then encourage him to learn something more about the era you just read about. Maybe he'd want to research the type of games kids played in that era, or the toys they had, or how people survived without electricity and technology. Then, rather than writing a report about what he learns, encourage him to reproduce a toy similar to what kids had in those days, and the two of you can play a game with it. Or suggest that he create an invention that could have made life easier for folks during that period of history.

By suggesting alternatives to doing worksheets and writing reports, you help him open his mind to other ways of learning. Over time, you may find that he learns more—and retains more—when he actively pursues areas that relate to his lessons. He has more control over what he studies and what he learns, he therefore has more interest in it, and, consequently, it has more meaning for him. From the above example, you better understand how your son's interests meld with his studies.

FACT

Some children learn better with a traditional school-like schedule. If you've given your child ample opportunities to try a less-structured schedule and he just doesn't take to it, then he's helped you to better understand his preferred learning style. Rather than trying to change your child to one style or another, let him show you how he learns best.

Scheduling Suggestions

In Chapter 1, we noted average times generally required to cover reading, math, language arts, social studies, and science in the homeschool each day. We'll recap them here:

- **Preschool and kindergarten:** 30 to 60 minutes
- **Elementary ages:** 60 to 90 minutes
- **Middle-school ages:** 1½ to 3 hours
- **High-school ages:** 2 to 4 hours

In a conventional school, a six-hour day is consumed by attendance taking, quieting the class, handling disruptive students, helping other students, lunch, recesses, physical education, showers, school assemblies, pep rallies, numerous minutes wasted between each class, and oodles of paperwork. In your homeschool, you won't need to schedule many of these events into your day. Plus, you won't be handling twenty-five or thirty children in your homeschool each day.

Therefore, rather than a six-hour school day, or even a four-hour school day, you can generally cover the required subjects within one to three hours, depending on your child's age. As mentioned earlier, some kindergarten-aged children can sit still for several minutes at a time, while others can't. Some can hold or move a pencil longer and better than others can.

Remember that your child is unique. Your kindergartner may only need thirty minutes of formal studies each day, or she may enjoy sixty minutes. Your thirteen-year-old may cover her lessons in two hours, or she may spend four hours on her lessons. Take time to observe your child, her interest in her studies, her attention span, the way she tires, or the way she seems to get a second wind later in the day. When you work with her capabilities, rather than trying to force someone else's schedule upon her, the homeschool day will proceed more smoothly.

Covering the Core Subjects

Even though math, language arts, social studies, and science are important subjects to be covered, you can build flexibility into your schedule. If it generally takes two or three hours to cover these subjects for a middle-grader, it doesn't mean they all have to fit into those daily two- or three-hour slots. Here's a summary of one way that could be used to cover lessons for a middle-schooler:

- **Monday:** In science, spent three hours reading about convection and conduction, performed several experiments under supervision with steam and heat vapors, and wrote a summary of what was learned.
- **Tuesday:** In social studies, spent two and a half hours reading about the Battle of Shiloh, learned more about General Grant's and General Johnston's roles, drew a map of the battlefield, and began working on a model of the battlefield.
- **Wednesday:** In language arts, spent four hours reading a story, rewrote it in a screenplay format, assigned characters to the parts, designed props, and made plans to perform the play.
- **Thursday:** In math, spent three hours working on a lesson in the geometry textbook, did logical reasoning puzzles in a software program, used foam models to draw accurate representation of cones and cubes, and used geometry concepts to help design and create model of Shiloh Battlefield.
- **Friday:** Worked on battlefield model more, began reading book by Gary Paulsen about the Civil War, got together with friends for games and experiments, began writing a story about a boy during the Civil War.

Although the above schedule may not be a conventional schedule, this middle-schooler spent about the same amount of time on each subject area over the course of one week as a child following a more typical school schedule. More important, he had special interest in each topic he participated in, had time to expand upon the topics or to put new knowledge into practice, and consequently retained the information longer, due to his interest and involvement.

Adding Variety Each Day

In addition to the time spent on required subject areas, such as math and English, you can keep a wellspring of ideas for other educational ideas for each day. Before or after the required subjects have been covered, children can focus on their special areas of interest, try a new hobby or craft, work on an ongoing project, or research new ideas.

One family cut up dozens of strips of plain paper, then began jotting down things they enjoyed doing, or things they'd like to do, on the strips of paper. They then folded the strips and dropped them into a plastic jar. On days when the kids couldn't think of anything to occupy themselves with, or they were simply bored, they would reach into the jar and pull out a strip of paper with an idea on it. If that idea didn't strike their fancy at that particular moment, they could always drop the paper back into the jar and select another slip of paper. Soon, the kids were immersed in motivating activities that they had forgotten about, that they enjoyed doing, and that helped to supplement their education.

Time Management Tips

When you have a family to take care of daily—perhaps a baby, a toddler, and a couple of older youngsters—and a house to keep tidy and errands to run, it may seem as though the day is gone before you've even had a moment to think about it. How will you incorporate homeschooling into such a busy schedule that already consumes the majority of your day? As often as we've heard it, it's still true: We *do* make time for the things we want to do in our lives. It just depends on how badly we want it.

If you want to watch a favorite television show each week, you usually find the time to watch it. If you want to read a chapter of a fascinating book each evening, you generally make time to do it. If homeschooling the kids is important enough to you, chances are you can find the time to do it.

As you've previously seen, you don't need to follow a school-at-home schedule. Simply allow your kids to learn, have an idea of what they "should" be learning, provide some guidance and ideas for them each week, and be there to help answer their questions, to provide direction, and to be a sounding board for ideas to bounce off of for input and feedback.

ALERT!

Remember: Homeschooling is not a "school at home." Don't confuse yourself or your children, thinking that it should be. You'll only make it harder on yourself. A *school* is an institution or a facility. A *home* is where you live with your family. *Homeschooling* is a way of living. It includes training and guidance in the home—a warm, comfortable, safe environment within the family unit.

Setting Weekly Goals

Goal-setting is the key to time management. Each weekend, decide the five most important things you want to accomplish in your homeschool during the upcoming week, and write them down. You have five days ahead of you to accomplish those five goals. Cross one off each day, or cross two off one day and one off the next. However you want to handle it, try to accomplish and cross off your five goals at some point during that week. Do this each week, and you'll be surprised at how much you are capable of accomplishing.

Try to focus on the most important goal, then move on to the next. The goals may vary from week to week. For instance, this upcoming week, your most important goal may be to cover three lessons in the math book. The least important goal this week may be to read about the Industrial Revolution.

When focusing on the math goal, determine the period of time during the day when your child is most alert and receptive to math lessons. This could be first thing in the morning or it could be at 4:00 in the afternoon. If the math lessons need your undivided attention, and you have babies or toddlers in the home, try to time those lessons with the younger children's naptime. If that's not possible, perhaps an older child can entertain the younger ones while you help your child with math lessons.

When there's work to be done, children often come up with innovative ways to get it done as quickly as possible. Rather than nagging the children, consult with them and ask for their ideas, then try them. When children are more inspired to help and are gratified to see you trying their ideas, the whole process goes more quickly. It could even turn into fun family time together.

Simplifying Housework

Each person living in the home has duties to fulfill within the family. A list of responsibilities for each person, children included, can be posted in plain view, so that no questions or squabbles arise. Each child can certainly be responsible for his or her room, bed making, linen changing, closet cleaning, polishing of furniture, vacuuming of floors (if capable), or general tidying up. In the rest of the house, everyone can take turns vacuuming, polishing furniture, and cleaning bathrooms. You may do it one week, the next week your daughter may handle it, the following week your son may be responsible for it, and so on. Or, you can all jump in together one afternoon and complete the housecleaning in an hour or two.

Here are some ways to streamline the chores:

- Prepare and cook several dishes, soups, or casseroles on Saturday or Sunday afternoon, then freeze them for the upcoming week.
- Enlist the help of children in daily meal preparations, mixing muffins, setting the table, clearing the table, scraping off dishes, putting away leftovers, and so on.
- Assign each child certain responsibilities in the home, or let them select, switch, or share chores with each other.

- Give each child a box or basket and send them through the house to pick up any items that are out of place.
- Play classical or pop music to make the cleanup time more enjoyable for all. Sing and discuss the music as you clean house, and you've just covered your music lesson for the day.
- Have children help on laundry day as they sort colors, remove clothes from the dryer, match socks, fold and hang clothing—all while you're discussing a history lesson.

Combine errands at one time, when possible, to save on driving time. Drop the dog at the grooming salon, make the deposit at the bank, drop the bills and letters at the post office, take your child to art or dance class, get a haircut, fill up the gas tank, do the grocery shopping, and pick up your child and your dog on the way home.

Timesaving Tips

Here are some timesaving tips that may be helpful in your homeschool:

- Keep all homeschooling books, supplies, records, and logs in one closet so they are easy to locate.
- Jot down weekly goals and lesson plans while having your morning coffee, watching the evening news, or nestling a baby in your lap.
- Have older children keep their own daily logs of books read, assignments done, and projects completed.
- Encourage older children to help younger ones with lessons and to record some of the younger children's activities in the daily log.
- Use colorful, stimulating books from the library to cover subjects that children tend to drag over.
- Incorporate as many skills as possible into a lesson plan, such as reading and writing skills, experimentation skills, estimation or calculation skills, and analytic skills.
- Include several periods of free time during the day, providing a break for the children and time for you to accomplish other activities.

Read to children and discuss as many topics as possible, rather than assigning chapters in textbooks. This reduces time spent dawdling over dry material and answering chapter questions. You also won't have to spend time grading papers when you engage in discussions. Plus, children retain more from lively discussions than from dry textbooks.

Time for Rest and Relaxation

Now it's time for some much-deserved rest and relaxation! Both are necessary components for a stress-free day, so be sure to allow time for them in your homeschool schedule. Each day should have a pleasant balance of active time and quiet time. The experiments, construction projects, nature walks, sports, and other physical activities should be interspersed with reading time, quiet playtime, and rest time.

If you find that a half hour of rest each day isn't enough, try an hour of rest and relaxation. If that still isn't enough to refresh you, or you feel stressed every day, it could be time for some extended rest and relaxation—in other words, vacation time! And that's one of the benefits of homeschooling—you can take a break or vacation whenever you need it. And when you return to your homeschool schedule, you'll have the energy to see you through until it's time to take another well-deserved break! Ⓔ

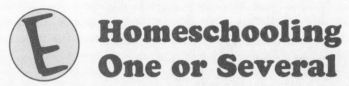

Chapter 9

Homeschooling
One or Several

If you're the parent of an only child, you may worry that he will be lonely if you homeschool him. If you have a larger family, you may worry that you won't be able to spend enough time with each child. Fortunately, there are solutions for each situation that will make your days flow smoothly.

Homeschooling the Only Child

Some families have received the mistaken impression that homeschooling an only child isn't a good idea. This idea probably resulted from the socialization concern, which, as we've already seen, shouldn't be a concern at all. Your only child can have as many opportunities to socialize as any child.

Both scenarios—an only child or several children in the family—may have their benefits and their disadvantages, depending on the viewpoint one prefers to take. What it comes down to, though, is the love, respect, and warmth that each family member feels for the other, regardless of how many people make up the family unit.

The decision to homeschool—or not—shouldn't be determined by how many or how few children are in the family. Rather, your reasons for homeschooling should focus on the desire to provide a good, well-rounded education for your child or children in a safe, caring environment.

View from an Only Child

Devin, now twenty-three years old, was a homeschooled only child. Today, he is a computer programmer with a company that prides itself on teamwork. Although he was raised and homeschooled as an only child, he's an integral part of this company's team, adept at working with others to solve problems on a regular basis.

"I didn't have the benefit of brothers or sisters as I was growing up," Devin admits, "but I had my parents and several close friends. I wasn't on the go all the time, but I also wasn't isolated. I went to my friends' homes, had my friends over to my house, took Tae Kwon Do and swimming lessons, as well as guitar and keyboard classes when I was younger.

"Sometimes, I'd go to work with my parents. I also helped out in a comic book shop from the time I was thirteen until I was seventeen. So, I've always had the opportunity to work with the public and see what it's like to work in offices and different types of businesses.

"I remember days at home when I'd start to feel bored, but I figured any kid would get bored from time to time. It was always easy to find something to do: work on a comic book I was writing; a piece of artwork; play my guitar; record some of my music on a tape, and later, on CD-ROMs; or do some programming on the computer."

Benefits for an Only Child

"I was always reading books on programming," Devin continues. "I started with BASIC back when I was twelve, then progressed to Visual BASIC, JavaScript, C++, and other programs. All that reading and programming definitely paid off now that I'm a programmer. Even today, I'll get the desire to learn a new type of computer code, get a book on it, learn it, and start creating a program in it.

"If it hadn't been for homeschooling, I'm not sure I would've had the time to spend on programming like I did. When I was in public school, it took up most of my time, especially with all the homework I had to do in the evenings and on the weekends. If I hadn't had the time to spend on programming, I doubt if I would've become a programmer. That's hard to fathom, too, because it's the thing I most enjoy doing.

FACT

Child development experts warn parents of only children to not be overly protective or to smother them with too much attention. Let the child find ways to entertain herself at times and to find things that truly interest *her*. Allow her to enjoy being alone when it suits her or to go places on her own, depending on her age.

"As a homeschooler, I did the regular subjects, but I had a lot more time each day to do the things that I really wanted to do, like programming, music, and art. I never really felt lonely; I kept myself busy, and a parent was always around. I was always close with my parents; I'd do things with them at home, go places with them, go on field trips or to happenings in the area. And we were always talking together, whether it was something trivial or something of great importance.

"Since I'm an only child, I can't really compare the experience with what it's like to grow up in a larger family. I know there were times when

I'd be at friends' homes, and their brother or sister would continuously get on their nerves, and I'd think that I was glad I didn't have to put up with that! But I'm sure that having brothers or sisters has its benefits, too. I just know that being a homeschooled only child made me feel pretty lucky, and it gave me the opportunity to become the person I am today. And, for that, I'm very thankful."

Socialization for the Only Child

Since socialization may still be a concern for some, we'll look at ways your only child can interact with others and build a network of friends. As mentioned in previous chapters, children can join playgroups or take gymnastics, music, or drama classes given at city parks and recreation departments. They can join clubs, scouting groups, or a ball team.

QUESTION?

How can I help my child get over her shyness?
Shyness is not necessarily a negative thing. But if your child's shyness causes her discomfort, strive to improve her self-confidence and self-esteem. Praise her qualities and capabilities and help her feel good about herself. Never push her into situations she feels timid about.

If you live in a rural area far from cities, towns, or neighbors, consider joining the closest church in your area. Country churches have long been meeting places for families, and they provide an opportunity to get together with others every week. Since the country church is somewhat isolated, they sometimes offer more events to bring the community closer together. They may hold country fairs, spaghetti dinners, fried chicken picnics, youth group meetings during the week, and family games or crafts on Saturday nights. They may even be able to introduce you to other homeschool families in your community.

Homeschooling Multiple Children

Mary and John homeschool their seven children, ranging in age from eight months to seventeen years old. They've been homeschooling since their oldest was six years old.

"Daniel was four when we began homeschooling Michelle," says Mary. "And Lauren was just a baby. That was nearly twelve years ago. Michelle went to kindergarten when she was five; Danny missed her terribly, and she didn't like being away from him. She had a hard time adapting to the kindergarten routine. When Lauren came along, I felt it'd be better for the whole family if I homeschooled Michelle that year. At that time, I didn't know we'd be doing it for the next twelve years!

"But, looking back now, I wouldn't have wanted it any other way. In fact, it doesn't seem normal to me, sending a child off to spend its day in a school building, day after day, year after year, having no control over the type of education she receives. It's not something I could ever do now.

"Oh, there were times when it was tempting!" Mary laughs. "There are days when I've thought I was trying to do the impossible, homeschooling five kids, chasing a toddler and trying to comfort a colicky baby. But those days are usually my own fault, not my kids' fault. It's because I'm trying to do too much in one day, trying to go too far in one direction."

Everyday Education

Like many families who homeschool several children, Mary and John view home education as a part of everyday life. "In the beginning," John says, "Mary had a schedule that she followed. But as the younger children became involved in the homeschooling process, the schedule was soon dispensed with.

"Mary would sit at the dining room table, doing lessons with Michelle and Danny, when Lauren and Jill would climb up on her lap and want to 'do school.' They were only toddlers then, but they'd get up on the table and doodle on paper with crayons, mimicking some of the things the older two were doing. It wasn't long before you started seeing A-B-Cs and 1-2-3s appearing on their papers—things they'd picked up from watching the older kids."

"Rather than following a schedule," Mary explains, "I just welcomed each little one as they expressed interest in what we were doing. I made sure there was paper and crayons available, and they started 'doing school' by the time they were two or three. I always read to the kids; oh, I've read so many books these past twelve years!"

Several Helping Hands

"We do have a routine or format that we follow nearly every day," Mary continues. "We have to, with nine people in the family, or we'd never get anything done! We'd just be bumping around into each other all day! So, we get the things done that need doing each day, and we learn a lot every day. The older kids are great with the younger ones; they always have been. I'm not sure I could've done this without their help. Yet, it's not like they're 'assisting,' really. It's just that we're family, and we care about each other, and we all help each other."

Assistance from Siblings

As evidenced by Mary and John's family, the older siblings were influential in the younger children's lives and learning. The younger children wanted to emulate their older siblings and "do school" along with them. And the older children enjoyed seeing the younger ones learn from them. This can be a great source of satisfaction for older children and helps to reinforce their own learning, as well.

Remember to show your appreciation to the older children, and never take them or their help for granted. In fact, reward them by allowing them some extra free time, or arrange a special time when they can just be with you, apart from the rest of the family.

Let your older children know that you don't expect them to teach the younger ones. However, you would appreciate them interacting with the younger ones, continuing to extend goodwill and kindness toward their brothers and sisters. If they could help entertain a younger child while you help a middle child with a lesson, it could make parts of the day go more smoothly and allow more time for everyone at the end of the day.

Observe your older children to see how they take to this. You don't want to see them develop a grudge toward the younger children. At the same time, every member is an important part of the family unit, and it's important that everyone gets along and respects one another.

ALERT!

There may be times when you need to sit down with each child and have a heart-to-heart talk. The chance to express oneself can be lost in the day-to-day action of family life. Let children know that you're always willing to listen to their concerns and feelings, and then share quiet times together when they feel free to talk with you.

If older children believe that they are being taken advantage of, or if they feel that they don't have enough time to themselves, take their concerns seriously. Try to create an arrangement that allows extra time for themselves and their friends. In most cases, they'll be happy to help out again in a few days, after they've had a break from the normal routine. Everyone needs a vacation now and then—even children!

Keeping the Schedule on Track

Even if you don't follow a strict schedule, most families have a framework they try to work within each day. This could be a loose unschooling format or an outline of what you want to accomplish during the day. In addition, you'll have your normal daily routine of meals, laundry, and housecleaning duties, so you'll want to keep those on schedule as well.

There are times, though, when an errant wind seems to blow through town, disrupting even the best-laid plans. And just like that, your good intentions for the day have been scattered. Try to not let it upset you. Understand that it's just one of those things that will happen occasionally, and tomorrow will be a better day.

Here are some ideas for helping your children stay on track:

- Consider a self-study program for some of the children if it seems to suit their learning style.
- Print out guidelines for each child's weekly educational goals or lesson plans, post it on their door or bulletin board, and encourage them to achieve the goals.
- Pair children up when they share certain learning styles, then work with two or three children at a time.
- Bring out new games, puzzles, or books to entertain some of the children while you're working with others.
- Try the unit study methods (described in Chapter 5), which can usually be adapted to all age levels.
- Set aside time every day when each child can have individual time with you (when others are napping, for example).

Time Off for the Teacher

Homeschooling can be stressful, even if you're homeschooling only one child. When you're trying to keep several children on track and taking care of a baby or preschooler at the same time, the stress can multiply. And this is something you definitely want to avoid.

Stress Reduction

Some of the main causes of stress in a homeschool are trying to do too much, planning to cover too much territory in a school year, and setting expectations too high for yourself and for your children. If you don't allow enough flexibility in your day, or you try to adhere too strictly to a schedule, this can compound the stress you're feeling.

Here are some ways to reduce stress in your homeschool:

- Don't try to be "SuperParent." When you overextend yourself, you overstress your body.
- Cut back on extracurricular activities. Your children don't need to attend every class that comes along.

- Reduce the number of topics you're trying to cover. There's always next month or next year for covering those subjects.
- Guide your children in self-directed learning. Provide books and resources that will help them to learn on their own.
- Seek support from other homeschool families. They've often found great ways of reducing stress and achieving a more balanced lifestyle.

Simplify Your Days

Try different ways to simplify your day: simpler meals, simpler housecleaning methods, more breaks during the day, more playtime. If nothing seems to be going right on a particular day, then stop while you're ahead and scrap the plans for today. Just as housework can always wait until another day, so can math or science. Nothing is as important as family and happiness within the family, so take the day off, go to the park or the beach with the family, and don't think another thought about homeschooling, lessons, or learning. Your mind needs a break and so do the kids.

Ask your children for input and ideas for simplifying homeschool and housework. They can look at things from a totally different angle and come up with some interesting solutions. Praise them for their suggestions and contributions, then try some of their ideas. They may just be the perfect answer!

As you relax and unwind, your children are busy playing and having fun. Don't forget that play is an important part of learning. Play provides time for children to learn on their own, to explore and experiment, to use trial-and-error, and to exercise choice and freedom in a fun and safe manner. So even as you relax and your children play, rest assured that learning is still taking place.

Mini-Vacations

Vacations can be long or short, helping you to regain your energy and sense of balance within your life. Frequent mini-vacations can be especially beneficial. You can homeschool Monday through Thursday, then Friday can be "free day." The children can select their own activities, and you won't need to create lesson plans for that day. It can be your "free day" as well.

Indulge yourself on your "free Friday." Take your time sipping your morning coffee or orange juice in bed or on the porch, where it's quiet and peaceful. Don't make any plans for the day, except for those that you'll find enjoyable.

Here's a great way to relax and renew yourself. Slip away on your free day into a glorious bubble bath. While the younger children are napping, or the older children are watching the little ones, treat yourself to a long, luxurious bath that will wash away your worries and rejuvenate your soul.

Getting Away

If it's a longer vacation you need, you can homeschool for three full weeks in a row, then take the fourth week off every month. Follow this cycle for twelve months, and you'll attain an average school year with thirty-six weeks. And you'll have a week-long vacation, every three weeks.

You can take longer vacations when following a traditional nine-month school year, with two weeks off during Christmas holidays, one or two weeks off around the Easter holiday, and most of the summer off. For longer holidays such as these, you might want to plan on getting away for a while, spending a week at a lake or beach cottage, staying in a cabin in a national park, or visiting with relatives in another city or state.

When you've had a chance to get away for several days, it's a wonderful feeling to come back home. And the entire family is usually re-energized and ready to get back to their normal routine once again. Ⓔ

Chapter 10

Typical Homeschool Days

One of the most common misunderstandings about a typical homeschool day is that there must be such a thing. Actually, each homeschool day is usually somewhat different from the day before. Therefore, the term "typical day" may actually be a misnomer. The point of sharing a "typical day" is mainly to provide insight into the fun, exciting life homeschoolers lead!

What Is a Typical Day?

A "typical homeschool day" is the name given to the description of a day in the life of a homeschooled family. As many families can attest, their days are not exactly typical. It's a little like trying to define an "average" family. What is average? How can average be measured or compared when referring to individuals?

The same is true for the typical day. What may be typical for one family may be impractical for another. When reading or hearing about others' typical days, don't feel that you should pattern your days after theirs. It's fun to hear about others' experiences, and we might even pick up some interesting ideas we hadn't considered before. But *your* homeschool day reflects *your* family's lifestyle and the things that work for you and your children. If it's working for you, there's no need to change it!

Recording Your Typical Day

When homeschoolers are registered with the school district in some states, they may be asked to submit a copy of their typical day. Of course, not every day is going to be the same, nor will it necessarily be "typical." Generally, homeschool officials simply like to know that your children are staying active, pursuing areas of study commensurate with their abilities, engaging in learning activities throughout the day, and spending time developing and furthering their skills and knowledge.

Timeline of a Homeschool Day

If you need to submit a typical homeschool day to your district at any point, you might ask them if they have a preferred format. Many are written in basic paragraph style, starting with events that first occur in your homeschool day. Others may follow a more structured timeline, such as the following:

- **8:00–9:30:** We had breakfast and talked about the things we planned to do that day. Son Number One wants to continue working on his airplane model. Daughter Number Two wants to try her hand at building a dollhouse. We put on music and sang together while cleaning the kitchen, making beds, and doing morning chores.

- **9:30–10:30:** The two older children did their math assignments in their Saxon math books. I worked with the two younger children, using math manipulatives for counting, sorting, adding, and subtracting.
- **10:30–11:30:** For science, the two older children took turns reading about magnetism. Then everyone gathered items for the magnetism experiments, from large magnets to magnetic shavings, from plastic items to metal items to try in the experiments.
- **11:30–12:30:** Lunchtime and time for early afternoon chores. Then it's time for reading and writing activities.

The rest of the typical day is recorded in much the same style, noting the books read, papers written, topics discussed, and so on. Obviously, the timeslots do not need to be as stringent, as some activities will take longer or shorter amounts of time. When you're done recording your day, you'll be able to provide insight into the various subjects your children study and the way in which they study them. This will be beneficial to homeschool officials, should they need this information.

Freeform Homeschool Day

Rather than a timeline like the one shown above, you can write about the things you did that day in paragraph format. Again, check with your homeschool administrator if they have requested to see a "typical day." They may prefer one style over the other. Based on the homeschool day outlined above, a paragraph style may read similar to the following:

We sat down to breakfast around 8:00, and the kids began talking about the things they wanted to do that day. Son Number One wants to continue working on his airplane model. Daughter Number Two wants to try her hand at building a dollhouse. We put on music and sang together while cleaning the kitchen, making beds, and doing morning chores.

By midmorning, our chores were done, and the two older children began working on their math assignments in their Saxon math books. I worked with the two younger children, using math manipulatives for counting, sorting, adding, and subtracting. As I was finishing with the younger children, the two older ones worked on the life-sized cardboard skeletal system they're creating in the playroom.

After this, we decided to do a few science experiments. The kids wanted to use their collection of magnets, so the two older children took turns reading about magnetism from a science book. Then everyone gathered items for the experiments: large magnets, small magnets, magnetic shavings, plastic items, metal items. This kept all four kids absorbed until lunchtime. I fixed lunch while watching their experiments and providing feedback. Around noon, we had our lunch, then straightened the kitchen and did our early afternoon chores. Now it's time for reading one of our favorite books and writing in our journals.

FACT

Keep track of homeschool activities by writing about the subjects you cover each day. Remember to describe some of the fun, surprising events that usually occur during a normal day. Not only will you have a record of a typical day, but you'll create an interesting daily log that your children will one day enjoy looking back on.

Breaking the Monotony

It may seem as if your typical days have turned into lifeless, uneventful days. Your family gets up, eats breakfast, does math, science, language arts, and social studies. So, what's there to write about?

Sometimes our days can fall into a rut, or we find ourselves with a case of the doldrums. That doesn't mean that it has to stay that way. Do something different or daring to jolt the very foundation of your homeschool day. Break away from the same old humdrum pattern by doing something totally unexpected. You can start by surprising the kids with your new "harebrained" idea.

Dare to Be Different

If you've been doing math every morning at 9:00, science at 10:00, social studies at 11:00, and so on, for the last several months, here's an idea: When the kids shuffle into the room to begin the 9:00 math lesson, tell them you don't want to see a math book for the next two weeks.

What!? Everyone will be aghast.

Yes, you'll tell them. Remove those math books from your sight, hide them, bury them if they must. (Just remember where they're hidden! Because you *will* need them again at some point. Just not for the next two weeks.)

Now, for the next two weeks, they—the children—will create and present math lessons, without the use of books. From their memory, knowledge, and comprehension of math skills, they will use math in some way each day to teach math lessons, to illustrate math concepts, or to simply prove that they can, indeed, do math without using a math book. You'll notice the kids eagerly looking forward to math over the next two weeks, rather than dully shuffling in, math books in tow.

Try handing the teaching part of homeschooling over to the children—the lesson planning, the educational activities, field trip suggestions, and reading and writing assignments. See how many creative ideas they can develop for learning. This will add some spark and excitement to the previously uneventful days.

Try an Atypical Homeschool Day

If your typical homeschool day seems okay, but it's become a bit too commonplace, try an *atypical* day. If you normally do lessons at the dining room table, inform the children that all lessons will be done outdoors today. If necessary, carry some chairs and television trays outdoors, and that's where the day's lessons will take place. You can take advantage of the outdoors by using it to assist with the day's lessons, from math to science to geography, and more.

Better yet, tell the children to pack a picnic lunch, because the day's lessons will be held at the park or the beach. It's not a day off, though, nor a mini-vacation. Not this time. This time, you'll do lessons just as you would at home, except you'll be in the fresh air all day and in new surroundings far removed from the dining table at home. Of course, the children can play once the lessons are finished, providing a perfect ending to an invigorating day. Now the whole family is animated and rejuvenated.

When you hold your lessons outdoors or at a park, you'll feel as though the fresh air has whisked through your mind and your home, blowing away cobwebs that had ensnared your family in dull, too-typical days. Try to incorporate atypical days into your homeschool schedule as often as possible, and enjoy the change of scenery.

Attaining a Well-Rounded Education

When you write down the events of a typical day, you're often surprised to see how many things are accomplished in one day. At the same time, it may become clear that some things are not receiving as much attention as others. Maybe you don't spend as much time on art, music, character education, physical education, or life skills as you had planned.

Now is a good time to reconsider your daily schedule and to determine how to work toward a more well-rounded education for your children. You don't want to overburden your day by adding more than it can hold, but you can spread subjects over the course of a week or a couple weeks. Then you'll open up a bit more time each day to include character education, life skills, or other topics that haven't received as much attention lately.

Remember when you attended middle school or high school? One semester or six-week period was devoted to home economics, one was devoted to shop, one to art, one to music, and so on. Similarly, you can find blocks of time for these and other topics, without having to squeeze everything into every single day. And at the end of three months or six months, when you look back over the subjects your child has covered, you'll be impressed with the well-rounded education she is receiving.

ALERT!

If you don't cover every topic every day, but you don't want homeschool officials to think you're skimping on lessons, try writing a "typical homeschool week." Jot down the topics, events, activities, field trips, and surprises that occur during the day, and keep track of them for a week. You—and they—will see how well-rounded your children's home education is over the course of a week.

Examples of Typical Homeschool Days

Here, families share examples of their typical days. Although they admit that not every day is "typical," they all agree that each day has its own special joys and rewards.

The Hamilton Family

We're early risers and gather for breakfast between 7:00 and 7:30. Dad has to leave for work at 8:00, so the kids, ages ten, eight, five, and two, get to spend time with him before he leaves. Today, after breakfast, I read to all four kids from *The Long Way to a New Land*. They always enjoy having me read aloud first thing in the morning; even the toddler plays quietly on the floor or couch as I read. Afterwards, I ask the kids what it might be like to leave their home and travel to a new country. We talk about the hardships they might experience, as well as exciting new adventures they might have.

Derek, age ten, wants to learn more about the country the boy in the book is leaving, so I help him find Sweden on the globe. Deanne, age eight, joins him, while Darcy, age five, spins the globe, and picks a place, asking, "What's this town?" or "What's this country?" She thinks it's especially funny when her pointer finger lands in an ocean. "What's this ocean? How many oceans are there?"

Derek is trying to determine how many miles the family in the book traveled from Sweden to Minnesota, and so our math class begins. Derek and Deanne are using encyclopedias, atlases, and maps from the bookshelf to measure and add the miles. Then they begin calculating how far the family travels in one day on a ship and how long it will take to reach the shores of America. Meanwhile, my younger daughter is still at the globe, trying to measure the distance of the oceans from Africa to New York, and from California to Japan.

FACT

At one point in our typical day, interest drifts from math problems to geography, and the kids decide to get out their "Take Off" geography game. All three of the children love this game. Danielle, my two-year-old, is too young, so she and I engage in finger-plays while the older ones fly their jets across the world and learn about the different countries.

After lunch, while Danielle naps and Darcy looks through picture books, I spend time with the older kids on spelling and vocabulary. They learn a new word each day, learn how to spell it, and they find ways to use it in a conversation. Some days, they write it in a paragraph. After this, the kids can usually play a while, draw, paint, get out the clay, or do puzzles, while I do some chores before Danielle awakes from her nap.

It's warmed up outdoors, so everyone puts on their jackets and we go for a walk around our yard to see what new things we might find. My littlest one always finds new things to explore, preferably with her mouth, so I have to watch her closely! Derek climbs into a tree and says he sees a dump truck hauling rock on the highway in the distance. Deanne can't see it and doesn't care to climb trees. So she digs under a pile of decaying leaves and finds some pill bugs that Derek immediately has to see, so he scoots down from his tree. Darcy doesn't like bugs but wants to find something, too; she picks a bouquet of flowers (mostly weeds) and wants to know the names of them.

The kids run around the yard, chasing each other a while, then red-faced and out of breath, they race each other to the house. We take the flowers (weeds) inside, so the kids can look at them under the microscope. I hear "ooos" and "ahs" as they dissect and view the magnified plants, each taking their turn at the microscope with only minor bickering. While they're absorbed, I take the opportunity to sit nearby and jot down what we've done today. As I review the day, I see we've had literature, history, geography, math, spelling, vocabulary, art, science, rest time, and outdoor recreation. A good typical day so far, and it's not even dinnertime.

The Reilly Family

Although I'm up by 7:00, the kids, ages sixteen, thirteen, and nine, get up a little later. Rachel, age thirteen, usually wakes before the boys and gets on the computer before breakfast. She has to read the news on CNN.com or MSNBC.com so she knows what's going on in the world first thing in the morning. Jared, age nine, is ready for breakfast as soon as he wakes, so he sits down to eat, then Rachel joins him after she's read the news. Matt, age sixteen, usually sleeps the latest. He comes to breakfast as we're cleaning up, and listens to Rachel fill him in on the news stories she read. He finishes cleaning up the kitchen after breakfast as we prepare for our school day.

FACT

I work part time at a landscape nursery from 2:00 till 6:00 during the week and all day on Saturday. My husband is home from work by 4:30 each day and is home all day on Saturdays, so the kids aren't on their own for long. This schedule works well for everyone, allowing the kids quiet time to themselves each day, as well as one-on-one time with their dad.

The older kids are mostly in charge of their studies. We never used a formal curriculum until the kids were older. Matt decided to enroll in a correspondence school affiliated with a university, and Rachel is trying a school that is Internet-based. I still homeschool Jared using an eclectic style that varies from day to day. Even so, we stay focused on lessons from about 9:30 until around noon.

At lunch, we all sit down together and discuss everything that the kids have been doing that morning. If any of them have questions or concerns about their daily lessons, this is when we discuss them. Then I can spend time helping them if necessary before I leave for work. On days when the kids are doing experiments, I request that they're done in the mornings before I leave for work, or that they wait until the evening when I'm home. You never know what might result from an unsupervised experiment!

Each child has lessons and chores to complete while I'm gone and before their father gets home from work. If they complete everything early, then Matt works on his computer, Rachel on music or writing, and Jared on art projects. Each of them must write down what they did each day, too. By the time their father is home, their school day is done, and they look forward to spending time with him. If they have meetings or games in the evening, he'll drive them.

When I arrive home, I take a shower and relax a bit, then we all pitch in to fix dinner around 7:00 most evenings. Sometimes, the kids and their dad will fix an early dinner, and I'll eat alone. Later, we gather in the living room and talk about our day. In this way, our entire family stays in touch with what each child is learning and any concerns they might have. After our family time, the kids go off to work on hobbies or talk with friends. Ours is a comfortable schedule that currently suits our family's lifestyle.

The Morrison Family

My girls, Courtney, age seven, and Kelsey, age five, start the morning in our playroom/schoolroom with the "Pledge of Allegiance." We then put on our CD-ROM of patriotic songs and sing, march, and dance around the room. We usually play a CD-ROM of other fun songs, such as the Wee Sings tunes, and sing and dance to them, too. By now, I have our books and lessons on the girls' worktable, and we sit down to start reading and writing. Courtney can read well, so she helps me in teaching her younger sister to read. After reading, Courtney copies simple sentences and underlines the subjects and circles the verbs in each. Kelsey practices printing simple words she can read.

While we're still content to sit still, we go on to the math practice workbooks. Courtney's is second-grade level and Kelsey's is kindergarten level. Courtney is having trouble with subtraction, so I take extra time to help her. Meanwhile, Kelsey goes over to the play center and starts playing with her dolls. Soon, Courtney is doing better, getting the correct answers to her subtraction problems, and she can leave the worktable and play house with Kelsey for a while.

I clear off the table and set out our science lesson. Right now we're studying insects in our life science book. We have a bugs and butterflies vinyl board set, with cling-on pieces, which the girls use while we're studying this section. The girls are eager to get outside now, so we finish with the lesson and take our bug-catching containers outside.

The plastic containers have air holes and built-in magnifying lids, so the girls can look at the insects up-close. Kelsey fills the containers with grass and leaves to make a soft bed for the bugs, while Courtney collects the bugs. After viewing the little critters, they always let them go exactly where they found them, because they don't want them to "get lost from home."

The neighbor kids see the girls out and come over to play. They all play together in the backyard until we go in to have our lunch. After lunch, we return to the playroom and take out our character education books and social studies workbooks.

FACT

Manners and social skills are important in our homeschool. Currently, we're learning about respect and citizenship. After reading the lessons, we take turns acting out ways to show respect and to treat others with kindness. The girls get colorful stickers for each way they can think of to be nice to others. They put the stickers on their citizenship posters on their bulletin board.

In social studies, we're using a book of multicultural crafts that contains arts and craft ideas while teaching about different cultures and lifestyles. As the girls continue working on a craft, I'll often read a book that relates to the culture. For instance, this week, they're learning about Mexico and working on a piñata, while I read *The Painted Pig,* a book about a Mexican boy who tries to make a piggy bank from clay.

After we clean up the worktable, the girls are free to play house, play with puzzles, build things, or do whatever else they'd like to do. On Tuesday afternoons, they go to dance class, and on Thursday afternoons, to gymnastics. On Wednesday evenings, they usually attend story hour at the library, while I pick out books to complement lessons for the upcoming week.

Keeping Faith Each Day

As we've seen, typical days can vary widely. Just as families and individuals have unique lifestyles and personalities, so do their typical homeschool days. Some days go smoothly and much is accomplished. Other days are not as easy and productive. But each day can still be enjoyable and worthwhile.

When your day doesn't go according to your plans, simply plan to go according to your day! Treasure the time with your kids, let them open your eyes to new ways of learning, and try new activities from time to time. Keep faith in your children's abilities to learn, and keep faith in your ability to help guide them each day. Ⓔ

Chapter 11

Record Keeping

Many states require that you keep records of some sort. Even if it's not mandatory in your state, homeschool records are still valuable tools. They'll help you keep track of lessons, monitor and assess your child's progress, provide verification of your child's education, and document the educational background of your child for college officials.

Planning Ahead

When you have short- and long-term goals for your homeschool, it becomes much easier to plan and record your lessons. In Chapter 3, you determined the educational goals and aims for your child. You can use that outline to plan your homeschool year and to break down your goals into monthly and weekly lesson plans.

Educational Objectives

Your family's educational objectives may include the following:

- Reading quality literature and classics.
- Improving speaking and writing skills.
- Improving mathematical and scientific abilities.
- Understanding world and national history.
- Enhancing musical and artistic skills.
- Functioning responsibly and respectfully as a citizen.

From these objectives, and others you may have, you can decide what subjects to study during the upcoming year to help achieve the goals for your family. You can select literary books to read, English and math textbooks you'd like to use, science and history activity books, music and art courses, and a character education program. Keep a list of the books or materials you may want to use for your homeschool. Research them or check with other families who have used those materials to determine if they'd be compatible with your educational aims.

FACT

If you intend to order books or materials, you'll need to plan ahead. If your homeschool is slated to start in the middle of August, you'll want your materials on hand a few weeks prior to your start date. Therefore, you may need to place your order in July. This means that June would be a good time to establish a plan for your upcoming homeschool year.

Charting Your Year

If you're using a curriculum guideline, such as the "Typical Course of Study" from World Book, Inc., or a guideline from a curriculum provider, you'll have a good idea of the subjects you plan to cover during the homeschool year. Another way to determine what you'd like to cover during the upcoming year is to check the table of contents in used textbooks for your child's grade level.

For example, a third-grade science book may list the following chapters in the table of contents: Animal Life Cycles; Plant Life Cycles; Environment and Habitats; Adaptation; Matter; Energy; Machines, Force, and Motion; Sun, Moon, and Planets; and Natural Resources. You'll see topics or areas to study listed under each chapter. Under Natural Resources, you may see topics such as air quality, air pressure, atmospheric gases, climatic changes, the water cycle, water sources, drinking water, pollution, and so on.

From reading the table of contents in textbooks, you'll gain a better understanding of the topics to cover during the year, and you'll be able to formulate more succinct ideas for lesson plans. With your ideas in hand, research the local library or Internet for materials to help present the lessons and activities. Make a list of the items you plan to use, and keep the list in your plan book.

By establishing long-term goals, you're able to consider each objective, or subject area, and break it down into bite-sized short-term goals. This enables you to design your curriculum and create lesson plans for each month or week of the year.

If you homeschooled the previous year and did not cover everything you had planned, you can work these areas into summer activities, or you can carry them over to the upcoming year. Be sure to list them in your plan book. Keep notes on areas that may need extra attention, too. Take these areas into account when planning lessons for the upcoming year.

Your Lesson Plan Book

In your lesson plan book, record descriptions of lesson plans for each day of the week. Write plans and activities to cover four weeks in a row, and you'll have your homeschool agenda planned for an entire month. This record of daily lesson plans serves as a timesaving map that will keep your family pointed in the right direction all year long so that you can reach your goals.

It's not necessary to purchase a formal teacher's plan book. You can create your own with notebook paper or copy paper. Using a ruler, divide the sheets of paper into columns, headed with the days of the week. Two sheets of paper provide adequate room for listing school days from Monday through Friday. Along the side of one sheet, list the subjects, such as math, language arts, social studies, science, and so on. Allow space for notes on special activities, goals, or field trips you may have planned for the week.

Make several copies of this template, and simply fill in the blanks for each day of the week. If there's a format that works better for your homeschool style, feel free to use it. Then place your lesson plan sheets into a three-ring binder or folder, and you have your lesson plan book.

QUESTION?

I'm running out of lesson plan ideas; what do I do?
For quick lesson plan ideas, look through homeschool supply catalogs and homeschool magazines, check lesson plan sites on the Internet, or browse the shelves of a nearby teacher supply store. You'll soon have new and exciting learning ideas for the upcoming week!

Saturday or Sunday afternoons are often a favorite time to create lesson plans for the upcoming week. Most of the week's work has been completed, and the kids are usually playing contentedly in the bedroom or backyard or spending time with friends. You can relax in the living room or at the dining table and spread out your notebooks and your thoughts, as you contemplate the week ahead.

You've already established your goals for the year, and you've created your short-term goals regarding the subjects you plan to cover. Consequently, you know what topics you'll want to cover in the upcoming week. Consult your stack of library books or look over the "Typical Course of Study" guidelines and begin jotting brief descriptions of lesson plans for each subject in your lesson plan book.

Depending on how much preparation has gone into your homeschool goals and how organized you are, writing up a week's lesson plans can take an hour or two. Therefore, writing up lesson plans for an entire month may require a few extra hours out of your afternoon. This may sound like a lot, but many homeschool parents find it an enjoyable and inspiring way to spend an afternoon.

Keeping a Daily Logbook

Many states require that homeschool families keep a logbook or other type of records. To check your state's homeschool laws, consult the coordinator of your school district's homeschool department or contact your state department of education. Even if you're not required to keep such records, the day may come when it would be beneficial to have documentation of your child's homeschool years, subjects studied, lessons covered, and other proof of educational activities. So, rather than feeling "relieved" that you're not required to keep records, consider the benefits of doing so and enjoy the process.

Creating a Logbook

The lesson plan book mentioned in the previous section helps to map out your curriculum week by week. It can also double as your homeschool logbook. If yours is a more freestyle unschooling format, you may not create actual lesson plans for each day. Therefore, the logbook is ideal for jotting down activities your child participated in during the day. A lesson plan book is generally prepared *in advance* of each day's lessons. The logbook is updated *after* the day's events have occurred.

You can purchase a weekly logbook for homeschoolers, or you can create your own. In many ways, it's like keeping a diary or journal. Once again, you can use notebook paper or copy paper. Put the day's date on the paper, and write brief descriptions of what your children did that day in each subject area. Then place the paper in your three-ring binder or folder. You could also use a pocket calendar or an inexpensive day planner with plenty of writing space to describe what your child accomplished that day.

Make quick work of recording your child's activities each day. Simply jot them down as they occur. While your child is preparing for science, write down what he did in math. As he switches from science to social studies, record the experiments and topics he covered while they're still fresh in your mind. This saves time at the end of the day.

Recording Materials Used

In addition to the daily or weekly logbook, some states want to see a list of books and materials used in your homeschool. On the back of our weekly log sheets, we had a section for recording the titles of books, as well as space for notes or activities related to lessons. This made it easy to keep everything together, week by week, in one binder. When the homeschool evaluator looked over the material, she could flip through the binder and quickly see what books and activities accompanied the weekly lessons.

You can create a similar chart on the back of your daily log sheets. Block off space for the title of the book or textbook, the author or publisher, and the date. You may even want to note how the book was used. The following is an example:

Title of Book: *The Young Naturalist*
Author/Publisher: Usborne Books/EDC Publishing
Date: 10/20/03–10/24/03
Notes: Used in science for identifying insects in a freshly dug patch
    of soil; identifying fungi on tree bark; creating a bottle garden; and

dissecting the parts of a flower and identifying under the microscope.

You can also list any educational videos your children watched or books they read for pleasure. This provides the homeschool evaluator more insight into your children's interests, or simply helps you keep track of books your children have read. If the books relate to lessons in any way, you can note that, as well.

Your Child's Learning Log

If your children are old enough, have them keep their own learning log. When they write about the projects and topics they learned each day, it helps to imprint them better in their minds, and they will retain the information longer. Keeping their own learning log will accomplish three things: it will save you time recording their activities, provide daily writing practice for language arts, and establish the habit of writing down notes, which will be helpful to your children's education in the years ahead.

Maintaining a Homeschool Portfolio

Some states require that a homeschool portfolio be available for inspection monthly or quarterly; others may request to see the portfolio annually or upon request, usually with a thirty-day advance notice. Even if your state does not require you to keep a portfolio of your child's work, it's often an important part of the annual evaluation process. Plus, it just makes good sense to have documentation of what your child is doing and achieving month by month, regardless of how formal or informal your homeschool is.

The portfolio can include the lesson plan book or weekly learning log, books used and read, attendance records, daily worksheets, creative writing assignments, book reports, and written evaluations or test results. You can also include examples of "typical days," artwork, scrapbooks of hobby projects, inventions or projects built, and descriptions or photos of projects, experiments, special activities, or field trips. Another good way to document your child's abilities is to videotape or record speeches, performances, concerts, sport competitions, trips, and other events.

ALERT!

Your child's portfolio can be helpful when it's time to apply to college. You may not need to keep *every* worksheet, assignment, drawing, or project for the portfolio, but maintain a good variety for each subject area. A well-rounded portfolio helps college officials gain a clearer picture of your child's homeschool years.

How Much to Keep

During our first year of homeschooling, we kept every worksheet and project, and we lugged everything into the homeschool monitor's office for the annual review. It took four trips to carry all the boxes and projects into the small office. The monitor was quite overwhelmed by it all and indicated that it wasn't necessary to bring in every item. If the inspector feels that the portfolio presented annually isn't complete enough, they can always request additional samples.

Check with your local homeschool officials in advance and see how much they expect you to bring when it's time to present your child's portfolio. Other items you may want to keep with the portfolio are copies of your child's immunization records, verification of your child's homeschool registration with your school district, or paperwork certifying that your child is enrolled with a private school or distance-learning program.

Attendance Records

Many states require you to keep attendance records. This may seem somewhat silly, considering the fact that your child is obviously in attendance in the home each day. But many states require that the child is homeschooled a specific number of days or hours each year, and they want to see proof of it. Check with your local homeschool division or your state department of education to determine their exact requirements for homeschool attendance record keeping.

Some homeschool officials consider the weekly learning log, which documents the activities and studies conducted each day, as an adequate attendance record. It shows the weekly dates, the number of days your child was involved in educational activities, and the hours your child was engaged in educational activities each day. Or you may be able to keep a simple calendar with your weekly learning log, and jot down the number of hours spent on home education each day.

Forms such as attendance records, learning log pages, lesson plan sheets, grade records, evaluation forms, and high-school transcripts are available on the Internet or in many homeschooling books. These are usually available for downloading, printing, or photocopying.

Other officials may prefer to see a traditional style of attendance record, documenting your child's name, grade level, the year, and the week, with each day of the week listed at the top of the page. Under each day of the week, from October 20 to October 24, for example, you would mark the number of hours spent on educational activities that day. If the time spent studying core subjects was three hours, and the time your child spent reading or pursuing other educational activities that day was three hours, you would record six hours for the day.

Assessment Alternatives

You'll need to have a way to determine what your children are learning and retaining each week. In conventional schools, tests or essay papers are a common method for assessing children's knowledge. In the home, you may prefer to assess your children's abilities based upon your close observations of them.

When you determine what your children already know or where their weaknesses lie, you can supplement the curriculum accordingly. There's no need to focus repeatedly on the Revolutionary War if your child already has a good understanding of it. Through your observations, you may find that he doesn't have a good grasp of the voting process or the branches of the government. Therefore, instead of studying the

Revolutionary War again this year, you can spend more time on the processes of the government or perhaps create a unit study around it.

Documenting Evaluations

Talk with your children daily about what they're studying and learning. Engage them in family conversations about topics they've read, researched, or been involved with. From general conversations and your child's responses to questions, you can easily determine what your child is learning. After a lesson, you could have your child explain what she gleaned from the lesson and have her elaborate upon it, perhaps recording her summary onto cassette tapes.

Your child could write a short paper about what she learned, or draw and label the parts of a plant cell and an animal cell, for instance, or match proper definitions with new science vocabulary words. She could do a project based on the lesson, such as creating a model of a plant cell and an animal cell from clay. You could also give her quizzes based on the information she just read or discussed and have her write down her answers.

Reporting Progress

From observing, listening, grading, or assessing your child's knowledge and abilities, you can compare them against your educational goals for your child. You'll be able to determine how he's progressing, and you can make improvements where needed before too many days or weeks have passed by. At the end of each semester, you should have an ongoing progress report to keep with your child's portfolio. You can refer to this report from year to year to refresh your memory of his progress. Plus, it will be helpful to homeschool officials who may want to assess your child's abilities.

Recording Grades and Credits Earned

It can be beneficial to keep a record of your child's grades or credits earned per subject, particularly as he enters high school. You can purchase a traditional grade book like the ones that teachers use. This could be a timesaver if you're keeping track of grades for several children. Or you can simply create your own grade book on notebook or graph paper.

ALERT!

Although grades can be an indicator of your child's comprehension of material, they are also a measure of the teacher's ability to convey information and guide the learning process. If your child is having difficulty grasping subjects, re-evaluate the teaching and learning styles within the homeschool, then try a new approach.

If you grade your children's papers—answer sheets are included in most workbooks and teacher edition textbooks—you can record their grades under each subject heading. To calculate grades, use a handheld cardboard grader, such as the E-Z Grader, to determine the score and letter grade on tests and worksheets. These sliding charts are inexpensive and are available at most teacher supply stores.

At the end of each six- or eight-week period, you can average out your children's grades. By acknowledging their grades *and* closely observing their daily performance or struggles with certain topics, you can help them improve on any weak areas.

Credits Earned

For high-school graduation, a child needs about twenty-four credits in most states. Check with your state to determine the exact requirements. You can keep track of credits earned by entering credits on a high-school transcript. A credit is generally based upon 130 to 140 hours of study in a particular subject. If a child spends 45 minutes on English for the 180-day school year, he'll have spent 8,100 minutes, or 135 hours.

In most cases, a half credit is earned in a subject in one semester, resulting in a full credit for a year's study in that subject. For instance, one semester of freshman English can equal one-half credit. The second semester gains another half credit. By the end of the child's freshman year, he has earned one full credit in English. At the end of four years, he should have earned four credits in English, as well as two or three credits in each of the other required subjects.

After four years in your homeschool high school, your child can acquire twenty-four credits. These could include four credits in English, four in math, three in science, three in social studies, two in a foreign language, two in physical education, and six credits in electives (art, music, computer courses, business courses, or special courses of interest).

Creating Transcripts

Keeping track of credits earned through the high-school years may not be mandatory, but if your child is planning to attend college, it's a good idea to keep a transcript. This is something your child can easily do. Create a transcript form by listing the subjects studied in the high school years. List the subjects by starting with the most important: English, literature, math, history, government, economics, science, and so on. List foreign languages and elective courses toward the end of the transcript.

At the end of the semester and the year, have your child record the number of credits earned in each subject or elective. Keep the transcript in a safe place with your child's other homeschool records, in case she should need to present a copy of it when applying for college.

Granting Awards and Certificates

Achievement awards and certificates can provide a sense of accomplishment and pride for your children. Educational supply companies have certificates available for nearly every situation: preschool awards, reading awards, science awards, honor roll and citizenship awards, high-school diplomas, and many more. Such certificates and awards serve as tangible signs of progress throughout the homeschool year. And your children will be proud to display them.

Chapter 12

Organizing Your Homeschool

With records to keep, paperwork to file, portfolios to update, books to shelve, and learning materials to keep on hand, an efficient organization system is essential. Your space should work for you and your family's needs, not the other way around. This chapter will help you organize the space in your homeschool to make it work harder and smarter for you.

A Place for Everything

Time is a major concern when homeschooling. Thankfully, the organization process will help you discover more time in your day. One of the most time-consuming activities is looking for misplaced items. We become acutely aware of this when time quickly slips away as we search for that certain book or lesson plan. We tell ourselves that we simply *must* become more organized.

"A place for everything and everything in its place" is one of the most helpful household rules to keep, and it will remedy this searching-for-misplaced-items problem. At the beginning of each homeschool year, eliminate the nonessentials to make room for the new. Sell, recycle, or give away those books or games you just don't use. If there are things that you haven't touched for over a year and that are not imperative to keep, it may be time to let them go. Once they're gone, you'll have more space available for organizing the necessities.

These items will help solve most storage problems:

- Bulletin boards for displaying notices or artwork.
- Dry-erase boards for noting important memos.
- Plastic or cardboard containers for folders or projects.
- Bins or baskets for textbooks, workbooks, or library books.
- Bookshelves for books, puzzles, and science equipment.
- Desks for pencils, paper, and writing supplies.
- Tall storage cabinets for miscellaneous supplies and materials.
- File cabinets for important documents or assignments.

Storing Homeschool Supplies

Keep all homeschool supplies in one area when possible. Many families devote a hall closet or linen closet to their homeschool materials. One shelf holds textbooks, another holds workbooks or folders of worksheets, another holds microscopes and chemistry sets, another holds arts and crafts supplies, and the floor holds boxes containing idea files, portfolios, binders, and other important homeschool documents.

Store portfolios and projects from past homeschool years by sealing them in plastic containers and labeling with your child's name and school year. Keep them in a well-protected area of the attic or basement, or on the upper shelves of a bedroom closet.

Cardboard boxes can be used for storing binders or books or to accommodate hanging file folders. Storage boxes with lids, drawers, or string-and-button closure systems are available in office supply stores. These usually provide adequate labeling space for noting the contents and the date.

Declutter Your Domain

If there are certain areas in the home where things tend to pile up—for instance, on the dining room table, a side table, or a section of the snack counter—consider ways to declutter those areas. Clear out the bottom of a dining room hutch or kitchen cabinet to hold books or notebooks often left on the dining room table. These cabinets are normally located near the dining room, and it will only require a few steps to transport the clutter from the table to the cabinet.

Baskets, Bins, and Bags

For items that stack up on a side table, use an attractive wicker basket that can easily slide under the table, leaving the tabletop clutter-free. If your snack counter bears the brunt of a clutter attack, create areas where family members can tuck things away. A spice rack with drawers can hold rubber bands, paper clips, staples, pushpins, map tacks, erasers, etc. A letter holder mounted on the inside of a pantry door can contain a pocket calendar, notepaper, pens and pencils, a box of crayons, or a roll of tape. Plastic vertical files (such as those seen on the doors in doctor offices), mounted on the inside of a hall closet door, can hold current lesson plans, file folders, worksheets, or other paper supplies.

Clear plastic bins are excellent for storing anything from library books to workbooks, paint supplies, or math manipulatives. You can easily see through the bin and determine what it contains, further reducing the time spent looking for things. Plastic storage bags with zip-style tops are convenient for storing puzzles and puzzle pieces, games and game pieces, magnets and magnetic wands, packs of flashcards, art supplies, and more. They come in different sizes to accommodate a variety of items.

Set up a color-coding system and label plastic storage containers and zip-top bags with colored markers for quick recognition. Math manipulatives could be labeled with a red marker, language arts games with blue, science accessories with green, and so on. Use masking tape as labels. It's easy to remove and replace when changing the contents of a container.

A Central Station

A desk or a table with drawers makes a convenient central station for homeschool supplies. Perhaps you have a family computer that can be set up on the table or desk. Place plastic organizers in the desk drawers to hold paper, pens, markers, crayons, paper clips, staplers, scissors, paste, glue sticks, rolls of tape, construction paper, index cards, and other supplies.

Place stackable letter trays on your desk or table to accommodate worksheets and assignments. One tray could be for daily assignments that need your attention or grading. One tray could be for artwork or miscellaneous projects the children have completed. Another tray could hold worksheets or project ideas for children to select and do on their own. More trays can be added as needed.

Manage Those Magazines

It won't be long before you begin receiving numerous homeschool supply catalogs, flyers, newsletters, and magazines in the mail. Dedicate a box or bottom of a file cabinet or closet to your supply catalogs. You never know when you might want to browse through them—either to order something or to spark fresh educational ideas. As new catalogs arrive to replace the old, remember to toss the out-of-date ones.

Store your magazines in a bookcase or in cardboard magazine files for quick access.

You'll probably want to keep your homeschool magazines for a while. Most include an index near the end of the year, so that you can easily locate helpful articles that appeared in previous issues.

Creating an Idea File

If you're planning to study oceans this month, browse through reference books or Internet sites for lesson ideas, jot down the ideas, and place them in a science idea file for this month. At the same time, you may come up with geography ideas relating to the study of oceans, or history ideas relating to early explorers who sailed the high seas. Place these ideas in the proper files—science, geography, history—then file those under "Oceans." You'll soon have a unit or theme study compiled for your study of oceans.

Index cards and a file box are great for jotting down and storing lesson plan ideas, reference books, or Web sites. Use the tab dividers to indicate the subject or topic areas, then file your notes in the corresponding sections. Store the file box alongside your idea file.

As you research lesson plan ideas for the upcoming month, you'll often come across ideas that will be great for the following months, perhaps on the environment, the solar system, or inventors. Jot down those ideas and place them in your idea files for the future. If you don't have time to record your ideas fully, note the book, page number, or Internet site that contains information on those ideas and slip the reminder sheet into a file entitled "Future Studies." Near the end of each month, review your notes and revisit the resource book or Web site, and delve further into those topics to create lesson plans.

Store your notes in color-coded files. For instance, math ideas could be stored in red file folders, language arts in blue, science in green, social studies in yellow, and so on. Or, if you use plain manila file folders, use different colored markers to label the different files. Color-coding labels, many of which are removable, are available at office supply stores. Soon, you'll see red and think "math," blue and "language arts," all helping to speed up the lesson planning process.

Activity Centers and Lab Stations

You can carve space out of your home for activity centers, reading corners, and homework tables, as well as areas to set up lab equipment for conducting experiments. The age of your children and their learning styles will determine how you arrange your educational areas. Spend time observing how they prefer to learn before you create learning spaces. They may decide to read and do projects at the dining room table, or sit at their own desk in their bedrooms, or sprawl across the living room floor. Ask for their input and ideas on activity centers.

Arts and Crafts Area

You may want to set aside a special area for arts and crafts projects. Consider the crayons, markers, and paints that may bleed through or spill across the table and onto the floor. We once thought a vinyl-coated paper cup would be ideal for holding paint thinner. Bad idea. Not only did it eat through the bottom of the cup and seep through the place mat below it, but it also ruined a portion of the finish on our dining room table.

In light of possible accidents, you may want to invest in an affordable folding table with a plastic or melamine top that is scratch- and water-resistant. Set it along a wall in the dining room or in one of the children's bedrooms. If the flooring below the table is of concern to you, you can position a clear plastic mat or runner beneath the table. Now the family has an area for art projects where they won't have to worry each minute about marker stains or paint spills.

The Science Lab

The science lab is another area that has special concerns of its own. Have no doubt—conducting science experiments is definitely one of the high points of homeschooling, so you'll want to spend many hours "in the lab." Most homeschool families consider the time spent experimenting and discovering the mysteries of science in the kitchen as some of the most treasured of their homeschool memories. Therefore, don't skimp on science experiments just because you're afraid you can't accommodate them.

Just to be on the safe side, you may want to protect certain surfaces in your kitchen when you set up the lab there. Sheets of hard acrylic can protect countertops. Plastic mats or runners can protect the kitchen floor around the experimentation areas.

The floor mats can remain in the kitchen by the sink and range when not used for protection. The sheets of acrylic can slide behind the dining room hutch or into a nearby cabinet, where they'll be out of sight, yet handy at the same time.

FACT

Many homeschool families change their educational areas from time to time. Others find an arrangement that works fabulously the very first year. As children grow and change, so will their educational activities. Remain open to new ways to set up learning stations in your home. Most important, use the setup that works best for your family, and be willing to adjust it as needed.

Store the chemistry set inside a kitchen cabinet (out of the reach of small children), along with a few good books containing science experiments. You may also want to store the microscope, Bunsen burner, petri dishes, beakers and test tubes, litmus paper, dissecting kit, magnifying glasses, and safety goggles in the cabinet.

And perhaps it would be a good idea to install a fire extinguisher in your kitchen, too. Even if you don't need it for a chemistry experiment gone wrong, you may become so absorbed in the science activities that you forget about dinner cooking on the stove.

Quiet Corners and Libraries

A daily homeschool schedule achieves a good balance when there are periods of recreation and activity, and periods of rest and quiet time. When you step onto the volleyball court or bring out the chemistry set, children gear up for the activity they anticipate, and their level of energy or enthusiasm increases accordingly. Likewise, when you retire to a quiet corner to read or curl up on the couch with a book or writing pad, children will relax and unwind.

A Reading Corner

By establishing a reading corner, you'll create a space that is settling and free from distractions. You can locate this area in a corner of a den or a bedroom. Add a bookcase and a couple of beanbag chairs or sleeping bags, and you've designed a welcoming and comfortable library for your children. If you have no extra space for a reading corner, mount sturdy shelves on the walls to hold books. Then add colorful pillows in different shapes and sizes to your children's beds. They can prop up several pillows against the headboard, stretch out their legs, and read to their heart's content.

FACT

A window seat is great for reading and storing books. Create one in each bedroom by sliding a toy chest or blanket chest beneath the windowsill. Add a cushion on top, and you not only have a charming window seat for reading and daydreaming, but also a large storage chest for books and supplies. If you're able to flank the window with bookcases, you'll create a cozy reading nook.

A Room for Writing

A desk stocked with adequate writing materials in a quiet corner of a room is ideal for encouraging writing. Add a good lamp to properly illuminate the desktop, clear the desktop of any distracting clutter, and provide a comfortable chair for the young writer. Place a dictionary, thesaurus, and reference books on writing and grammar nearby. And, if possible, ensure that there is a door that can be closed for peace and quiet.

Writing requires one to focus mentally on the task at hand. It's not something that can be done well when others are chattering, playing music, or watching television. The mind must formulate ideas, grapple with ideas, process the ideas, and construct them in a manner that can be captured on paper. It can be quite a mental challenge for anyone, young or old. However, it can be an extremely enjoyable activity when the writer has the quiet and the environment he needs for producing pages of wonderfully written words and stories.

The Library

One of the most-used areas in your home will probably be the "library." Yours may not be the library of your dreams, with floor-to-ceiling bookcases lining all four walls of the room. Yet, all of us treasure the collection of fiction and nonfiction books, textbooks and activity books, reference books and picture books, on our own bookshelves, no matter how large or small they may be.

The library in your home—which you may want to incorporate into your reading corner—should contain a few choice books to help your children learn and to encourage their interest in reading. The dictionary and thesaurus, as previously mentioned, are important tools, not only for writers, but for any reader. A set of encyclopedias is also a wonderful asset to the home library. These can be found reasonably priced at garage sales, consignment shops, or used-book stores.

Picture books for young homeschoolers might include *Allison's Story: A Book About Homeschooling* or *Kandoo Kangaroo Hops into Homeschool,* as well as traditional, exciting picture books, and first reader books. Books for older readers could include homeschooling books such as *Real Lives: Eleven Teenagers Who Don't Go to School, The Teenage Liberation Handbook,* and *A Sense of Self: Listening to Homeschooled Adolescent Girls.*

And, of course, any classics, popular books, or nonfiction books that interest your children are always worthwhile investments. These can be found reasonably priced at used-book stores, so visit them often. When you glance into your child's room and see him completely absorbed in another book, knowing that he's developed a true love of reading, it's a rewarding and heartwarming feeling for any homeschool parent.

ALERT!

Everyone needs a chance to dissociate themselves from the homeschool environment during evenings and weekends. By dedicating specific areas to the learning activities, you leave other areas of the house free for the daily activities of eating, sleeping, relaxing, playing, or simply conversing with family and friends.

Keeping Home and School Separate

The time may come—generally sooner rather than later—when the homeschool begins to overtake and, eventually, overrun, the home. If you've applied some of the tips in this chapter, you will hopefully stay fairly well organized. But even the organized areas may begin to infringe upon your family's living space, until it seems as if there's no place left to escape the influence of homeschooling. Or, when company comes to visit, you sometimes wish that wall of overflowing, floor-to-ceiling bookshelves in the dining room wasn't quite so prominent.

If you're fortunate enough to have a separate "schoolroom" or playroom, it would, of course, be an ideal location for worktables, bookshelves, and storage closets. Some families can create such a space in an attic or basement. If you're tight on space, though, you can set up an activity center in a corner of your child's room, or use attractive partitions, available from department stores, to separate a portion of the family room.

As often noted, homeschooling is a lifestyle and not a school at home. You needn't reproduce a classroom in your family room, a chemistry lab in your kitchen, a cafeteria in your dining room, or a gymnasium in your garage. Your family can easily live and learn in your home, using what is conveniently available to them. (E)

Chapter 13

Homeschooling and the Single Parent

Single parents face special challenges, but this doesn't mean they can't home-school their children. With a host of home-school options available to you, including preplanned curriculum packages, correspondence schools, online schools, independent study programs, and unschooling techniques, children can attain a quality education in the single-parent home today. This chapter will show you how.

Single-Parent Homeschools

Single parents handle issues daily that are unique to their situation. The single parent doesn't have another adult in the home to share feelings or experiences with, bounce ideas off of, or to engage in conversation. Of course, there are times when two-parent families feel the same way. Due to hectic work schedules, there never seems to be time for a couple to sit down together and talk. The difference is that the two-parent families know they *could* sit down and have a heart-to-heart if they could get a better grip on their schedules. The single parent, on the other hand, faces the reality that there's *not* another adult in the home on a regular basis. And simply knowing this can contribute to the stress and aloneness that the single parent feels.

Add to this stress the loss of one's partner through separation, divorce, or death, and we begin to understand the pressure single parents feel. You would like to share your feelings with someone, yet you want to shield your children from any pain or stress you're feeling from your loss. It's no wonder that single parents become such strong, self-sufficient individuals. They realize that the success and happiness of their family depends solely upon them, and they manage to stand up and meet that challenge head on.

Interactive support for single homeschool parents is available online at ✍ *www.vegsource.com/homeschool/singleparent.* Yahoo! Groups has message boards such as HomeschoolingSingle, while America Online has the Single Homeschooling Parents forum. The Web site ✍ *www.singlemoms.org* (for both moms and dads), also provides information and advice for single parents.

Setting Priorities

It can be difficult to work and keep the home, plus homeschool your children, spend recreational time with them, and attend homeschool support meetings or gatherings. Flexibility and balance are the keys to success. Avoid setting your expectations too high and over-scheduling your days. Maintain a flexible routine that allows time for activities, recreation, and relaxation.

Remember that it's not imperative that you do everything. Set priorities, and don't worry about the little things that there's just no time for. Housework and yard work will always be there. Your children won't. Make your children, their childhood, and their home education your priorities. Soon, they'll be grown and on their own. Then you'll have plenty of time to spend on that housework and yard work.

Your health and your state of mind are also priorities. If you don't take care of yourself, your health and happiness can suffer. You want to be able to enjoy your children while they're young, and to joyfully participate in their home education experience. Set time aside for yourself just for relaxing and rejuvenating. You'll be more valuable to your children when you have a refreshed and re-energized frame of mind.

Keeping the Other Parent Involved

If you're separated from your partner or spouse, hopefully he or she will be supportive of the decision to homeschool and eager to assist. Your former partner can spend quality time with the children while you're at work. He or she can encourage the children to share what they've studied and learned, help with lessons and ongoing projects, and contribute learning activities and ideas.

ALERT!

If your former spouse has visitation rights every other weekend, and you rely upon weekends for homeschooling, try to arrange a more flexible schedule. Maybe he or she could have the children over during the week, rather than on weekends. If not, perhaps he or she could follow the lesson plans, do science experiments, or arrange field trips that relate to current topics.

Strive to keep the lines of communication open with your former partner, so that you both can work together for the good of your children. Avoid letting any personal feelings intervene, add stress to your life, or disrupt your goals for your children. Stress and unhappy feelings deplete your energy and good intentions. Don't allow outside influences to knock you down; instead, rise above such problems and stand tall and firm. Your top priority is the happiness and education of your children. Always keep that uppermost in your mind, never allowing unrelated issues to deter you from that goal.

Educational Options and Alternatives

Remember that a wide range of homeschooling options are available. Home education doesn't require that you sit at a desk or kitchen table for hours each day, teaching the children. (See Chapter 4 on the different types of homeschooling that are available.)

Unschooling, unit studies, or an eclectic style of schooling may provide the most flexibility. Curriculum providers or schools may cost a bit more, but they can offer timesaving services, such as assignment preparation, grading, tests, evaluations, record keeping, and teacher assistance. Internet-based schools, also called cyber schools, correspondence schools, or independent study programs, may work well for some children, particularly if they're working to achieve credits for high-school graduation as they prepare for college.

Homeschooling Time

Some states set attendance requirements of 180 days per school year, or 900 to 1,000 hours per school year. This works out to approximately five or six hours per day. Check with your state department of education to determine their homeschooling requirements. If your state has similar attendance laws, you should have little difficulty meeting the requirement.

For example, if you work during the day, you could spend two or three hours each evening, helping your children with new lessons and reviewing previous lessons, reading history books or biographies together, and playing educational games. While you're at work, your children can spend two or three hours a day on "homework" papers, finishing assignments, reading ahead to new lessons, and working on homeschool projects. A sitter or day-care worker could monitor your children to be sure they're doing their assignments and staying educationally entertained during the day.

Let others know that you're homeschooling. When enrolling your child in community courses or clubs, inform instructors that your child is homeschooled. If there are special skills or knowledge they can convey to your child, tell them you'd be appreciative. If they spend a little extra time with your child, show your appreciation by rewarding them with a small gift of thanks.

Together Time

When the weekend comes, you can spend additional quality time on science experiments, hands-on projects, and real-life lessons. Some of the best learning takes place when you're running errands together, shopping, going to the zoo or museum, or on other family activities. Together, you can experience these lessons, discuss them, and expand upon them, taking the knowledge or experience even further or in new directions to contribute to a comprehensive education.

Interestingly, homeschooled children tend to experience more quality educational hours than do their conventional-school counterparts. This is mainly because homeschool parents regularly capitalize on the educational opportunities that arise, seeing them for the knowledge or experience they can convey, rather than considering them a "normal part" of daily life. What may seem normal or mundane to us, may be new and exciting to our children. Making the most of everyday events helps our children to understand and learn from such events, ultimately helping them to better prepare for their own life experiences.

Year-Round Homeschooling

If your state requires a specific number of hours per homeschool year, and you can only homeschool a few hours per day, you can try the year-round approach to homeschooling. Since homeschooling is basically a way of life, you and your child shouldn't feel as if you're engaging in school all year long. Instead, you'll eliminate those boring days of summer when the kids think "there's nothing to do." With challenging homeschool projects to do all year long, your family can enjoy daily activities that keep the kids busy, motivated, and learning.

Staying Within a Budget

As a single parent, you are the main breadwinner in your family, and it can be crucial to live within your budget. Therefore, you may feel that you don't have the extra money to invest in homeschooling. Contrary to what one might believe, it needn't be costly at all. Your children can receive a fine, quality education, even with limited funds.

Take advantage of these homeschool money savers:

- The library and all its wonderful resources.
- Used-book stores, for buying and selling books.
- Consignment shops, for buying and selling educational items.
- Used-curriculum fairs and book sales.
- Borrowing a book (or video) through homeschool support groups.
- Trading or sharing books and equipment with other homeschoolers.
- Free, complete lesson plans and worksheets available on the Internet.
- Regular household items for science experiments, art, and educational fun.

Special One-on-One Time

Whenever you spend extra one-on-one time with your children, you and they will benefit. You'll become closer to your children and more in tune with their interests and thoughts. And they will develop a closer, stronger, more trusting relationship with you. In all likelihood, they will continue to open up and share their feelings more frequently as the months go by. Behavioral problems will most likely diminish, and a more mature and capable child will emerge.

Take advantage of the time you spend together at the dinner table. Children learn and retain information by talking about the things that interest them and by engaging in lively discussions. This is an excellent time to review topics studied during the week in an interesting, not drilling, way. You don't want dinnertime to turn into teaching or test time. Rather, you want to hear what your children gleaned from lessons in a casual way. This not only gives children the opportunity to expound upon their lessons or areas of interest, but it also allows you to observe and evaluate the progress they are making.

FACT

The benefits of developing good lines of communication between yourself and your children—and keeping those lines open—will prove themselves over and over in the years to come. The more that children and parents interact, the more learning that takes place, and the closer the family unit becomes.

Weekend and Evening Homeschooling

When dinner is over, the chores are done, and the day has been discussed, parent and child still have time to play games outdoors, read books together, do science experiments in the kitchen, work on educational projects, play board games or do puzzles together, look over assignment questions, or discuss concepts and subject areas for the next day. And it need not take all night to do this.

Evenings are also a good time to attend community classes and social events, such as art, music, sports, concerts. Your child can attend one or two classes or events a week, when you're able to drop him off and pick him up. The other evenings during the week can be spent on educational activities at home. Weekends can be similar to your evening routines, but with more flexibility and free time for fun and recreation.

Don't feel that you should spend *all* your evening or weekend hours on home education. That's simply not necessary. If you're concerned that you're "falling behind" or there's a subject you weren't able to cover this past week, discuss the topic with your child, encourage her to think about it and share thoughts or feelings on it, and artfully weave it into an hour or two of your time together.

As mentioned throughout this book, homeschooling isn't school at home. You needn't stand in front of a desk and chalkboard to teach and instruct. Your role is to help your children learn, to be aware of what others their age are learning, and consider what you feel is important for your children to learn. You can then provide the guidance, resources, assistance, and encouragement to start them on the road to an enjoyable educational experience.

Flexible Work Options

Even though homeschooling can work well for single parents, you might wish that you had more time to spend at home with your children. You could speak with your employer about a more flexible work schedule, consider telecommuting, or look into establishing a home business.

FACT

The Woman's Work Web site offers advice on finding flexible jobs. Visit the site at ✍ *www.womans-work.com* to view the job board, search available freelance jobs, home business opportunities, or to determine wage and salary comparisons. Just browsing the variety of jobs listed could provide you with a moneymaking idea of your own.

Support from Employers and Coworkers

If it's your hope to stay employed in your current job, speak with your employer about your career goals, as well as your educational goals for your children. Have a plan firmly in mind before approaching your employer. Stress your desire to continue contributing to the good of the company. Offer to arrive at work an hour earlier and work through your lunch hour. As a result, you could leave two hours earlier than normal and have extra homeschooling time in the evenings with your children.

Not surprisingly, the workplace can be similar to conventional schools. Much time can, unfortunately, be lost or wasted in a normal workday. What may take eight hours for some to accomplish can be done by an industrious person in four hours.

Time at work is often lost by waiting for others in meetings, taking breaks to chat about the previous day or night, gathering around the water cooler to discuss favorite television shows or movies, gossiping about employees in various departments, and taking more breaks to chat about the upcoming day or night. Each of these breaks interrupts the productive flow of the day. A worker who avoids these time-killers and focuses on work alone can accomplish as much in a four-hour day as the worker who spends eight hours at work but who stops to talk or take breaks throughout the day.

Observant employers and coworkers can recognize the person who is willing to work hard, who focuses their mind and their skills on the job at hand, and who honestly does a good day's work. As a result, you'll often win their support and admiration when you can accomplish as much as you do in a day and still manage to educate your children, too.

Telecommuting and Working from Home

If it's simply not possible to shorten your normal workday, suggest telecommuting or taking work home a few times each week. You may be able to work from home on Fridays or even a couple days per week. If your place of business is computerized, you can access files from home via PCAnywhere, GoToMyPC, or other remote access programs. Just imagine how much time you would have with your children if you had an extra day or two at home each week!

FACT

Consider starting your own business. The Small Business Administration (SBA) offers Women's Business Assistance Centers that can help women start their own business. Visit the SBA's Women's Business Center at *www.onlinewbc.gov* for information on training, counseling, financing, and marketing a business.

Taking Children to Work

Several homeschool parents have successfully taken their children to work with them. This works well for parents who have a separate office within the building. Your child can sit at her own workspace and complete lessons, occasionally asking questions or for input from you. You can take your lunch break together and follow it with a nature walk before going back to the office. In the afternoons, she can read, draw, or work on homeschool projects. Depending on her age, she may be able to assist with simple duties around the office.

Other Flexible Jobs

Your lifestyle may not be suitable to a regular nine-to-five job. If you'd prefer to have more control over your hours or to work at home, here are some moneymaking opportunities to consider:

- Home day care.
- Tutoring, music, or art lessons.
- Substitute teaching.
- Medical transcription or data entry.
- Graphic or Web design.
- Copyediting or proofreading.
- Newspaper routes.
- School-bus driver.
- Errand-running or catering service.
- Home, party, or wedding organizer or planner.
- Sewing, alterations, or laundry services.
- Office cleaning service.
- Home health aide.
- Tupperware, Pampered Chef, Avon, or Mary Kay.

Single-Parent Support Groups

Support from other adults is a major boost for single parent homeschoolers. When possible, set aside time to attend local support group meetings. The experiences, perspectives, support, and understanding from other homeschool parents will center you, inspire you, and boost your morale. If you can't make it to all the group meetings, stay in touch via telephone or e-mail. A group of single homeschool parents may even want to meet separately on Saturdays or Sundays once a month.

A local homeschool cooperative could provide educational advantages and social contact for your children. Consult with other homeschool families in your community to see if they are interested in starting a co-op. If you're unable to participate during the week, offer to hold a science, art, English, or writing class for a couple hours on Saturdays, which their children could attend along with yours.

Help from Family and Friends

Relatives may be the first to say "Have you lost your mind?" when you tell them you're planning to homeschool your children. But they're often the first to boast to others about you and your children, and they are soon eager to lend a hand. Don't be too proud to accept help from them.

Sometimes as a single parent, you may experience tight financial situations that require you to temporarily live with parents or friends. Although this arrangement may not be ideal, it enables you to have a closer circle of support around you and your children while you're getting on your feet. Try to make the best of the situation. While living with family or friends, encourage them to contribute their special abilities and knowledge to help further your children's education or to take an active part in their home education.

Grandparents are wonderful sources of information, ideas, and inspiration for your children. They come from a time when they had to create their own forms of entertainment and learned beneficial skills at an early age, and they have often experienced a half century of history firsthand that they can share with your children. The relationship your children develop with their grandparents may leave an indelible mark on their childhood that they'll always treasure.

Child-Care Options

The younger the child, the more challenging single-parent homeschooling can be. Some children may be mature and responsible enough to stay alone for a short time during the day as they focus on their studies. However, always try to avoid leaving your child alone for very long, regardless of his or her age. Young children should, of course, never be left alone.

A viable and successful homeschool arrangement can usually be found, no matter your child's age. It may take a few tries to hit upon the best solution for your family, so don't give up. Since you're homeschooling your children, the thought of placing them in a day-care facility may not set well with you or them. However, some day-care centers may be homeschool-friendly and understand your unique needs. Always research any day care, speak to other families whose children attend, and see if day-care employees are open to supervising your children's homeschool assignments. Most are accustomed to making sure that after-school children complete homework assignments, so they should be able to do the same for your children.

An in-home sitter or relative is often the preferred choice for homeschool families. This person should also be open to helping your children with lessons or projects and making sure that they stay busy and challenged while you're away at work. You don't want your children sitting around all day, watching television or playing video games.

FACT

Some sitters or child-care workers have special talents they could demonstrate to your children, so encourage them to open up and share. Due to their interest in working with children, most enjoy the opportunity to help children learn. Some have taken early childhood development courses and are working to become certified teaching assistants. They could be a valuable influence on your children's education.

Remember that homeschooling *can* work for you and your family. With a little creative inventiveness, and the understanding that homeschooling or unschooling is a natural part of everyday life, your children can enjoy the benefits of a quality education and a close family unit.

Chapter 14

Homeschooling and the Two-Career Family

When both parents work, daily life may seem overfull and chaotic. In addition to working and homeschooling, you have a family life to maintain, relatives to visit, appointments to keep, events to attend, pets to care for; the list goes on and on. Don't despair! There are ways to streamline your schedule to better fit your family's lifestyle.

Balancing Work and Family

If homeschooling occurs at your house, then children are obviously in your home. And they, like you, have responsibilities to the family. To carve out the time you'll need for homeschooling (and it is much less than you might imagine), everyone can share the responsibilities and chores. Many working parents have successfully homeschooled their children, and, with a little help and insight, you can, too.

Flexibility at the Office

Similar to single working parents who want more time at home with the kids, you might talk with your employer about a flexible work schedule. Emphasize that you want to continue working for the good of the company, and you believe that you can do that, even while you educate your children. Devise a plan that would be beneficial to the company, as well as to your home life, and present it to your employer. Maybe you could go to work earlier and work through your lunch hour. Then leave a couple hours early to spend time with your children.

When you have the company's interests in mind, employers can tell that you are sincere and hardworking. They will see that you're capable of accomplishing a full day's work in half the time it might take other employees. You have set priorities in the office and for your family.

Sharing the Homeschooling

Unlike the single-parent family, the two-career family has a partner who can help share the home education responsibilities. If Dad goes to work early in the morning and is home by 5:00, he can take over some of the homeschool activities when he arrives home and begins dinner. If Mom goes to work later in the morning and arrives home around 7:00, the family can have dinner together and discuss the homeschool projects that have been covered that day. After everyone has helped to clean up after dinner, Mom can sit down with the kids to read, go over lessons, or look over projects. The following morning, she can present lessons for the upcoming day, before she leaves for work around 10:00 or 11:00.

Consider the Age of Your Children

Of course, the schedule you establish will need to take the ages of your children into consideration. Younger children may require more one-on-one time as they learn concepts, attempt to comprehend the lessons, and work on completing assignments. If you're not able to be alongside them throughout each step, you'll want to ensure that your partner, a relative, or sitter will be available to help them through the processes.

ALERT!

Teenagers may be mature enough to self-direct their education, update daily learning logs, and keep themselves on track. They may have spent more years homeschooling, be familiar with the routine, grasp concepts fairly quickly, or be able to complete lessons with less supervision than a younger child. Give them more responsibility for their studies, then evaluate their response to this challenge.

For instance, you may spend a couple hours in the morning before work, helping with English, history, and science lessons. You have just enough time to introduce the math lesson and go over the necessary concepts, but you realize that your son, Alex, doesn't grasp the lesson or needs additional practice before proceeding. Before heading to the sitter's home, leave a note for your partner that Alex needs more help on Lesson 10. Or, take the math book and note along to the sitter's home or day care, and ask that they help Alex with parts of Lesson 10 when they have the opportunity. You can establish a relationship with the sitter or day care ahead of time, so that they understand your home education schedule and are willing to help when possible.

Other Work Options

If it proves too difficult to keep your current career position and homeschool your children, other options are available. Perhaps you could move into another position within the company, where you can telecommute, work from home a few days a week, or work on computer files via a remote access program. When you take breaks from your office in your home, you can check on your children's lessons or spend your lunch hour on science experiments.

FACT

The Small Business Administration, at ✎ *www.sba.gov,* provides information on starting and financing your business, plus other helpful resources. The BusinessTown Web site, ✎ *www. businesstown.com,* includes business ideas, along with start-up costs, marketing tips, and business planning advice. Home business advice on working from home and financing and promoting your business can be found at Power Home Biz, ✎ *www.powerhomebiz.com*

Flexible Work Schedules

Flexible work schedules can ensure that one parent is home while the other is at work. For instance, you may work from 10:00 A.M. to 4:00 P.M. and your partner may work the nightshift from 11:00 P.M. to 7:00 A.M. In this way, a parent is always at home with the children, ensuring one-on-one time with the kids while overseeing the education process.

In this scenario, you may have some quiet time with your partner in the early mornings before the kids awaken. Then, after breakfast and before you go to work, you could start the kids on the lesson plans for the day. While you're away, your partner can help them with projects or questions, making sure they're staying on track. When you return in the late afternoon, you and your partner can spend more time with the kids, working on lessons and projects before it's time for the next work shift. This provides a great opportunity for children to have time alone with each parent, as well as time with both parents together each evening.

Of course, the parent working the nightshift will need to sleep at some point during the day. If your children are mature enough to handle themselves properly while a parent is sleeping, they should be capable of completing lessons on their own with little supervision. If the children are too young to be on their own while the parent sleeps, they can go to a relative's or sitter's home or to a day-care center when you work the dayshift.

FACT

Regardless of how you arrange the schedule, your children can still receive a solid education in the home by studying important topics, taking part in daily learning activities, regularly sharing information and knowledge with parents and other family members, going on educational field trips, and spending time on experiments and projects on weekends.

Homeschooling Dads

Dads are becoming more and more involved in their children's education at home. If they can't be home all day with the kids, then they take advantage of the learning opportunities during the hours they are at home. And in some cases, Dad stays at home with the kids, while Mom goes to work.

Dave, a homeschool father from Texas, made the decision along with his wife to homeschool their two children. As a nurse, Cindy chose to remain in her position at the local hospital, while Dave took over the primary homeschool and household duties. Three years later, the arrangement still works for the family, and the kids love the time they have with their dad.

"It doesn't feel like school," says twelve-year-old Josh. "We do fun things every day. Dad makes it fun. We act silly a lot, but we still learn a lot. Even when Dad makes it fun, he's still serious about it. I mean, if he thinks we're just goofing off, well, it's not funny then. As long as we keep learning, Dad lets us have fun while we learn."

Dads can bring a different perspective to learning and education, as well as new and varied ideas. Their enthusiasm can be contagious, energizing the whole family. "Nick is more creative than I am," Dawn, another working mom, says about her stay-at-home husband. "Not only is he artistic and accomplished at inventing handy gadgets and tools, but he can come up with unique ways of looking at the most mundane thing. Thanks to his way of thinking 'out of the box,' he's got the kids thinking in new and creative ways."

Involving Relatives

As busy as you are, you may overlook the benefits of involving grandparents, aunts, and uncles in your children's education. Grandparents can often provide firsthand knowledge of historical events that have occurred over the past fifty or more years. When you visit grandparents, encourage them to share memories of special events, the way life was when they were young, mementos from the past, or skills they have learned over the years.

Ashleigh, age thirteen, spends one week each summer at her grandparents' home in North Carolina. Over the years, she has not only grown closer to her grandparents, but she has learned much about their lives when they were children, as well as learned the family tree on both sides of the family, all the way back to the early 1700s. She has helped put together the scrapbook that includes pictures, newspaper articles, birth certificates, letters, and documents from ancestors who lived two and three centuries ago.

From her grandmother, she has learned to bake biscuits from scratch, fix meals, plant a healthy garden, can fruits and vegetables, and to make soap and candles. From her grandfather, she has learned to carve boats out of wood, personalize them with a wood-burning kit, make hand-painted signs (she's thinking of starting a sign-making business one day), how to change tires and oil filters, how to organically fertilize a garden, and how to get water from a hand pump.

No doubt, Ashleigh's aunts and uncles could share many of their skills with her, too. Is your brother or sister a banker, computer wizard, musician, writer, attorney, or cattle rancher? Then they have knowledge and skills they could share with your children. Does your brother or sister have a knack for electronics, landscaping, painting, making speeches, or selling things? Encourage them to share their skills and talents with your children, broadening their horizons and illuminating the possibilities that await them in the world.

Dividing and Organizing Responsibilities

It takes everyone in the family pulling their own weight to make each day a success. By the time a family decides to homeschool, it's usually a unified decision. In the beginning, it may have been Mom's idea, and she may have sought feedback from other family members. Or it may have been Junior's idea, and he may have had to work especially hard convincing Mom and Dad. It required research and homework, discussions and considerations. Then it probably required additional research and homework, and discussions and considerations!

ALERT!

When you first embark upon the homeschooling journey, be sure that everyone comprehends and agrees with the goals and what it will take to reach those goals. When *everyone* works toward a common goal, you'll have enough time for a quality education in the home, as well as time for family fun and recreation.

One thing that may be overlooked in the initial stages, however, is the division of responsibilities in the home. No matter whose idea it was, the full weight of the homeschooling process shouldn't fall upon Mom (because it was *her* idea) or Junior (because it was *his* idea). If Mom happens to be able to stay home full time, she may have more time to be involved in the entire homeschooling procedure. But Dad can take part in the evening reading sessions, look over completed assignments, determine how the math skills are progressing, and take over the science classes in the evening or on weekends.

Taking Turns

If both parents work, each can take turns with the evening reading sessions. Then one parent may focus on English and history lessons, while the other may prefer to be in charge of math and science. Art, crafts, music, physical education, and life skills can be shared between the parents.

When both parents are working, each can also take turns with the daily household chores. Some people may be better suited for certain tasks. For instance, Dad may be the better cook, so he's the preferred chef each night. Mom may be more cognizant of the grounds around the home, thereby taking over the weekly mowing chores, planting, pruning, weeding, and outdoor upkeep.

Everyone Is Equal

Everyone's tasks go quicker when everyone pitches in to clean up the kitchen after the meals, to haul yard clippings or trash to the curb, to set out or put away utensils and tools, to help parents, to help each other, and to pick up after one's self on a daily basis. The earlier this is learned (during preschool years), and the longer it is maintained (as long as people occupy the home), the more responsible, mature, and adept each child will become.

If family members tend to forget which tasks they are responsible for each week, post a "chores chart" in plain sight of everyone. Allow columns for the name of the task-doer, the task, and the day the task is to be done.

This does not mean that children should be servants within the home, nor does it mean that Mom or Dad should be subservient to their children or to each other. It only means that the people who live within a family should act in a proper and responsible manner, each contributing equal weight to the good of that family.

The To-Do List

A lot of folks believe they can remember what needs to be done each day, and they don't need to write it down. That may be true. However, one of the major benefits of a to-do list is to free up space in your brain. When a dozen things are needling the back of your mind, they interfere with your focus and productiveness. Once you get those dozen items onto a to-do list, something surprising happens: Your mind immediately becomes clearer and more focused.

Your to-do list can be a small three-by-five-inch notebook that you keep in your pocket, purse, car, or by the phone. Or, your to-do lists can be written on slips of paper cut from scrap paper, then attached to the refrigerator with magnets or to a wall calendar with removable tape. Reminders jotted onto different-sized sticky notes can be adhered to computer monitors, telephones, cabinet door interiors, dashboards, calendars, or mirrors. Whatever your preferred method, getting those pesky to-do thoughts out of your mind and onto paper, where they are conveniently in sight, will enable you to think and focus more clearly each day.

A Daily Planner

A daily planner may be better than the to-do list for some. These usually provide separate spaces for noting appointments on a daily, weekly, and monthly basis; calls that need to be made; jobs that are due or deadlines to meet; bills to pay; birthdays, anniversaries, and special events; shopping lists; address and telephone numbers; and your own weekly goals, along with recreational plans.

Free daily-planner pages are available at ✑ *www.digital-women.com*. Click on the Free Daily-Planner link, choose the pages you'd like to print out, then place them in a handy three-ring binder. Or you may prefer to organize your day electronically with PDAs or programs such as Lotus Organizer or Microsoft Outlook.

Homework by Day, Homeschooling by Night

If you and your partner must work an eight-hour day, then you'll probably want to homeschool in the evenings. Even if you're away from the home from 8:30 A.M. to 5:30 P.M., that's only nine hours out of a twenty-four-hour day. If you sleep for eight hours, you still have seven hours left to accommodate the time necessary for individualized homeschooling.

FACT

The actual one-on-one time you spend with your child directly on lessons could range from one to two hours per day (kindergarten and early elementary) to three or four hours per day (middle to high school). A six-hour day requirement doesn't mean you must stand in front of your child, teaching for six hours straight. Learning occurs at all hours of the day.

You and your partner can spend a couple hours in the evening after the dinner meal working with children on their lessons and projects. Then, rather than having your children do "homework" in the evenings, as the schools do, your kids can do their assignments during the day while you're at work and they are with relatives or a sitter. When their "homework" assignments are completed, they can work on other educational activities, such as reading, doing research, working on construction or art projects, or playing music or stimulating learning games. In this way, children easily attain the six-hour educational day that some states may require.

When the family is together again in the evenings and on weekends, you can all work together on projects: discuss them; contribute thoughts, ideas, and input; and brainstorm together on new ideas, themes, or unit studies to pursue. As a result, you'll stay in close touch with what your children work on each day. You'll encourage them, and you'll inspire them to think of new educational avenues to explore.

Weekend Learning Activities

Save those in-depth science experiments for the weekend. Then you can break out the chemistry set, lab equipment, Bunsen burner, microscope, and other science tools. You'll be able to spend hours on various experiments, learning and having fun at the same time. This is a great time to create volcanoes, landforms, and erosion demonstrations, and study soil, rocks, and fossils. You could even grow crystals, construct a water cycle model, create a tornado in a bottle, or build electronic devices.

Keep science experiment books on hand or pick up new ones regularly from the library so you'll always have new projects to try. The *Hands-On Science Activities* and the *Science for Every Kid* books offer hundreds of experiments and projects.

Weekends are a good time to watch science or history videos, too. The *Tell Me Why* video series and the *Nova Adventures in Science* videos are fascinating. The *American Adventure* history videos, PBS documentaries, and National Geographic videos are also excellent.

FACT

LibraryVideo, at ⌕ *www.libraryvideo.com,* carries science experiment videos, such as the Dr. Science set, as well as educational videos on nearly every topic imaginable. The members of your local homeschool group may want to chip in to purchase a few and maintain your own video library. Families can check out the videos and then return them in a timely fashion so that another family can view them.

Family Field Trips

Educational activities can be rolled into family field trips to museums, zoos, nature centers, aquariums, or planetariums. In addition to field trips to bakeries, restaurants, grocery stores, and other businesses, consider areas that welcome spur-of-the-moment field trips. Spontaneous stops could include such things as visiting a honey bee factory, an alligator wrestling contest, Native American craft shows, a medieval fair, log cabins, a fire lookout tower, a magic show, an eighteenth-century cemetery, wildlife sanctuaries, and an artists' colony.

Others places and events to be on the lookout for include the following:

- Local exhibitions or cultural events.
- Historic homes or sites.
- Farms or orchards.
- Beaches, streams, and tide pools.
- Canoe or boat rentals.
- Boat, ship, or submarine tours.
- Air shows or warplane tours.
- Wildlife refuge or national parks.
- Gardens and landscape nurseries.
- Circuses and petting zoos.
- Rodeos and horse shows.
- Visits to nearby towns and communities.

Local homeschool groups also hold field trips throughout the school year. Unfortunately, many of these are held during the week, while working parents are on the job. Try to set up a few group field trips for the weekends when possible. Or arrange to work on a Saturday, so that you can take a day off in the middle of the week to participate in homeschool field trips and get-togethers.

ALERT!

Keep field trips fun. You don't want to turn the event into a school lesson or threaten a quiz when the trip is over. Remember that learning occurs and lasts longer when activities are presented in fun, relaxing, and interesting ways.

When taking part in field trips, reinforce the educational aspects by discussing the destination in advance. Discuss any questions your kids may have and encourage them to research the areas you plan to visit. Take notebooks and sketch pads along on the trip. Children can draw maps to the destination, sketch the scenery or buildings you visit, and jot down thoughts and events as they unfold. Ⓔ

Chapter 15

Homeschooling in the Early Years

Your child can guide you in home-schooling during the early years. Follow the joy and enthusiasm that bubbles from within him or her each day. If they love to run and tumble, join in the fun as you sing alphabet or counting songs. If they love to color and paint, discuss the many shapes and colors they create. Through play, learning occurs naturally every day.

Toddlers and Preschoolers

Parents sometimes ask how soon they should begin homeschooling their toddler. As soon as your baby is born, you're "homeschooling." In other words, you're interacting with the new addition to your family, playing with him and helping him to learn about the world around him. This process of interacting with children and guiding the learning process continues through the toddler "homeschool" years and through the high-school "homeschool" years. Homeschooling is simply a way of life.

Early Learning Activities

With babies and toddlers, you'll want to engage in visual, auditory, and sensory activities to stimulate all five senses. Include lots of music and dancing in your home, moving along to the rhythm of the tunes. Talk with your child as you go about your day, and carry on conversations, pointing out objects in the home or yard and describing the places you visit. Read to your child, no matter how young or old she is—recite poetry, nursery rhymes, and lyrics to songs.

Count out items on a daily basis; for instance, "One finger, two fingers, three fingers; one Cheerio, two Cheerios, three Cheerios; one block, two blocks, three blocks," and so on. Perform fingerplays with your young child, gently moving his hands and fingers for him in time to the rhythm of the song. Besides talking and interacting with your child, allow him to interact with himself in a mirror as soon as he's able to focus. He'll also enjoy looking at photos or picture books of babies and toddlers near his age, and may carry on "conversations" with their pictures.

FACT

Toddlers learn quickly through simple songs and fingerplays. For lyrics and descriptions, visit *www.preschoolrainbow.org* and click on "Rhymes, Songs, and Fingerplays." For more fingerplays, rhymes, and lullabies, visit *www.zerotothree.org/brainwonders/ EarlyLiteracy* and click on "Activities Infants and Toddlers Enjoy."

Ideas for Activities

You can also learn new activities to do with toddlers and preschoolers by attending mommy-and-me programs at community centers, or story time or puppet theaters at libraries or bookstores. Browse the local school supply store or the educational section of the toy store, too. A multitude of ideas are available from these. You can also get ideas on how to make similar educational toys and games with household items at little or no cost.

Toddler Activities

As your child's ability to walk improves and he begins to explore his surroundings, his level of curiosity will increase. Provide texture boards or boxes for him to touch and respond to. Discuss the concepts of soft, hard, furry, rough. He'll love to pour and fill items, so engage in these games with him, using plastic pitchers and balls. Count as the pitcher is refilled with balls, and count as he pours the balls into plastic bowls, mimicking the way you pour drinks into glasses.

Copying the actions of grownups or older siblings is one of the main ways that children learn. Babies and toddlers are fascinated by all the things that older siblings and adults can do. They constantly strive to be like you or an older brother or sister. Allow them to do the things you do, within reason and at their own skill level. Discuss the activities they work at or perform each day. Talking and discussion is just as important for reinforcing learning with babies and toddlers as it is with older children.

Active Learning

As your toddler's mobility increases, so will his desire for more activity. Help him develop his gross motor skills with rolling, throwing, and chasing soft rubber balls, climbing on pillows and cushions, hopping and jumping, all with supervision, of course. Enhance his fine motor skills with finger-painting, roller-art, peg-style puzzles, fitting pieces into slots, and putting jumbo beads together. Remember to talk, count, and sing during these activities to add more meaning to the learning process.

Books such as *Bright Start* by Michael Meyerhoff or *Preschool Play and Learn* by Penny Warner provide ideas and simple directions for games and learning activities for little ones. Also visit ✐*www.enchantedlearning.com*, ✐*www.perpetualpreschool.com*, or ✐*www.totcity.com* for preschool activities.

Learning Through Play

Don't underestimate the learning benefits that result from playing. When a child is engaged in a playful environment where he's using his imagination, pretending, exploring, and discovering, he focuses his thinking and problem-solving skills on the moment at hand, inevitably learning from these firsthand experiences. This is true whether he's involved in fantasy play or building a LEGO village. When you remove him from this environment to sit him at a desk, you abruptly interrupt the learning process he is thoroughly engrossed in.

Suspended Between Two Worlds

While his mind is in another realm, absorbed with the situation there, he's focused on problem solving and bringing resolution to the world he's playing within. When he is placed at a desk with worksheets to do, he feels suspended between two worlds where nothing makes sense for a few minutes. He has been torn from the world he was previously making sense of, only to have his imagination and creativeness suddenly turned off. His brain must quickly readjust to this drastic change of events as it struggles to shut down its imagination process, its creativeness, and its problem-solving mechanisms. The child strives to comprehend what the worksheet in front of him has to do with the world he had so recently been captivated by.

Schedule Time for Play

Even though lessons and worksheets may be important, there is a time and place for everything. It's imperative to your child's intellectual growth, as well as his physical, emotional, and social development, that he has plenty of time and space for playing. Set aside blocks of time each day for uninterrupted play, which will allow your child to explore his world, use his imagination and creativeness, and be an active participant in his own life.

Gently provide advance warning of when that playtime is about to come to an end, due to the need to work on lessons. When he has fifteen or twenty minutes to bring resolution within his world of play and draw things to a close, he'll be better able to make the transition from play to lessons.

FACT

According to Bruce Duncan Perry, Ph.D., an authority on brain development in children, "It is through play that we do much of our learning. We learn best when we are having fun. Play, more than any other activity, fuels healthy development of children— and the continued healthy development of adults. An hour of 'educational' television does not have the same power as an hour of creative play."

Creating a Stimulating Environment

A variety of activity centers will further your child's social skills, reading and language skills, and math and science skills. In your child's room or playroom, create areas that allow for dramatic or pretend play, a dress-up corner, a kitchen play area, music area, and a library or quiet corner. You can use cardboard boxes and the imagination to serve the purpose for these areas.

The presence of stuffed animals or dolls allows for the care and nurturing of animals and infants. Arrange other toys and hands-on manipulatives appropriate for your child's age on shelves that are accessible to him. Make learning activities available that stimulate the sensory, visual, and auditory senses, such as physical touch, reading, playing, singing, dancing, and talking.

Create a place for art and crafts projects, painting, clay, puzzles, and games. Display the artwork your little one creates on a bulletin board in the kitchen or hallway. Hang colorful pictures or educational posters where your child can see them. Discuss the pictures on the posters from time to time; point out and read the words, too.

Spend lots of time together, looking through picture books and discussing what your child sees. Include your child in daily outdoor activities, such as walking the dog, feeding the birds, getting the mail, or planting and weeding a garden. You'll round out your child's daily education and enhance their mental, social, and physical growth by including dramatic play, music, reading, art, discussions, and recreational play each day.

QUESTION?

Can I use educational software with my toddler?
Some researchers believe that children age three and under should not spend time on computers. They feel that children in this age group learn best through movement, personal interactions, and using the senses. The sedentary basis of the computer is therefore not as beneficial to their development. However, three- and four-year-olds are generally ready to begin experimenting with age-appropriate educational software.

Overcoming Stranger Suspicion

Young children may go through a shy stage of "stranger suspicion," where the only people they are comfortable with are their parents or siblings. They may resist making eye contact with others, pull back from others' touch, or hide behind Mom or Dad. Most children will outgrow this stage, so there's no need to force your child to interact with those he's presently not comfortable with.

Rather, allow your child to observe friends or relatives from a safe distance until he's ready to venture forth at his own pace. When he watches the way you interact with others, how you meet and greet people, the way you smile or laugh, and the comfortable and natural relationship you have with others, he'll begin to open up and mimic your positive, friendly, and sociable behaviors.

Arrange to attend story time at libraries or bookstores and mommy-and-me programs where he can simply watch, rather than participate. Provide opportunities for him to observe other children at play in the park or in preschool or kindergarten groups. Over time, the reticence and suspicion he feels will begin to subside, and he'll become more relaxed and able to enjoy, and look forward to, opportunities to socialize with others of all ages.

Ready for Kindergarten

Many preschool activities carry over into kindergarten but with emphasis upon strengthening various skills, comprehension levels, and reading readiness abilities. Continue to talk with your child about everything going on around him, engage in discussions about topics of interest to him, and encourage him to always ask questions about anything on his mind.

For kindergarten ideas, consult books such as *How to Prepare Your Child for Kindergarten* by Florence Karnofsky and Trudy Weiss and *What Your Kindergartner Needs to Know* by E. D. Hirsch and John Holdren. Or you can visit *www.childfun.com* or *www.kinderstart.com* for learning activities and crafts.

As with preschool children, repetition is an important tool for learning. Kindergarten children still enjoy hearing rhymes, songs, and stories repeated over and over. Due to their unique sense of humor at this age, they often like to switch the lyrics or stories around in a silly manner, just to see if you can catch the discrepancies.

Important Skills to Learn

By now, children will need to know critical information about themselves, their families, and their homes, such as full names, addresses, and telephone numbers. Their ability to communicate is a high priority, not only for communicating with family members, but with sitters, doctors, police officers, and other adults. Yet they must be cautioned against talking with strangers.

They will need to be able to follow simple directions, then increasingly complex directions suitable for their age. Manners and showing respect are important, along with proper social skills. They should understand how to take turns and share, and they should know that hurting others is not acceptable behavior.

You'll want to help your child improve his fine motor skills, such as handling pencils, cutting and pasting, and tying shoes. You'll also want to encourage him to practice gross motor skills, such as hopping on one foot, pumping a swing, or riding a bike. Emotional growth shouldn't be overlooked, either. Outbursts or temper tantrums need to be curbed, as well as whining or crying when things don't go one's way.

For a list of preschool and kindergarten skills and activities, see World Book's Typical Course of Study at ✍ www.worldbook.com. Click on "Parents," then "Typical Course of Study," and select the grade level, such as preschool or kindergarten.

Getting Ready to Read

Reading readiness includes the ability to listen attentively to stories, tell or retell stories, make the connection between words on a page and the story they tell, understand that letters create words, and identify signs and labels in the community. You can help your child prepare for reading by surrounding him with picture books and storybooks, reading to him regularly, and asking him questions about his thoughts or feelings on stories.

Read to your child from anything that has words on it: the cereal box, milk carton, labels on cans or jars, newspapers, calendars, posters, or anything else around the home. Show him the letters that spell "Cheerios" or "milk." Repetition in this manner will help him make the connection between the item, the letters printed on it, and the spoken word.

Reading Field Trips

When you're running errands, continue to point out letters and words on signs, logos, and at the grocery store. It can be helpful to engage in "reading field trips" on a regular basis. Walk or drive around, pointing out the letters and words on signs and in grocery stores. Then go to the library and sit down at a table with a few favorite books and continue to point out the letters and words in books. Back at home, read a favorite story and, again, point out familiar letters and words. He'll soon see that words are everywhere, and reading is an important skill to possess.

Show your child how you can write a simple short story, using letters and words that he may be familiar with. Allow him to watch you create and print this short story on paper. Then read it back to him. He'll make the connection that he, too, can put letters and words on paper, then read them to you.

Varied Learning Rates

Of course, not every child will learn to recognize letters or words, or learn to print or read, at the same time. Not every child learns to walk or talk at the same age nor learns to ride a bike or tie his shoes at the same age. If your child does not show interest in letters or words, don't force it on him.

FACT

Children mature at varying ages, emotionally, physically, and mentally. If your child experiences difficulties in certain areas, don't pressure him. Wait a week or two and try again. A young child can easily accomplish certain feats when he's had a few more weeks to mature and practice his skills.

You don't want to exhibit frustration or associate negative feelings with reading or writing. Simply continue to read and point out words and signs, but don't quiz him on them or force the issue. As long as you make reading an enjoyable activity, it's only a matter of time before he makes the connection.

Daily Educational Activities

In a traditional school during kindergarten and first grade, a report card will cover social and emotional capabilities. Areas they cover include the ability to pay attention in class, listen well to the teacher, play well with others, stay on task, and exhibit self-control. Cognitive skills on a report card can include the ability to recognize or print the alphabet and numerals, count objects, associate sounds and letters, use appropriate vocabulary, and demonstrate problem-solving skills. As your child matures, she will continue to work on these skills as they become increasingly more challenging.

You can help your child work toward similar goals by continuing to talk and read to her daily, sing and recite rhymes together, tell and retell stories, and create and print your own stories. Play educational board games and recreational games together, visit the library and check out a variety of books and tapes, and go on field trips and various places of interest on a regular basis.

Free worksheets for preschool and kindergarten skills are available at Web sites such as ✍ *www.edhelper.com,* ✍ *www.first-school.ws,* and ✍ *www.learningpage.com.* You can print the pages out for your children to complete, color, and display.

For busywork, judge your child's interest in kindergarten-level to second-grade-level workbooks or worksheets. You may want to purchase a reading workbook and a math workbook that interests your child. If you have Internet access, you can download and print age-level worksheets from children's Web sites.

Kindergarten Activities

The following activities will help enhance fine motor skills, visual discrimination, auditory discrimination, classification skills, sequencing skills, reading readiness, and math readiness.

- Tracing straight and curved lines and letters.
- Cutting and pasting shapes and puzzle pieces.
- Determining same and different.
- Determining same sounds and rhyming words.
- Recognizing and matching colors and shapes.
- Determining what comes first, second, and last.
- Recognizing upper- and lowercase letters.
- Pattern and color matching.
- Measuring and estimating size and distance.
- Counting and adding objects.

First-Grade Activities

The following activities will help to improve fine motor skills, printing and composition skills, phonics and decoding skills, independent reading, and math skills.

- Printing short sentences.
- Creating and printing stories.
- Organizing ideas and sentences logically.
- Reading and comprehending short stories.
- Making inferences and drawing conclusions.
- Counting, adding, and subtracting.
- Matching shapes and patterns.
- Using charts and graphs.
- Measuring objects and counting money.
- Telling time and using calendars.

Length of School Day

The time you spend on formal learning activities will depend on your child and her abilities and attention span. Once her fingers have grown tired of holding a pencil, or her mind can no longer grasp the concept of adding two objects to three objects, it's time to quit for the day. Next week, she may better understand the concept that two things placed with three things equals five things. Or, next month, she may have attained better control of the pencil and will have an easier time printing sentences.

For now, if ten minutes is all she can spend on tracing letters or printing sentences, that's fine. If ten minutes is all she can spend on listening to a story, recalling some of the details of the story, and summarizing it for you, then that's enough. If ten minutes is all she can concentrate on the names of community helpers, maps of your neighborhood, or safety rules, it's time to allow her a much-deserved break.

Be happy with all she's absorbed in thirty minutes today. She's actually learned a lot and practiced important skills during that time. The rest of the day, she can continue learning through play—independently, with you, or with siblings or friends. Tomorrow will offer plenty of opportunities for additional learning, practice, and playtime. E

Chapter 16

Homeschooling in the Elementary Years

You can be sure that exciting adventures await you just around the bend. The elementary years are some of the most entertaining and inspirational of the homeschool experience. This chapter will discuss the basics and offer suggestions for a fun-filled educational homeschool.

Teaching a Child to Read

Some parents may not trust their ability to teach their child to read, but it's not as difficult as you may think. With practice and patience, you'll soon have your child on the road to reading success.

The Phonics Method

The phonics method of sounding out and deciphering words provides beginning readers with the tools they need to sound out a multitude of words. When a child has learned the sounds of the consonants and vowels, and is able to sound out the word *cat*, for instance, she will be able to sound out a dozen more words rhyming with the *at* sound. When this method clicks in your child's mind, and she realizes the key to reading is to sound out words, there will be no holding her back.

Of course, there are those words that defy logic and the rules of phonics. You have *ate* and *eight*, and *through* and *though* and *trough*. The pronunciation of "sight words" such as these will be learned in time, with practice and with patience. Good reading skills result from good reading habits. The more a child reads and becomes familiar with sounding out words, and the more she recognizes words that don't adhere to basic phonics rules, the more adept she'll become at reading.

Reading to Your Children

Once your children become good readers, don't slack off in your reading to them. Continue reading aloud every day from favorite books, classics, bestsellers, biographies, or textbooks. Continue reading bedtime stories, as well. Even after children have learned to read, they will pick up proper pronunciation of words, voice inflection, the sound of dialogue, and add to their vocabulary skills as you read aloud to them.

Continue to expand your child's world of books and reading. Visit the library often to select books at your child's current reading level and determine her abilities with higher-level books. While at the library, sit down together and have your child read a few lines from the selection of books. In this way, you both will be able to determine if the books are too easy for her, or whether she's ready to move on to the next reading level.

Ready for Math

Basic math, or arithmetic, includes counting, adding, subtracting, estimating, measuring, and calculating. As your child progresses through the elementary years, additional mathematical skills will be introduced. When your child has grasped the basics, you'll be able to help her build upon a solid mathematical foundation.

Mastering the Skills

Unfortunately, the math skills introduced in traditional schools move along so quickly, if a child doesn't catch them the first time around, they've often lost that window of opportunity. In the homeschool, however, if you see that your child is still struggling with basic subtraction, you won't want to move ahead to more complex problems until she has mastered the basics. Fortunately, you can spend weeks on basic subtraction alone, if you'd like.

When she has finally achieved true comprehension of subtraction and the ability to perform the calculations flawlessly, then she can move on to the next lessons. You will know without a doubt if she has truly mastered the skills she needs before moving ahead. With this solid foundation, she is ready for multiplication and division, fractions and decimals, estimation and measurement, problem solving, and increasingly challenging mathematical equations.

Hands-On Manipulatives

By using concrete examples of math problems, children will better understand the abstract concepts that are introduced. You can use any objects for counting, adding, and subtracting, from buttons to beans to plastic animal counters. You can also use an abacus or counting frame with plastic beads.

Educational supply stores carry a wide variety of math manipulatives. However, you can often make your own. From poster board or construction paper, you can create coin-sized counters, pattern blocks, fraction circles, fraction bars, cardboard clocks, mathematical charts. You can also make rulers, number lines, geometric boards, play money, and flashcards. And your children will enjoy the cutting and creative activities, too.

ALERT!

Every math book or program incorporates methods unique to its principles, so research each carefully and compare notes with other homeschool families. Most important, consider your child's learning style. A math program that one family loves may do wonders for their child, but its method may be in direct contrast to your child's learning style.

Everyday Math

Textbooks and math programs are one way to learn and practice skills. But everyday situations present excellent ways to put those skills to regular, logical use. In a normal day, your family can practice telling time as the minutes and hours go by. You and your children can estimate, then measure ingredients when cooking on a daily basis. Practice counting and money skills by setting up a "store" in your home. Have children put prices on items gathered from the pantry, or on toys or books gathered from their room. Make purchases, have children add up the total costs, pay with play or real money, and have children count out your correct change.

When you're grocery shopping, children can keep running tabs of the items you're purchasing and see how close they come to the actual total. At the gasoline station, they can calculate the cost of your tank of gas. Then, based upon how many gallons of gasoline are in the tank and how many miles your car gets to a gallon, they can determine how far this tank of gas will go. Every day offers mathematical problems that can be fun to solve, clearly showing children the importance of learning and applying math skills in real life.

FACT

Activity books such as *Fabulous Fractions* by Lynette Long, *Hands-On Math* by Frances McBroom, *Math Wise* by James Overholt, *Real-Life Math Problem Solving* by Mark Illingworth, and *Real-World Math for Hands-On Fun* by Cynthia Littlefield all provide interesting, down-to-earth activities that help your child understand and relate key math skills to everyday life.

Living History

For decades, children have complained about reading long, dry chapters in history textbooks, then answering the even drier questions at the end of the chapter. There are no fascinating experiments to do, no stimulating challenges, and little creative license allowed with the lessons. It's just facts, and more facts, which can quickly take on a dull, repetitive tone, with little correlation to the child's life today. So what can you do to make history fun?

Dramatize Historical Events

Now is a good time to bring dramatic play back into lessons. If you're studying the era of the Revolutionary War, for instance, along with the signing of the Declaration of Independence, enlist the help of the local children's librarian. Seek colorful books written about that era or biographies about prime characters, such as George Washington, Thomas Jefferson, and John Hancock.

Then have your children bring the historic period to life by dramatizing the events. Each family member can take a part, speaking the dialogue, and adding to it as they further develop the performance. They can use their creativeness to design their own costumes to the best of their ability. If they don't have boats or a nearby stream to illustrate Washington's crossing of the Delaware, they can make a cardboard skiff and place it upon blue bed sheets spread upon the living room floor, representing the river. If they don't have powdered wigs or quill pens lying around to use when signing the Declaration, cotton batting can adorn their heads and a feather can be inserted into their pens.

Advantages of Re-enactments

Nearly all historic events or periods can be dramatized, and children are generally eager to re-create those periods, using whatever props they have at hand. Such props, no matter how simple, can pull children into a particular era, making them feel as if they're actually living the events. Not only does this manner of re-creating history inscribe the events into their mind better than simply reading about them, but it provides the opportunity for children to memorize and deliver parts of important documents or speeches, such the Declaration of Independence, the Gettysburg Address, the Mayflower Compact, the Magna Carta, and many more.

Encourage children to create a short book on their historical presentations. They can write and illustrate the steps they took in researching, designing, and performing parts of the living history lessons. They can also include the script they developed and followed for the performance. Bind the book with string or staples and add it to their portfolio of homeschool memoirs. Include photos or videotapes of the performance, as well.

Scientific Explorations

History can easily be carried through into science lessons, as both are intricately intertwined. Scientific and medical discoveries, inventions and machines, have all contributed to the progression of historic events in our world. One can hardly learn about the invention of the telephone, light bulb, or radioactivity, for instance, without learning the history of Alexander Graham Bell, Thomas Edison, or Marie Curie.

Science Biographies

Short biographies on scientists and inventors help children zero in on the person and their accomplishments. Such biographies sometimes include suggestions on scientific experiments that children can explore at home. The relation between the scientist, the experiments, and that period in history helps to pull events together in a logical way. When a child thinks of an experiment she did involving a battery and a light bulb during a study of Thomas Edison's life, she's more likely to remember the fact that Edison was nearly deaf, that he lived through the Civil War era, and that he not only developed the incandescent light bulb but also the phonograph and movie projector.

Backyard Science

Engage in science experiments and hands-on projects several times a week. Take advantage of your backyard, your region, and your seasons and climate. It may be the time of year when mushrooms, fungi, and spores are prolific and available for observation.

It may be the rainy season or the dry season, offering insight into the season's impact on soil, crops, gardens, leaves, harvests, streams and rivers, heat, and humidity. Birds and rabbits may be making nests, or teaching their young ones to fend for themselves. All of nature, throughout the seasons, offers opportunities for hands-on learning and projects right in your own backyard.

Science Experiments

Science books can provide knowledge, methods, theories, and principles for the topics you study. These are helpful for establishing the background or foundation of experiments your children will conduct. But it's the actual experiments or hands-on projects that provide real understanding of the reasons and results of the projects, or the cause and effects of the experiment.

The Exploratorium at ✎ *www.exploratorium.edu* provides virtual visits to the Antarctic, the Observatory, Sports Science, Brain Explorer, and Math Explorer. Visit Questacon at ✎ *www.questacon. edu.au/kids.html* for science shows, illusions, activities, and puzzles. Numerous science and math lessons are also featured on Discovery School's site at ✎ *www.school.discovery.com/lessonplans.*

Art and Music

Unfortunately, art and music programs have begun to suffer in some schools, due to a lack of funding or mismanagement of school budgets. Yet, art and music are fundamental parts of even the earliest education. Rhythmic moving and dancing come naturally to youngsters as soon as they are able to stand in their crib. Coloring and doodling are the first exercises that children attempt when they pick up a crayon, whether they have paper before them or not.

Art and music are an integral part of human beings, helping to enhance thinking skills, creativeness, and imagination. Such skills should, therefore, never be discounted or relegated to one or two days a week. Rather, they should be an essential part of every day.

Artistic Creations

Art brings out the creativeness and inventiveness in children, as well as provides ways for children to illustrate, convey, and communicate feelings and perspectives from their point of view. You'll want to focus on the creative *process* of hands-on arts and crafts projects, rather than the *outcome* of the project. It's the involvement and action of creating art that makes it so enjoyable. Being overly concerned with the end result can extinguish the creative spark before it ignites.

Harmonizing Body and Mind

It's fascinating how we can remember the words to a song we haven't heard in twenty years. Yet, we can't remember what we wanted to pick up at the grocery today. Perhaps we should set our grocery lists to music.

Similarly, children can have difficulty learning the alphabet, the months of the year, or the countries of the world, but put them to music, and suddenly they can sing them in the correct order. Music has this ability. Music brings the mind and body together in a splendid harmony of sound, rhythm, words, and brainwaves. Research has shown that music increases spatial-temporal reasoning skills, which are especially helpful in grasping some mathematical concepts.

FACT

For fun ways to incorporate music and art into your curriculum, browse the lesson plans at ✎ *www.lessonplanspage.com/ Music.htm* and ✎ *www.lessonplanspage.com/Art.htm.* The music section includes lesson ideas on rhythm, melody, tempo, mood, composition, and instruments. The art section has lessons on artists, art history, crafts, collages, drawing, painting, sculpture, and more.

Even if your children are not necessarily musically or artistically inclined, they will still reap the benefits of artistic creation and the sound of music. Welcome both into your lessons every day.

Testing and Test Results

Testing can be a "testy" subject with some homeschoolers. In schools, testing has been a way to determine what each child has learned, or, as some say, how well the teacher has taught the child. Due to the close, one-on-one interaction in a home-based education, parents can clearly see how well their child is progressing and what areas may need additional attention. They also understand that the mere idea of a test can set anyone on edge, which can result in adverse or misleading test results.

However, some states require testing as part of their evaluation process, so it may be something that your child will need to deal with at some point. The good news is that homeschool-friendly testers are usually available to administer the tests. These are certified teachers who are authorized to give tests, and many of them are also homeschool parents.

Standardized tests include the California Achievement Test (CAT), Iowa Tests of Basic Skills (ITBS), and Stanford Achievement Tests (SAT), among others. The *Get Ready for Standardized Tests* books, designed for each grade level, provide practice exercises, preparation tips, and test result explanations.

When you have a friendly, state-certified tester in your home, administering the test to your child at the dining table—and allowing your child to take breaks, go outside for fresh air to clear the mind, and have lunch or a snack in the middle of the test—it makes for a less stressful test environment and truer test results. Some homeschoolers prefer to gather in one location and have the test administered as a group. Again, breaks from the testing and a more casual atmosphere will enable children to be more relaxed and to perform better. Check with your local homeschool support group regarding standardized tests in your region.

Socialization Opportunities

Children in this age group, from six to twelve years of age, usually have little trouble making friends and socializing. In most cases, they've already developed friendships with other children in the community.

To broaden their circle of friends, you can join the local homeschool support group, where you can attend regular gatherings and take part in picnics, field trips, bowling, miniature golf, and similar group activities. Invite homeschoolers near your child's age to your home and allow your child to visit their homes.

Enroll your six-year-old in swimming lessons, your eight-year-old in violin lessons, and your ten-year-old in sculpture classes. Next semester, enroll the children in skiing lessons, voice lessons, and painting classes. In addition, sign the kids up with a theater group, musical band, sports team, or 4-H to encourage group interaction and teamwork. Not only will your children learn new skills and improve upon previous skills, but they'll continue to meet new and old friends, as well. Ⓔ

Chapter 17

Homeschooling in the Middle Years

As your child enters middle school, his educational, emotional, and social skills will take on deeper meanings. The high-school years are just around the corner, the emotional and physical changes of adolescence are on the horizon, and closer alliances are formed with friends. This chapter will show you how to make this transition time a smooth and enjoyable experience for all.

Moving at Your Child's Pace

In the homeschool, your child should be allowed to move at a pace that remains challenging, yet allows for thoroughly grasping concepts and skills. Unlike a traditional school, it's not necessary to keep all lessons moving along on the same time schedule. In other words, you needn't feel that you must complete a history lesson in thirty minutes, a science lesson in thirty minutes, math and English each within a thirty-minute time frame, then repeat the process again tomorrow.

If your child can do his English lesson in thirty minutes, that's fine. But if he has difficulty in math, struggling with ratios and percents, for example, then the time allotted for math class may need to be extended. In fact, there's nothing wrong with spending a couple hours learning a new concept, as long as your child is inclined to do so.

If he simply cannot make sense of the lesson today, then it's okay to set it aside and work on it another day. A couple weeks from now, he may be able to easily comprehend the relationship of ratios and percents.

ALERT!

If you find it necessary to skip certain lessons for a few weeks and go back to them later, note the fact in your lesson plan book or mark the pages with sticky notes. You don't want to reach the end of the school year and realize you forgot to cover some of the lessons.

Focusing on Weaknesses

If you've homeschooled your child for a number of years, you have a good understanding of his strengths and weaknesses. Because you have been so in tune with him, you've been able to help him overcome most of his weaknesses over the years. However, if you've recently withdrawn your child from school, you may notice gaps in his education.

Bringing Life to Subjects

Donna withdrew her son from school after the seventh grade. Although he could read and write well, he couldn't tell a subject from a verb, let alone a preposition from a conjunction. To this day, Donna still has no idea why this wasn't determined through his assignments or test papers. Perhaps he "learned" the skills long enough to pass the tests, but promptly forgot what he had learned.

Even though he was a middle-schooler and seemingly "too old for silly nonsense," Donna and her son used props to dress up as the subject of sentences and acted out the action of the verb. For instance, if a sentence stated: "The mouse ran up the clock," then Donna and her son would find a way to dress as mice, and they would perform the action, running up an imaginary clock.

Their props were simple, close-at-hand objects, which added to the silliness of the exercises. They admit that they spent many hilarious hours learning subjects and verbs, along with other parts of sentences. Now, over six years later, Donna's son can still name any part of a sentence without hesitation. And he declares with a laugh that he will never forget the antics he and his mother engaged in as they gave "sentence performances" during his homeschool years.

Inherent Weaknesses

Keep in mind that some weaknesses are a result of gaps in the education process or of your child missing certain nuggets of information. Other weaknesses may be a part of your child's unique personality. Some people are better talkers than others, some better writers, some better at math, and some better artistically. There are some things you can't change.

If your child isn't as strong in math as his brother, father, or mother, then it's probably a trait that is unique to his character. He may possibly be stronger in art, science, or music than his brother, father, or mother. Everyone has strengths and weaknesses, some of which can be improved, and some which cannot. Knowing that you've done your best and knowing that your child will be a success, thanks to the many other strengths he possesses, will be reward enough.

Enhancing Comprehension Skills

One of the best things you can do for your child is to continue encouraging his interest in reading. As children approach their preteen and teenage years, their focus begins to shift. They may interact with their peers more and want to be more like them, which means developing new interests in music, movies, or the latest fads. With their attention focusing elsewhere, they may conclude that they don't have enough time to read anymore. However, reading, literacy, and comprehension should remain a top priority in the homeschool.

FACT

A recent survey by the National Assessment of Educational Progress (NAEP) found that only 40 percent of adolescents can read well enough to comprehend high-school textbooks. Researchers have found that, although teens may be able to read the text, they aren't always able to make inferences from the material, draw conclusions, summarize what they've read, or relate what they've read to other applications.

Choosing to Read

In the homeschool, your child may spend two to three hours each day on "school" topics, but during the rest of the day, he is free to think, read, and learn about the things that genuinely fill him with enthusiasm. As a result, he has more time for reading, is more likely to *choose* to read books on subjects that interest him, or to research and read related topics on the Internet, and visit the library and bookstore more often.

FACT

When reading and research are a result of a child's own interest in a subject, he doesn't feel as if he's being forced to do something that has little meaning for him. Therefore, he's not averse to additional reading of magazines, newspapers, or the latest fiction book, just for the pleasure of it. When you resist the temptation to force the reading issue, you'll often be surprised by the positive results.

Encouraging Reading

If your child's interest in reading still seems to have waned, invest more time in reading, yourself. Avoid nagging your child to read.

Instead, casually turn off the television and radio, pick up a book from the collection you keep on the side table or bookshelf, and spend an hour quietly reading. It can be helpful to spread a few books or magazines on a coffee table, too.

Sometimes, reading can seem like too much of a "chore" to a child. If this appears to be the case, get things moving by reading the first chapter of a book to your child, or take turns reading chapters aloud. Even though they are now middle-schoolers, kids still enjoy being read to, whether they want to admit it or not.

Reading for Pleasure

When reading for pleasure, you don't want to drill your children on what they've read. However, it's helpful when family members discuss books they've read or are reading. When children hear you describe a special passage from a book, the events unfolding in a novel, or the surprise ending of a mystery, their interest is aroused. As you continue to comment upon the story day after day, the characters and events take on a more realistic quality. Your kids may see how wrapped up you are in the story, how deeply it affects or excites you.

QUESTION?

How can I determine which books would appeal to my child?
Read book reviews together at Web sites, such as
www.bookmuse.com or *www.bn.com,* to see which books might interest him. Then visit the library, leisurely browse the shelves, and ask your child to select a half dozen books that look interesting, fiction or nonfiction. Take turns reading and discussing the books at home. You and he will both soon discover the books that excite him.

When they become engrossed in a book, they'll be more likely to share the story or events with you, just as you shared your comments with them. Make the discussion of books and stories as normal and routine as discussing a sit-com or movie. By relating what they've read in a book and how it made them feel, children are demonstrating their comprehension skills. And by listening to your book discussions, they have a better idea of the themes that can run through a story, the inferences that can be made, clues to watch for in stories, conclusions that can be drawn, and how events in books can relate to real life. These are critical reading and comprehension skills that can be applied across the curriculum in all subject areas.

Exploring and Learning Together

The middle years are great years for pursuing special interests and exploring educational topics together, doing research together, writing reports together, and learning together. When your child sees you select a book to read and to write a report on, he's more likely to select his own book and write a report on it, right alongside you. If he doesn't know how to write the bibliography page, and you've forgotten, you can both research it together. When it's time to stand up and give the book report from notes, you can do it together, in front of family, friends, or relatives. Learning together helps a family stick together.

Allowing Time for Educational Interests

During the middle school years, children may need to spend an average of two to three hours per day on core curriculum subjects. Some days may require more; some may require less. The remainder of your child's waking hours should be spent on exploring, thinking, reading, playing, discovering, creating, composing, exercising both the mind and body.

Finding One's Niche

Always encourage your child's current interests or hobbies. If your daughter is presently fascinated by computer art, for instance, allow her to attend computer art classes and experiment with digital art software. She may enjoy reading numerous books and articles on three-dimensional computer animation and spending hours creating her own computer art or animated clips. She might also enjoy visiting local artists or graphic design businesses.

If your son loves taking apart computers, printers, or small engines, and putting them back together again, give him plenty of opportunities to do so. He can have access to the many discarded computers that end up at recycling centers and work on rebuilding them. He can use his special skills and instruction manuals to help him repair your VCR, the lawn mower, or water pump. He would no doubt enjoy visiting computer-repair businesses or small-engine repair services in your area.

Making the Most of Talents

If your daughter loves music, allow plenty of free time for practicing the piano, guitar, violin, and any other instruments that interest her. In school, she would probably be able to choose *one* instrument to learn to play. At home, she can choose to play the flute, *and* the clarinet, *and* the trumpet, *and* the drums. And she will have the time to become accomplished on all four instruments, as well as the time to compose her own music and record her compositions.

FACT

At this point in their lives, as they approach adolescence, children begin to "search for themselves." Psychologists refer to this as "identity formation." It's an integral part of making the transition from child to adult. Seeking a sense of independence, and focusing on things that interest them, is therefore the natural order of things.

If your son is captivated by the politics of our times, is stimulated and motivated by debates aired by political analysts, often has his nose buried in political science books, and speaks strongly of his own views and platforms, he may be headed toward a legal or political career. He may be energized by debates he witnesses, driven to deliver rebuttals on viewpoints expressed by others, and feels the most alive when he can listen to facts and opinions supporting diverse viewpoints, then articulate his own feelings. He will need plenty of time to absorb these areas of interest, reflect upon them, hear your views on them, and consider his own feelings regarding them.

Turning Hobbies into Careers

When children are able to devote much of their time to special areas of interest, they are actively developing their skills for the career that awaits them. The child with an interest in computer art may become a graphic artist; the interest in putting together computer parts may result in a computer-repair business; the musically inclined child could become a musician or open a recording studio; the politically motivated child could become a state representative, working for the good of the people.

Self-Directed Learning

It may be difficult for some people to understand that children naturally teach themselves. We, as parents, can share information, share our own experiences, provide guidance, answer questions, and suggest ideas, but we can't get inside our children's minds and take over the way they process, absorb, or retain information. We can help them, we can be of assistance, we can observe the manners in which they seem to learn best, but we can't force them to learn according to our own styles or timetables. Forced learning will usually result in a lack of learning.

Self-directed learning leads to self-motivation, self-confidence, and self-reliance. A child who experiences freedom in learning and exploring also experiences more purpose and joy in each new day. The positive power of self-directed learning greatly influences the child's happiness and success in all areas of his life.

Children acknowledge, absorb, and retain information through their own experiences, research, and discoveries. When they have some control over what they are learning, and have the freedom to delve into ideas and concerns that interest them, they have a sense of purpose and identity.

Self-directed learning, or freedom to pursue their own interests, is one way to help children begin to acquire their independence. The desire for more freedom in self-directing their learning should be supported and encouraged by parents, who can keep a watchful eye on their children and guide them when they need assistance.

Socialization Skills

These are the years when children begin to go through emotional and physical changes, and socialization can take on more importance. It's a good time to reinforce proper etiquette, social skills, morals, and values. Children may begin to be away from home more than they've been in the past, visiting with others, going to a movie or to the pizza parlor. Your children will need to select friends based upon the values and character education you have passed on to them during their homeschool years. And they'll need to make informed decisions based on the solid moral training you've provided.

Here are some wonderful books for reinforcing and improving manners and moral behavior:

- *365 Manners Kids Should Know,* by Sheryl Eberly.
- *Book of Virtues for Young People,* by William Bennett.
- *Building Moral Intelligence,* by Michele Borba.
- *Gift of Good Manners,* by Peggy Post and Cindy Post Senning.
- *Rules to Be Cool,* by Karla Dougherty.
- *Teach Your Children Well: Helping Kids Make Moral Choices,* by Don Otis.

Extracurricular Activities

As your child's social life begins to pick up, he may become more active in art or drama clubs, writing or book clubs, youth groups, environmental groups, sports, bands, or other organizations. His circle of friends will expand along with his interest in hobbies and community events. These are important social times for him, allowing him to interact with others, use his social skills and manners in real situations, work as a team on projects, and use his logical reasoning and problem-solving skills in the real world.

As your child matures and spends more time with friends or in extracurricular activities, continue to be there for him. Keep the lines of communication open, answer any questions he may have, observe his behavior and his friend's behaviors, and help him find ways to resolve conflicts he may encounter. As much as he wants independence, he also needs to know that he can always turn to you for support.

Volunteering in the Community

Volunteerism is a form of entry into the working world and society. It provides a sense of responsibility to one's community and to the world we live in. Volunteering in hospitals, nursing homes, animal shelters, senior citizen programs, day-care centers, or homeless shelters offers insight into situations and lifestyles that your children may have previously been unfamiliar with. It broadens their vision of the world and the many walks of life that exist.

Children may also want to volunteer in a business or service that parallels their passions: computer, art, music, or book stores; woodshops or repair shops; science or nature centers; museums or libraries; summer camps or after-school programs; political headquarters or newspaper offices. Volunteering in certain businesses may eventually lead to a part-time, paying job. And what a thrilling and motivating experience that is for a youngster—being paid for something he already loves to do! Ⓔ

Chapter 18

Homeschooling in the Teen Years

Congratulations! You've reached the teenage years in your homeschool! Or perhaps you're just beginning your homeschool odyssey with the teen years. Either way, it's sure to be a voyage that you'll remember and treasure for all the years of your life. Of course, you'll want your child to remember and treasure these special years as well, so read on.

Living with Teens

Some parents may dread the teenage years. Surprisingly, homeschooled teenagers often seem to escape many of the stereotypical problems associated with these years. They are excited about the direction their lives are going, the things they're learning and pursuing, and the activities they're involved with. They're overflowing with ideas, plans, and goals for their lives. It's a joy to see and feel such energy and happiness from these young adults. Their boundless excitement is positively contagious.

FACT

For help on raising teens in today's world, consider these books: *10 Best Gifts for Your Teen,* by Patt and Steve Saso, on maintaining strong relationships and providing guidance; *Parent's Guide to the Teen Years,* by Susan Panzarine, about teen pressures and the importance of support systems; and *Raising Responsible Teenagers,* by Bob Myers, on helping teens become mature, considerate adults.

There may be times of moodiness or irritability, which, as you may well recall, are all a part of the teenage years. Hormones are still fluctuating, occasionally wreaking havoc physically as well as emotionally. In many ways, you're sharing your life and your home with another adult now—a young adult, who may still waver between behaving as an adult and behaving as a child.

These can be challenging years, but they can also be exceedingly wonderful years. Enjoy them, treasure and savor them, for when they're gone, your child will be off and away.

Teaching High-School Courses

Yes, you can teach high-school courses. As we've noted several times before, teaching in the homeschool is a form of *guiding* your child and assisting her in finding the answers and resources she needs to help her learn. It's important that your child experiences and understands the concept of *learning to learn*. Just as she must learn to be responsible for her actions, she must learn how to learn on her own. This is a major skill that will benefit her the rest of her life.

Educating Oneself

Today's fast-moving technology and way of life demand that children, young people, and adults all be capable of learning new skills, enhancing their own knowledge base, and continually expanding their education. A child who has sat through school, expecting others to teach her what she needs to know, or who expects that the education process is over after high school or college, may not advance as far in the workplace as the person who has learned how to educate herself.

FACT

Teens may become more secretive and touchy about others "prying" into their lives, so be careful how you approach them. Most important, keep the lines of communication open. Though they may have nothing to say for days on end, when they know you're there for them, the floodgates can open at any moment, and a deluge of thoughts and feelings may stream forth.

As you progress through the high school years, you'll want to reinforce the importance of learning on one's own, while still helping to guide your child through her studies. Now is the time for your child to keep track of her grades and credits earned, particularly if she's planning to attend college. She should keep a list of books she's read each year, the daily learning log complete and up to date, her portfolio of assignments completed, book reports, essays, science projects, and proof of other activities she's involved with.

Correspondence Schools

Keep in mind that your child can attend independent study programs or correspondence schools as she works toward her graduation. Some of the schools that offer diplomas include the following.

- Abeka Academy: *www.abekaacademy.org*
- Alger Learning Center: *www.independent-learning.com*
- Alpha Omega: *www.aop.com*
- American School: *www.americanschoolofcorr.com*
- Clonlara High School: *www.compuhigh.com*
- Indiana University High School: *http://scs.indiana.edu/hs/hsd.html*
- Keystone National High School: *www.keystonehighschool.com*
- Laurel Springs School: *www.laurelsprings.com*
- Malibu Cove Private School: *www.seascapecenter.com*
- Oak Meadow School: *www.oakmeadow.com*

Subjects Required for College

As your child prepares for college or a career, it's a good idea that she take four years of English courses (including grammar, composition, and literature) during her high-school years. In addition, she should take three years of math (including algebra and geometry); three years of science (including biology, physical science, and lab experiences); and three years of social studies (including U.S. history and government and economics). If she's applying to college, she'll also need two years of a foreign language, a computer technology course, and at least two years of electives.

FACT

Many of these electives are actually life skills that every parent would want their child to learn. Most can be studied and experienced in six- to eight-week courses at the local parks and recreation department or community college. The number of credits your child may need for electives can add up quickly.

Fun with Electives

Electives are the fun part of school. These can include art, music, dance, drama, filmmaking, broadcasting, sculpting, computer science, computer programming, accounting, business practices, business law, journalism, speech, agriculture, forestry, woodshop, auto shop, drafting, mechanical engineering, electronics, health and nutrition, cooking, family living, parenting, philosophy, and psychology, among others.

Handling Difficult Subjects

Along with the fun subjects, the high-school years can hold some challenging subjects, as well. It may have been a while since you took Algebra I or Algebra II, and you didn't like it the first time around. How, you may wonder, will you be able to help your child with those subjects? There are several ways.

The Saxon Math books are excellent. They are designed for the user to teach herself, by reading easy-to-understand lessons, building upon previous lessons, and continually practicing and refreshing her skills. Their set of math textbooks (ranging from basic math to pre-algebra, advanced algebra, advanced math, calculus, and physics) may not be for everyone, but they worked wonders in our homeschool math program. Of course, we supplemented the textbooks with lots of math games and software, logical reasoning skills, problem solving, and working with basic, everyday math problems.

Many other math programs are also available, as well as videos that clearly explain and illustrate math concepts and exercises. Library Video, at *www.libraryvideo.com*, carries numerous videos on nearly every mathematical topic. If your homeschool group has several homeschoolers approaching the high-school years, you may want to pitch in and purchase a few videos to share over the upcoming years. If your group has a couple of parents who are especially interested in math, they may want to work with a group of teens on weekends. This type of group learning, use of videos, or educational software can be helpful in any of the subject areas: foreign languages, government and economics, biology, or electives.

Educational math software, such as that carried by Cognitive Technologies Corporation, *www.cogtech.com*; Intelligent Tutor, *www.mathtutor.com*; or Math Media, *www.mathmedia.com*, provides practice in geometry, algebra, and advanced math.

Help from Tutors and Mentors

Sometimes you just can't teach certain things to your child. If you took French in high school or college, you may not be the most helpful when your daughter decides she wants to learn Russian. When certain subjects prove to be too difficult for your child, it can be a good idea to seek a well-trained and experienced tutor. Don't hesitate to help her find the resources that will help her learn best.

Colleges and libraries often keep a database of tutors, along with their specialties, such as foreign languages, calculus, chemistry, physics. These tutors tend to be language majors, math majors, accounting majors, or computer science majors. If you're still unable to find tutors or mentors in your community, don't forget your local school district. They will have a list of tutors who may be able to help your child.

Driver Education

Getting one's license is a huge milestone in a teenager's life. It's the moment when she may feel she's attained true independence. Now she can experience one of those privileges that adults get to enjoy. But, as we all know, everyone must earn that privilege and follow the rules in order to keep that privilege. An obvious level of maturity, responsibility, and consideration for others must be displayed before a child can get behind the wheel of a car.

ALERT!

If your child must complete a driver education course of study, you may want to look into programs such as the National Driver Training Institute's program (✍ *www.nationaldrivertraining.com*) or Keystone High School's Driver Education course (✍ *www.keystonehighschool.com*). However, check with your local department of motor vehicles first to see if they accept these courses.

Contact your local department of motor vehicles to determine your state's driver education requirements and restrictions, as they will vary from state to state. Some states allow homeschooled children to enroll in a high-school driver education course. Or they may require that your child enroll in a driving school. Some states require teens to take a drug and alcohol awareness program, which is usually offered locally, before they can obtain their learner's permit or enroll in a driving course.

The Social Life

During these high-school years, teens have busy lifestyles. Social events take on even greater importance, and many teens volunteer their time, serve apprenticeships, or work part-time jobs. They might begin to experience more stress as they take on more responsibility, have fuller schedules, and work hard to complete their high-school studies.

For help in teaching social skills, manners, and values to your teens, check out *Six Steps to an Emotionally Intelligent Teenager,* by James Windell; *Emily Post's Teen Etiquette,* by Elizabeth Post; and *What Teens Need to Succeed,* by Peter Benson.

As she ventures further into the world, your child must realize that the choices and decisions she makes during these years can have lasting results. If she chooses the wrong group of kids to spend her time with and that group gets into trouble, she could feel reverberations from her unwise choice for many years to come. If she chooses to spend her spare time on college prep courses, and she's able to enroll in college a year early, this, too, can have an impact on her life. As she teeters on the threshold of adulthood, she must understand and accept the relevance and responsibility of preparing wisely for this important phase of her life.

Decision-Making Skills

To help your child, you'll need to remain steadfast in your beliefs and morals. When she comes to you for support, you can help her see both sides of an issue. If she chooses this path, *this* could happen. But if she chooses the other path, *that* could happen.

As in the past, you don't want to force your feelings upon her; rather, you want to help guide her in finding the right decisions. This helps her work through the decision-making process, keeping your beliefs in mind while considering her own. The day will come when she is on her own and will have to make her own decisions. Now is the time to help her work her way through the process.

New Challenges and New Joys

New opportunities and experiences will present themselves during the teen years. In addition to boyfriends and girlfriends, dates and dancing, working and socializing, teens still need to focus upon their studies, possibly more than they have at any time in the past. Prospective employers or college administrators will be interested in seeing proof of capabilities when meeting with the young adult. Your child will need to have a solid background to present to them.

Volunteering and Apprenticeships

Volunteering is an excellent opportunity for your child to meet and interact with others, work as a team on projects, and feel a tremendous sense of satisfaction and personal achievement by making a difference in the lives of others. If she has special interests or hobbies, she may want to volunteer in an area that corresponds to that interest. For instance, if she loves books and reading, she may want to volunteer in the library. If she loves animals, she could volunteer at the animal shelter, nature center, or wildlife refuge.

FACT

Teens face new challenges, rocky relationships, and difficult decisions as they approach adulthood. These books provide insight and guidance for teens on their journey: *The Seven Habits of Highly Effective Teens,* by Sean Covey; *Life Strategies for Teens,* by Jay McGraw; *Stay Strong,* by Terrie Williams; and *Teen Esteem,* by Pat Palmer and Melissa Froehner.

Encourage your child to call or visit areas of interest. She can express her enthusiasm and offer her time and desire to help in any way. If they currently don't need extra assistance, have her check back from time to time. Watch your local newspapers for notices regarding volunteer groups and opportunities, too.

Volunteering in Businesses

Your child can also volunteer her time and help in general businesses. At age thirteen, Brad volunteered to help in a comic-book shop, and eventually became a paid employee and store manager. While working there, he spent time improving his artistic skills and went on to become a book illustrator. Heather loved fashion and jewelry design and chose to help the owner of a clothing consignment shop; she then opened her own boutique while taking fashion design courses. Amanda volunteered to run errands and do filing in a newspaper office at age fourteen. She soon began writing articles and is now a newspaper reporter. Volunteerism can help your child obtain real-life experience in the retail or business world, or it may even lead to a lifelong career.

Apprenticeships and Internships

Apprenticeships aren't as popular in the United States as they are in some countries. However, colleges or vocational schools often try to match up students with employers in apprenticeship or internship programs in many regions of our country. Many communities and organizations, such as 4-H, YMCA, or the Boys and Girls Club, also offer work experience or mentor programs.

Working Part Time

Your child's first paying job is another milestone in her life—another step toward independence and becoming an adult. In addition to earning her own money, she experiences a new form of satisfaction when helping others run a business or service, which enhances her self-esteem. She takes on the responsibility of exchanging her skills and time for money, while agreeing to put her best efforts into her work.

Whether she works in a fast-food establishment, a video rental store, or a gift shop, this is a great experience for a teen. She learns how to meet others' expectations by delivering what she promised when taking on the job, being punctual, and getting along with supervisors, coworkers, and customers. At the same time, she will need to continue her studies as she works toward college or her career. Just because she now has a job, it doesn't mean she can slack off on her educational responsibilities or that she should forget her long-range goals.

ALERT!

Working ten to fifteen hours a week is usually enough for a teenager. As she nears the end of her high-school years, she may be able to increase her work hours or switch to a job that offers more hours and advancement opportunities.

College Preparations

If your child is planning to attend college, the early high-school years are the time to begin preparations. She'll want to focus on the subjects that are required for college, as well as her grades and credits earned. Her volunteerism and part-time jobs also come into play. Most colleges recognize the benefits of real-life experiences, so your teen will want to document all these experiences and include them with her college admission package.

The College Board provides a wealth of information on planning ahead for college, considering careers, planning courses, choosing majors, SAT preparation, how to apply to colleges, seeking financial aid, and much more. Visit their Web site at ✍ *www.collegeboard.com*.

College Entrance Exams

She'll also want to begin preparing for SAT or ACT tests if she plans to take them. These are only given at certain times of the year, so she'll want to be prepared well in advance and register ahead of time. To find out when and where the tests will be given in your area and how to register, contact your local school district. They can also advise you on ways to prepare for the test, the costs, and any other information you may need. Although there are no age restrictions, students usually take the SAT or ACT tests during the eleventh or twelfth grades.

Scholarships and Financial Aid

Many books and Web sites are devoted to helping you locate scholarships or financial aid for college expenses. You needn't pay a service to do this research for you. However, you do want to be on the lookout for scams regarding scholarships and aid. Once again, look to your local school district and library to help guide you in the best directions for information and advice on applying to colleges.

QUESTION?

Are college scholarships available for homeschooled children?
Just as colleges are now more open to homeschooled students, scholarships are becoming more available, too, as long as certain requirements are met. For more on homeschool scholarships, visit *www.eho.org/hsscholarships.htm* and *www.hsadvisor.com/scholarships.html*. Financial aid and student loans are available, as well. For information on applying for student aid, visit *www.finaid.org* and *www.fafsa.ed.gov*.

High-School Transcripts

For homeschoolers, the high school transcript is an important tool for gaining entrance into college. You or your child will want to keep track of all the subjects she covers, her grades, and credits earned from the ninth through twelfth grades. This information will be recorded in the high-school transcript that many colleges require.

Generally, a half credit is earned in a subject in one semester, providing your child with a full credit for a year's study in that subject. For instance, one semester of science can equal one-half credit; the second semester earns another half credit. By the end of the freshman year, your child will have earned one full credit in science. As indicated earlier, your teen will usually need twenty-two to twenty-four credits to meet traditional graduation requirements. These credits can easily be attained in each of the core subject areas and electives during the four years of high school.

High-School Graduation

When my son graduated from our homeschool high school, we had a celebration that equaled my own graduation from traditional public school. In many ways, it was more enjoyable for everyone. We arranged a schedule that was convenient for everyone attending, it was much less formal, there were no huge crowds, everyone knew each other, and everyone was more relaxed and, consequently, enjoyed themselves more.

Although ours was a private affair, many homeschool organizations across the country hold graduation ceremonies, complete with invitations, commencement speeches, caps and gowns, the handing out of awards and diplomas, and yearbook signings and class rings. Homeschoolers can enjoy their moments in the sun just as much as any other child, and, often, they even enjoy them more! Ⓔ

Chapter 19

Homeschooling Special-Needs Children

As with every homeschooled child, individualized attention in a safe, caring environment pays huge dividends. In a home environment, you can help your special-needs child benefit from learning at his own pace, on his own terms, and in his own style. This chapter will show you how.

Learning Disabilities

Unfortunately, "learning disabled" labels are placed upon children quite readily these days. Just because a child learns at a slower pace or learns differently from others, it doesn't necessarily mean that he's "learning disabled." It's one thing to diagnose a child with special challenges; it's quite another to unfairly label or categorize a child. Always seek second opinions from professionals regarding your child's abilities.

Two "Reading Disabled" Girls

Several years ago, I tutored two seven-year-old girls who faced learning challenges. Each attended separate schools, but both came to me with "reading disabilities," according to them.

"I have a reading disability," each girl informed me. I thought that "disability" was a rather large word for a seven-year-old.

"What makes you think that?" I asked each girl separately.

"My teacher told me," each girl replied.

I didn't ask if either knew what a "disability" was. Inwardly, I was appalled by the label placed upon these two little girls, who, as it turned out, had no disability.

Amy, the Decoder

Amy was an amazingly meticulous decoder, working diligently to sound out each letter and word phonetically. But she was afraid of sounding out a word incorrectly. She had little or no confidence in her ability to read a sentence, let alone a paragraph. As she read, either aloud or silently, she became mired in the process of sounding out words. She became extremely frustrated, sighed continually, and often gave up. She comprehended very little from her reading book, social studies, or math books. Her grades suffered across the entire curriculum.

From my library shelves, I chose books at a lower reading level and presented them to Amy. She read through them with fervor and animation. Now that I'd found her comfortable reading level, we had a base to build upon. I gradually added stories that were a bit more challenging, but we always previewed new or unfamiliar words before attempting the stories. Within a couple months, this "reading disabled" girl was reading at her grade level *and* comprehending what she read. All she had needed was assistance, practice, and self-confidence in herself.

QUESTION?

How can I instill self-confidence in my child?
Exhibit a great depth of patience with your child, and cheer her on with meaningful statements that tell her she can do it and that you have faith in her abilities. Allow plenty of opportunities to do things on her own, no matter how trivial they may seem, so that she frequently feels a rewarding sense of accomplishment.

Kristen, the Mover

Kristen was quite different from Amy. She was overly confident, did not want to sit down to read, and couldn't understand why she should have to sit down *or* read. When I first tried to determine what she could read from a story in her reading book, she flipped open the book cover with a bang, placed her nose ridiculously near the text, and spewed some words that were far too fast for me to catch, and which she obviously couldn't have seen, let alone read. A second later, she was an airplane, roaring through every open doorway.

It soon became clear that Kristen learned best when she was moving around. I'd finally pinned her down to reading a passage to me, but she struggled with it desperately, fidgeting in her seat, swinging her legs, complaining that she *could* read, but she just didn't *want* to. When she came to me for tutoring, she, a very active seven-year-old, had just spent several hours confined in a classroom. So before we attempted any reading exercises, we exercised. She did jumping jacks, hopped on one foot, raced around the yard, and became an airplane.

This physical activity didn't wear her down or tire her out; rather, it seemed to nourish her body and stimulate her mind. She didn't come to the reading table ready to sit down and read. But she was ready to learn, which she did best by standing up, though not standing still. She couldn't just read a story. She had to dramatize it with great flourishes, sweeping arms, dancing legs, and a voice that took on the tone of many different characters. She could handle reading assignments quite well—when allowed to stand and perform.

The Learning Disabilities Association of America, ✍ *www.ldanatl.org*, provides information on homeschooling children with learning disabilities. The site also offers resources, articles, and updates on various types of learning disabilities, including ADD/ADHD, dyslexia, reading disorders, and speech and language disorders.

Of course, I knew that in school she wouldn't be allowed to read in such a manner, at least not on a regular basis. So, we continued our dramatic, exuberant reading sessions as long as she agreed to sit still and read a short story with me at the end of each session. It wasn't long before she sat by my side, though, and eventually snuggled against me as she read quietly and contentedly from her reading book.

Helping Learning-Challenged Children

Sometimes, all that mildly learning-challenged children need is someone to understand their style, who is in tune with them, and who can help them make the most of their learning styles. In the homeschool, you have the ability to focus on your child's unique abilities, you can progress at his own pace, and you have the flexibility to work with him when he is at his best. Some special-needs children require more structure than others. Provide the amount of structure they are comfortable with, while remaining flexible enough to take advantage of special learning opportunities as they arise.

If your child's learning challenges are more complex or difficult for you to handle on your own, ask your child's pediatrician to recommend a therapist or special-education expert. Seek their advice and suggestions on improving your child's learning skills and helping you to make the most of your home education program.

ALERT!

Some states may have certain regulations regarding homeschooling a special-needs child. Check with your state department of education to see what regulations, if any, may apply to you. Access to special-needs services also varies from state to state, so check the availability of such services within your local school district.

Input from Your Child

Every child and every family is different. What works for one may not work for another. A professional therapist and special-education program may be perfect for your child, or it may be frustrating and unproductive for your child. Most important, you want your child to be happy and learning in an environment that is comfortable for him.

If he's not happy with the environment he's in, is frustrated by the activities he's trying to do, or feels he's not learning the way that best suits him—whether it's through you, a therapist, or a special-education program—listen to what he has to say. Knowing that you care enough to listen can make all the difference to him. Ask for his input and what he'd like to learn, and how he'd like to learn it.

FACT

Schwab Learning, ✐*www.schwablearning.org,* provides support and information for parents of children with learning differences, such as ADD/ADHD, dyslexia, and reading problems. Articles focus on learning strategies and the emotional and social impact of learning disabilities. This site also includes college resources for learning-challenged students.

Talk with other families, speak with the experts, and contact organizations dealing directly with your child's situation. Then apply all you've researched and learned toward determining what you feel is best for your child.

Creating Your Curriculum

You can create your own curriculum by determining your educational goals and objectives for your child. Based upon your goals, you can then design an educational program as discussed in Chapter 7. When designing a curriculum, consider your child's individualized needs, learning style, and his special areas of interest. Steer the curriculum and activities toward those areas. For additional learning opportunities, contact community centers, museums, libraries, and bookstores about classes or events they offer.

You'll also want to consult with your child's pediatrician, therapist, or special-education teacher to consider their advice and suggestions on working with your child. They have the training, knowledge, and experience to help you assist your child with his learning. In some cases, the school system may provide speech therapists, physical therapists, or occupational therapists to help with your homeschool program. Through the homeschooling process, continue to closely monitor your child to determine the learning style that seems to work best for him, how well he's adapting to the educational program, and the progress he's making.

Ask for Input

As you incorporate an educational program in your home, do so at a pace that is comfortable for your child. Allow him time to adjust to this new routine and method of learning. He may become distracted or disoriented if there's not enough structure in his day. Or he may become overly anxious and stressed if he senses pressure, or if there's not enough free time to enjoy the things he likes to do.

FACT

An IEP (individualized education program) is used by special-needs teachers to create a curriculum for a child, record the objectives and goals for that child, and to document any specific programs or instruction he may require. To learn more about IEPs, check the articles at LD Online, *www.ldonline.org/ld_indepth/iep/iep.html.*

Every few weeks, have another heart-to-heart discussion with your child about his learning program and encourage him to continue sharing his feelings. His feelings on the program may change as he learns and matures. The way he learned six months ago may no longer feel right to him, and he may be ready for something more stimulating, or perhaps he needs something less challenging for a while. The beauty of homeschooling is the ability to change and adapt, according to each child's learning styles and preferences. This can be especially beneficial for your special-needs child.

Support and Resources

Support from others is extremely beneficial. No one knows what you're going through better than another family in circumstances similar to yours. Support groups for families with special-needs children will provide insight, encouragement, and strength as they share their personal experiences.

LD Online, ✎ *www.ldonline.org*, a Web site for parents and teachers of learning-disabled children, includes message boards on homeschooling LD or ADHD students. The online bulletin board also provides strategies on teaching reading, math, and using educational software with learning-challenged children. America Online also offers homeschool support for Parents of Differently Abled children.

Online message or bulletin boards also provide support and can sometimes put you in touch with families in your community. Those with experience in homeschooling special-needs children can help with the ins-and-outs of the process or share particularly useful resources they've tried with their children.

Resources for Children with Special Needs

Check the following companies for resources that may be helpful to you or your child.

- Don Johnston, *www.donjohnston.com,* carries books, software, and other products for children with learning disabilities.
- IntelliTools, *www.intellitools.com,* creates computer products and software for special-education needs.
- Parent Pals, *www.parentpals.com,* has numerous resources and links on a wide variety of learning challenges facing children.
- Special Education Products, *www.iser.com/specialproducts.html,* includes auditory tools, videos, reading helps, and books on working with your children.
- Wrightslaw, *www.wrightslaw.com,* provides information on homeschooling rights and special-education needs.

Books for Homeschooling Special-Needs Children

These books provide guidance for families of children with special needs:

- *Homeschooling Children with Special Needs,* by Sharon Hensley.
- *Homeschooling the Child with ADD,* by Lenore C. Hayes.
- *Learning Differences Sourcebook,* by Nancy Boyles and Darlene Contadino.
- *Right-Brained Children in a Left-Brained World,* by Jeffrey Freed and Laurie Parsons.

ADD and ADHD Information

Children with Attention Deficit Disorder (ADD) and Attention Deficit Hyperactivity Disorder (ADHD) are better understood and treated today. One of the leading nonprofit organizations, Children and Adults with Attention Deficit Hyperactivity Disorder (CHADD), provides support, guidance, and up-to-date information for families. They discuss multifaceted treatment approaches, which incorporate parent training, educational and behavioral modifications, and medical treatment. You can visit their Web site at *www.chadd.org* and click on your state to locate a chapter near you.

The Attention Deficit Disorder Association, ✍*www.add.org*, has added ADD coaching guidelines as a way of helping those with Attention Deficit Disorder. They cite research suggesting that current methods of treating ADD/ADHD individuals, such as behavioral, psychological, and medical treatments, aren't always successful. They include an in-depth look at ADD coaching, how it works, and the principles behind it.

Dyslexia Support

Dyslexia becomes apparent through single word decoding difficulties. Usually, no other types of developmental disability are evident. The International Dyslexia Association's Web site, ✍*www.interdys.org*, offers updates, research, a message board, and links to branches throughout the United States and Canada. Techniques for overcoming reading and writing difficulties are included on the Dyslexia Web site at ✍*www.dyslexia.com*, along with learning strategies, articles, and a forum for networking with other families.

Teaching LD, ✍*www.teachingld.org*, has articles and information on reaching children with learning disabilities in reading, writing, and math. They also offer links to lesson plans, discussion forums, and other helpful resources.

Autism Assistance

For many families, the calm, comfortable surroundings of home make homeschooling the preferred educational alternative for their autistic child. When parents are able to discover their child's unique learning styles, homeschooling becomes fun and the child begins to blossom. To share experiences, parents can subscribe to an online homeschool-autism list that discusses the education of autistic children, teaching methods, curriculum, and more at ✍*www.isn.net/~jypsy/home-aut.htm*.

The Autism Society of America in Bethesda, Maryland, also includes information on educating children with autism, as well as treatment options. They list state resources and support groups on their Web site at ✒ *www.autism-society.org.* Families for Early Autism Treatment (FEAT) offers support for families, along with field trips, gatherings, and other events within their state chapters. Visit their Web site at ✒ *www.feat.org.*

Down Syndrome and Special Needs

The National Challenged Homeschoolers Association Network (NATHHAN) got its start when the mother of a Down Syndrome child contacted the mother of another child with Down Syndrome in an attempt to find support for those with learning-challenged children. The NATHHAN Web site at ✒ *www.nathhan.com* includes experiences from parents of children with Down Syndrome, autism, hearing and vision impairments, and other physical handicaps and challenges.

FACT

If you decide that you'd prefer to try a local private school or individualized program dealing specifically with your child's learning challenges, ask your child's pediatrician or therapist for their recommendations. They may even know of an in-home tutor specializing in special needs, which may better suit your child.

The National Association for Child Development, Inc., ✒ *www.nacd.com,* helps to design individualized home education programs for learning-challenged children and adults, including those with Down Syndrome, Tourette Syndrome, and Rett Syndrome, as well as ADD/ADHD, dyslexia, autism, cerebral palsy, and other developmental and physical conditions.

Vision-Impaired and Hearing-Impaired Help

The National Organization of Parents of Blind Children, ✒ *www.nfb.org/ nopbc.htm,* provides the Homeschooling and Blindness Network for families, along with a magazine, seminars, and workshops. Yahoo! Groups maintains an active message board, Blindhomeschoolers, where parents can share experiences and support.

A Web site for homeschool families with deaf or hearing-impaired children, Another Path at ✍ *www.pacinfo.com/~handley*, provides articles, tips, and resources for homeschooling your child. Yahoo! Groups has an active message board for parents of homeschooling deaf children, called Deafhomeschool, where parents can exchange information.

Gifted Children

Gifted children look at things from a different perspective, learn and process information differently, may read or do math at a higher level, and/or seem mature for their age in some situations, yet childlike in others. They realize they have different abilities, and they, like any child, need to understand that it's okay to be different.

When homeschooling gifted and talented children, you'll want to locate educational resources that meet your child's level of interest and will continue to stimulate and challenge him. Gifted children are creative, innovative, enjoy brainstorming and exploring. They're good at self-educating themselves, due to their curiosity and interest-driven desire to know more. The challenge in the homeschool is to ensure that your child remains enthusiastic about his areas of study and that he's continually motivated to use his talents.

Resources for Homeschooling the Gifted

Check these Web sites for educational games, books, and materials designed for gifted children:

- Castle Heights Press, ✍ *www.castleheightspress.com*, offers unit studies, as well as science and lab books for gifted children.
- Gifted Education Press, ✍ *www.giftededpress.com*, carries books on teaching and parenting gifted children.
- Gifted Psychology Press, ✍ *www.giftedpsychologypress.com*, has a

variety of books on gifted education and homeschooling gifted children.

- Hoagies Gifted Education, ✐*www.hoagiesgifted.org/parents.htm*, carries educational games and toys.
- Prufrock Press, ✐*www.prufrock.com*, offers activity books on enhancing thinking skills, math, science, and reading abilities.

FACT

Stanford University's Education Program for Gifted Youth (EPGY), *www-epgy.stanford.edu*, offers distance-learning courses for kindergarten through advanced-undergraduate levels. The Westbridge Academy distance-learning school for gifted children, ✐*www.westbridgeacademy.com*, accepts students at kindergarten through twelfth-grade levels, based upon their abilities.

Associations for the Gifted

The National Foundation for Gifted and Creative Children, ✐*www.nfgcc.org*, includes a message board for parents, as well as articles on natural learning and gifted education. The National Association for Gifted Children, ✐*www.nagc.org*, lists enrichment programs and schools, along with state-based gifted associations. America Online also offers homeschool support for parents of gifted and talented children.

Books for Homeschooling the Gifted

These books provide guidance for families of gifted children:

- *Creative Home Schooling for Gifted Children,* by Lisa Rivero.
- *Helping Gifted Children Soar,* by Carol Strip and Gretchen Hirsch.
- *Helping Gifted Children Succeed at Home,* by James Carroll.
- *Homeschooling Your Gifted Child,* by Lee Wherry Brainerd.

Chapter 20

Veteran Homeschoolers and Burnout

Burnout is usually a result of trying to do too much or trying to stick to an old format. It can be a sure sign that it's time to try something different, to broaden your horizons, and to make changes not only in your homeschool, but in your lifestyle. Change can help us keep growing and lead to many happy years of exciting, rewarding homeschool experiences.

Encouragement for Your Homeschool Journey

Burnout can occur after ten years of homeschooling or it might happen after just two years. Parents may feel that they have exhausted all the ideas that once seemed so fabulous and endless. After a few years of homeschooling, the kids might not be as excited about the homeschool experience as they were in the beginning. Trying to get them to open a book or finish an assignment seems like a losing battle.

Eliminating Stress

Stress is one of the main causes of burnout. Parents may find themselves trying to fill two full-time roles in the home—as a parent and as a schoolteacher—which adds unnecessary stress to their lives. As indicated in previous chapters, learning is a natural part of living, and homeschooling should be a natural part of your family's lifestyle. You needn't turn it into "school at home" or make it more difficult than it should be. Teaching your children is simply a part of parenting.

Burnout also comes from setting expectations too high, then trying to reach them, day after day, and finding yourself falling short. Your expectations may be emotional ones, intricately interwoven with how well your children are learning. If you feel you'd be a "better teacher" if your children were ready for learning every morning at 8:00 A.M., dove into their lessons with glee each day, stayed on task throughout the morning and afternoon, achieved 100 percent on all their papers, and were able to deliver the Gettysburg Address over dinner, then you're only setting yourself up for disappointment.

If you, on the other hand, feel you're accomplishing your goals when your children enjoy most of their lessons, like to delve into things that interest them, are learning new information and skills each week, and can deliver the Gettysburg Address by the end of a school year, then you and your kids are probably enjoying the homeschool process, and you won't be as likely to burn out.

Preventing Burnout

As they say, an ounce of prevention is worth a pound of cure. Lower your expectations for yourself and for your children, and you will lower your feelings of stress and chances of burnout. It's true that you'll want your children to attain certain goals, so you naturally have some expectations of them. Just remember that you have an entire year to reach those goals. And then there's next year, too, and the year after that.

When you begin to get that nagging feeling that maybe you're not doing enough in your homeschool, or read or hear about the fantastic adventures of other homeschool families, take some moments to step back and look at your own family. Consider the happiness and well-being of your own children. Consider how much they've grown, how much they've learned since you began homeschooling.

ALERT!

If your children are exhibiting signs of boredom, then they may not be challenged enough. Set the learning rail a little higher for them—just enough to entice them to try a little harder. But not so high that they become frustrated, which will lead to feelings of frustration and burnout for everyone.

Less Structure and More Flexibility

Remember that childhood is a time for being a child, not for squeezing hundreds of extracurricular activities into their lives. Remind yourself that childhood is a time for being curious and explorative, for daydreaming and thinking, playing and learning, having fun and being happy. The child who has plenty of time for these simple activities will grow into a happy adult who enjoys the freedom and fun of learning.

Rekindling the Fire

If you've gone from burning with enthusiasm to burnout in your home-school, it's time to rekindle that fire. Try to determine what has lost its appeal. Perhaps you are bogged down by record keeping and constant updating of learning logs. If your children are old enough to print, hand that duty over to them. You may need to spend a few days helping them record their activities, but they'll quickly get the hang of it. As you're preparing the next lesson or activity, they can update their learning logs and reading lists.

Streamline Record Keeping

If your children are unable to handle the updating of the learning logs, streamline the record-keeping process. You're no doubt keeping records because your state requires it or because you want documented proof that your child has covered certain materials. But this doesn't mean you must write daily essays on your child's homeschool experiences. Imagine a teacher writing descriptive analyses for each of her thirty children every day! Simply write the chapter or page numbers of textbooks you used that day in social studies, jot down the Cuisenaire Rods math lesson, the Super Spellicopter spelling game in language arts, the nature walk in science.

FACT

A picture is worth a thousand words. Keep your camera handy and snap photos of ongoing lessons, activities, and projects. These can reduce the need for in-depth documentation in the learning log, remind you of projects you've done, and be placed in your child's portfolio.

Reduce Lesson Planning Time

Are you spending too much time preparing lessons? This can cut deeply into the best part of homeschooling: the fun, interactive learning activities. You really shouldn't have to keep a lesson plan book *and* a daily learning log. If you keep a lesson plan book, but don't get around to that lesson, erase it and move it to another day. If you do something in place of that lesson, jot that down.

Rather than developing in-depth lesson plans, note what you hope to cover and what you plan to use to cover it. The point of a lesson plan book is to help you be prepared, saving time over the long run. Use an hour or two on the weekend to glance ahead in any textbooks and note the topics and their page numbers. On your next "field trip" to the library, which probably occurs every week or two, check out books that help convey lessons and subjects in fun, colorful ways. Jot them down in your lesson plan book, too. Skim through your homeschool idea books and your favorite Web sites on the Internet for supporting activities and experiments. Jot them down, and you're ready for the week ahead—plus you've got your learning log filled out in advance!

Staying Motivated and Inspired

When you stay genuinely motivated and enthusiastic about homeschool, your children will stay motivated and enthusiastic, too. However, the time may come when the wind has gone out of your sails and you begin slowing down and not billowing with as much enthusiasm as before. Your children are quick to pick up on this.

ALERT!

Avoid using reward systems that focus on end results, that is, reading to appease a parent, completing an assignment as quickly as possible, striving to get the best grades on a test. For a child, or adult, to remain enthusiastic about learning and education, they must enjoy the *process of learning.*

When learning has meaning and is enjoyable, your children will be inspired to continue learning. Here are some strategies to help motivate your children to learn:

- Allow children to choose topics they'd like to study and ways in which they'd like to learn.
- Have children think of new ways to promote learning, using games, arts and crafts, hands-on projects, recreational pursuits, and field trips.
- Be sure that learning activities have real meaning to your children and are genuinely interesting to them.

- Provide plenty of free time for children to become deeply involved in the learning activities that interest them.
- Pursue family hobbies or studies you might never have considered as a way to stimulate new interest and goals.
- Encourage children to follow those areas of interest that branch off from the path they're currently traveling.
- Praise children for specific skills they've developed, information they've learned, and efforts they have made.

When a child enjoys the learning process and has the desire to learn, very little can hold her back. Her curiosity will abound, her knowledge will increase, and her desire to continue learning will expand. This desire to learn is a form of self-motivation. Because there is something that she *wants* to learn, she *will* learn. Motivation and enthusiasm are key ingredients in successful learning.

Reconsidering Curriculum Choices

If you've been using a certain type of curriculum or teaching style, but you've noticed a lack of interest in your child or an obvious resistance to homeschooling, it's time to make a change. Try unit studies for a while (these are lots of fun for everyone) or explore the concepts of unschooling (a wonderfully natural way of living and learning). Your children will love you for it, and they'll be bubbling over with excitement once again.

It can be difficult to release your hold on a curriculum (whether it's one you designed or a prepackaged plan) and adopt an unschooling form of education. It can be difficult to trust your children to learn in their own way. But it can be done—and successfully.

Try an eclectic approach to learning by using a textbook from one publisher; a couple of activity books from another; unit studies for certain topics; learning games from the Internet; board games, construction sets, and hands-on projects; and lots of books from the local library for inspiration and ideas.

Evolving into Unschooling

We did a lot of pigeonholing of activities as we tried to follow a specific course of study. We'd decide that this learning activity could be classified as Science, that one as Social Studies, another as Logical Reasoning Skills, and yet another as Life Skills. Finally, it clicked. They are *all* Life Skills, Logical Reasoning Skills, Social Studies, and Science, because they are *all* a part of life, and *life is made up of all these skills*. When the light finally came on, when that connection finally clicked, the need for pigeonholing every activity and fitting it into a specific subject area no longer seemed as important. That's when "unschooling," or natural learning, became a normal part of everyday life.

For us, it wasn't a conscious decision to unschool. It just evolved that way, and it suddenly made the most sense. When I first heard of "unschooling," I didn't give it a lot of thought. It seemed like a very unusual way to get an education, and I gave it no further consideration at the time. I probably would have doubted the ability to learn anything through unschooling, anyway.

Trusting Interest-Led Learning

As things evolved in the unschooling direction, and I eventually realized that ours was, indeed, a form of unschooling, I was past the point where I would have had doubts. I was already in the process of seeing the actual results of my son's learning and improvements in all areas of his education through his own style of unschooling, or interest-driven learning.

Today, Devin is a professional computer programmer in a highly reputable company. He went to college and excelled in class and on tests—even though he hadn't been in a class or taken a test in years. Most important, he developed the desire to learn, to follow his true interests, and to self-educate himself—as much today as he did when he was twelve years old—a skill that will benefit him the rest of his life.

Unschooling may not work for every child or family. However, a modified version may work for yours. Try incorporating certain aspects of unschooling into your program, while relying upon your main curriculum as a foundation as you test the waters. *The Unschooling Handbook,* by Mary Griffith, provides hundreds of examples of unschooling experiences from dozens of unschooling families.

Looking to Your Child for Direction

As previously noted, it can be hard to relinquish your dependence upon a curriculum. And if your child is truly motivated and stimulated by it, happy and enjoying the learning process, then there may be no need to change directions. But do keep in mind that children will not be following curricula the rest of their lives.

How well they'll learn and how productive they'll be in college will depend upon them and their desire to learn. No one will be helping them through a packaged curriculum at that point or leading them through pre-established guidelines. Their success in college and beyond will depend upon their level of self-motivation, fostered by their enjoyment of learning.

Therefore, even if your homeschool curriculum still "works" for your child, strive to introduce interests and learning challenges not included in the current homeschool program. Most important, encourage your child to explore areas that interest her, to follow the many paths that may branch out from those areas, to spend plenty of time learning on her own and in ways that work best for her.

New and Refreshing Ideas

If you just can't make the switch to an unschooling or unit studies method of learning, you can still add renewed enthusiasm to your homeschool program. By now, you've probably incorporated some of the tips mentioned earlier on motivating your children and helping them to regain the joy of learning. You've encouraged them to pursue new hobbies, follow new directions of interest, create new ways of learning, and to spend plenty of time exploring their areas of interest.

QUESTION?

How can I trust my child to teach herself?
Your child's ability to teach herself is one of the most pleasant surprises of homeschooling! Give her the freedom to learn, and look to your child for direction and guidance. Observe her style of interest-led learning, self-education, self-motivation, and learning enjoyment. She will delight in sharing the things she's learned with you and the rest of her family.

Provide new resources and tools for learning, different or more advanced scientific experiments to try, interesting books to look through or to read, stimulating toys and games to play, new music or artwork to try, educational field trips, and community events to take part in. If these items or events don't necessarily excite your child, she'll usually come across something in the process that leads to a different area of interest that neither you nor she had considered. As a result, she has achieved a new or special interest, which leads to interest-driven learning, self-motivation, and self-education, the skills that are necessary for continuing education throughout her life.

Handling Unexpected Challenges

What if your child loses her interest in learning? What if she becomes resistant to homeschooling? Try the motivation strategies mentioned earlier. If that doesn't work, sit down and talk about the situation. As always, ask for her input and suggestions. What does she not like about her lessons? What would she rather be doing? How can the two of you come to a resolution on her feelings?

If your child is bored with her lessons or no longer has interest in them, tell her that's okay and that you'll set them aside for a while. You may need to go back to those lessons later, or, in the meantime, you or she may find an interesting way to use those skills in a way that isn't directly related to lessons.

Resisting Learning

If your child is resisting the home education process, hand it over to her for a while. Tell her you understand her need to be in charge of her own learning and that you admire that in her. Jot down a few topics or skills you have planned for the next few weeks, such as learning about the kingdoms of classification; studying the Mayans, Aztecs, and Incas; plotting coordinates on a graph; and composing music on a staff. Then ask her to devise a new and innovative way to learn those skills in a way that is enjoyable to her. She may find the challenge exciting and freeing, or she may find that she prefers the guidance you've provided in the past. Perhaps she'll find that a little of both is just right: freedom in learning her own way with some guidance and suggestions from you.

Flavorless Lessons

If your child has lost her desire for some of her lessons, find out why. What is it that she doesn't like about them? Answers you may hear could include: "They're boring; too easy; too hard; there's no reason to learn those things; they have nothing to do with *real* life."

Take what she says to heart. If a lesson is too boring, jazz it up. Better yet, ask *her* to help you jazz it up. If it's too easy, then it's definitely time to move on to the next level. If it's too hard, then it's time to back up and refresh previous skills. If refreshing skills is too boring for her, find *real life* ways to sharpen those skills. Then she'll see how those lessons apply to her life, how they do make sense, and how there is a reason to learn them, after all.

Tired of It All

If your child has simply had it and doesn't enjoy anything at all about learning at home, have her share her reasons. Maybe it's not what she thought it would be. Ask her what she thought it would be like, then agree to try those ideas.

ALERT!

Keep in mind that unschoolers can become bored, too. If your child unschools every day and she needs a change of pace, maybe she'd like to attend a class a few hours a week. See if she'd be interested in enrolling in a course at your parks and recreation department or a nearby community college.

Maybe she'd rather be fishing instead of homeschooling. Then go fishing. When homeschooling or daily life becomes uninteresting for your child, it's time to make changes. It's important to find at least one thing that interests her. If fishing truly is the only thing that sparks her enthusiasm, then fishing it is. Learn about life together on the bank of a bubbling stream. If cooking is the only thing that interests her, spend time together in the kitchen, concocting seven-course meals and seven-layer desserts. The time spent together—doing, talking, sharing, laughing—results in quality learning experiences, helping to bring both parties closer together, in a greater understanding of each other.

Explaining Goals

You'll get better results, and children will learn more, when you explain the goals of each lesson, what the "learning outcome" is to be, and the steps required to reach the goal. For instance, the purpose of a specific geometry lesson could be to determine the perimeter and area of a room, knowledge that is useful and understandable to children. Geometry is a study of shapes and space. Our world is made up of shapes and space, and geometry helps us to better visualize those shapes, measure the space, and see two-dimensional objects in 3-D. When children understand why they are learning a subject or skill, how it relates to the real world, and what they can expect to learn from it, their mind is better focused on those principles and objectives, helping them to acknowledge and absorb the critical information.

Taking Time Off

This is the beauty of homeschooling—being able to take breaks when it best suits you and your family. Do you need an extra day off each week? Then have a Fun, Freaky Friday or a Mild, Mellow Monday, where everyone does what they want that day, within reason.

Maybe you want to homeschool for four or six weeks at a stretch, then take an entire week off. Knowing that you have a week off every month or two helps you maintain a better frame of mind during the homeschool weeks. If you prefer to keep your schedule closer to that of regular schools, then have a Wild, Wacky Week every four to six weeks. That week can still be homeschool week, but it can be quite different from your normal schedule. During that week, your children are in charge of lesson plans, or they take on the role of teacher, or together, you come up with a fun, unusual way of learning.

You can also simply stop homeschooling for a while. Schedule a vacation for a couple of weeks from now (so that you have time to look forward to it!) and tell everyone that school will be out for a two-week period. No teaching, no lesson plans, no attendance logs, nothing but free time to do whatever you'd like.

A Happy and Successful Homeschool

Do something special each day with your children and your partner. And do something special for yourself, as well. When you lie down at night, you'll feel much more satisfied with your day. If you didn't get to Lesson 12 in the math book as you had hoped, but you *did* play tag with the kids this afternoon and joined in their laughter and jubilation, then this makes your day worthwhile. If dinner wasn't on the table at six o'clock sharp because you spent an hour sitting with your partner, engaged in meaningful conversation, then your day was still worthwhile. If you didn't get the curtains laundered today as you had planned, but you were able to soak in a bubble bath for twenty minutes, which was much more restful, then your day was worthwhile.

You still accomplished several things today. Plus, you were able to enjoy time with your children and your spouse, and to indulge yourself in a little relaxation time. The time for doing Lesson 12 in the math book, for getting dinner on the table, for laundering the curtains, will be there another day. But for today, and for every day, your children, your partner, and your self should take priority. You will be happier, your children will be happier, and your homeschool—and joy in your homeschool—will flourish as a result.

Chapter 21

College and Beyond

From Ivy League universities to community colleges, homeschoolers have a wide range of choices available to them. As you consider your child's goals, unique personality, spiritual beliefs, and life principles, you can research and find a college that will benefit your young adult as he or she embarks upon the journey to higher education.

Colleges Welcome Homeschoolers

Many colleges today not only welcome home-educated students, they actively seek homeschoolers. Impressed by the level of maturity, independence, well-rounded education, and self-directed study habits of homeschoolers, more universities continue to open their doors to homeschoolers. As Jon Reider, a Stanford University admissions officer, stated: "Homeschoolers bring certain skills—motivation, curiosity, the capacity to be responsible for their education—that high schools don't induce very well." Michael Donahue, Director of Admissions at Indiana University–Purdue University (IUPUI) in Indianapolis, adds: "Homeschoolers are well prepared. They're self starters. Faculty, in general, enjoy having them in class because they know how to do things independently."

If your children are set on going to college, they can usually get into the college of their choice by planning ahead, taking the recommended courses during high school, preparing for the college entrance exams, and obtaining scholarships.

FACT

Although your child might be enthralled by the idea of attending a popular, large state university, don't overlook community colleges or private colleges. These often have less-stringent requirements, have a smaller and closer-knit student base, are located closer to home, and are less expensive. From here, your student can transfer to the larger university if he's still interested when the time comes.

Searching Online

To begin your college search, try some of the following Web sites. The Online College Fair, *www.onlinecollegefair.com,* hosted by the National Association for College Admission Counseling (NACAC), provides the opportunity for children and parents to connect with college representatives of over 180 colleges and universities. National College Fairs are also held around the country at more than fifty locations. Check

NACAC's list of fairs, locations, dates, and times at ✍ *www.nacac.com/exhibit/fair.cfm.*

Many Christian colleges are especially open to homeschoolers. The Christian College Search site, ✍ *www.christiancollegesearch.com,* allows you to search by name or criteria. The College View site also lists Christian colleges, along with information on life at college, at ✍ *www.collegeview.com/college/niche/christian.* Additional listings of Christian colleges and general college information for the homeschooler are included at ✍ *www.aaronacademy.com/aares/rescol.html.*

Homeschool-Friendly Colleges

Here are just a few of the hundreds of colleges and universities that have accepted homeschooled students. Don't hesitate to contact the college your child has his heart set on. Chances are, it will be open to homeschoolers, as the following colleges and universities have been:

- Auburn University, Auburn, Alabama: ✍ *www.auburn.edu*
- Baylor University, Waco, Texas: ✍ *www.baylor.edu*
- Brigham Young University, Provo, Utah: ✍ *www.byu.edu*
- Bryn Mawr College, Bryn Mawr, Pennsylvania: ✍ *www.brynmawr.edu*
- Christendom College, Front Royal, Virginia: ✍ *www.christendom.edu*
- Clemson University, Clemson, South Carolina: ✍ *www.clemson.edu*
- Cornell University, Ithaca, New York: ✍ *www.cornell.edu*
- Dartmouth College, Hanover, New Hampshire: ✍ *www.dartmouth.edu*
- Georgetown University, Washington, D.C.: ✍ *www.georgetown.edu*
- Harvard University, Cambridge, Massachusetts: ✍ *www.harvard.edu*
- Indiana University, Bloomington, Indiana: ✍ *www.indiana.edu*
- Johns Hopkins University, Baltimore, Maryland: ✍ *www.jhu.edu*
- Mary Baldwin College, Staunton, Virginia: ✍ *www.mbc.edu*
- New York University, New York, New York: ✍ *www.nyu.edu*
- Northwestern University, Evanston, Illinois: ✍ *www.northwestern.edu*
- Ohio State University, Columbus, Ohio: ✍ *www.acs.ohio-state.edu*
- Patrick Henry College, Purcellville, Virginia: ✍ *www.phc.edu*
- Rosemont College, Rosemont, Pennsylvania: ✍ *www.rosemont.edu*
- Texas A&M, College Station, Texas: ✍ *www.tamu.edu*

- Thomas Aquinas College, Santa Paula, California: *thomasaquinas.edu*
- University of Arizona, Tucson, Arizona: *www.arizona.edu*
- University of California, Berkeley, California: *www.berkeley.edu*
- University of Colorado, Boulder, Colorado: *www.colorado.edu*
- University of Florida, Gainesville, Florida: *www.ufl.edu*
- University of Georgia, Athens, Georgia: *www.uga.edu*
- University of Pennsylvania, Philadelphia, Pennsylvania: *www.upenn.edu*
- University of Minnesota, Twin Cities, Minnesota: *www.umn.edu*
- University of Washington, Seattle, Washington: *www.washington.edu*
- Yale University, New Haven, Connecticut: *www.yale.edu*

A Homeschooler in College

"I'm a schoolteacher! Can you believe it?" Jennifer, a homeschooler, now twenty-five years old, laughs jubilantly. "I teach third grade in a small school. I loved homeschooling; I loved learning—reading, math, everything. When I was thirteen, I volunteered at a day-care center, and it was such a good feeling to work with kids. That's when I knew I wanted to be a teacher. I enrolled in a distance-learning school during high school, and I got my diploma through them.

FACT

The best time to begin planning for college is during the freshman high school year. Real-life experiences, volunteerism, part-time jobs, community involvement, and activities, especially those that relate to your child's chosen field of study or special talents, will play an important role in his preparation for college. College administrators will want to see documented proof of such activities, so keep up-to-date records throughout the high school years.

"During my senior year, I also took part in the dual-enrollment program offered by the local community college. That helped me get additional credit hours for high school, as well as credit for college. I took the SAT during my junior year. With my high-school diploma and SAT scores, I had no trouble getting into college.

"I wasn't sure I'd like college, but since I've always liked learning, the experience was great. It took a little adjusting to sit in a classroom and handle the required coursework. But help was always available if things got too tough. The counselors were friendly and ready to offer advice at my school.

"I didn't live on the campus; I thought that would be too distracting and expensive. I lived at home, worked in a preschool part time, and took the certification courses required to work there. Everything I did seemed to revolve around my desire to be a teacher. I'm glad I was homeschooled, and I'm glad I went to college. As homeschoolers, we can have the best of both worlds: freedom in learning and formal education, too."

College Considerations and Preparations

The preparations begun during the high-school years should culminate in a solid college application package. And the real-world experiences of the homeschooled years should make an outstanding impression on the college admissions officer. As your child begins to prepare for college, speak with him candidly about his expectations and goals for college.

Take a Tour

Encourage him to speak with others who have attended and graduated from the college he's interested in, as well as acquaintances who are currently attending. Contact the admissions office to arrange a visit to the college and take a tour. Your child might find these books helpful reading as he considers the college life that awaits him: *ABC's of College Life*, by Vicki Salemi; *Making the Most of College*, by Richard Light; and *Orientation to College Learning*, by Dianna Van Blerkom.

Subject Requirements for College

Most colleges require that your child take four years of English courses, which should include grammar, composition, and literature, during his high-school years. In addition, he should take three years of social studies, including American history and government and economics; three years of math, including geometry and algebra; three years of science, including biology, physical science, and lab experiences; two years of a foreign language; a computer technology course; and at least two years of electives.

The College Board, ✑ *www.collegeboard.com*, provides information on planning ahead for college, considering careers, selecting courses, choosing majors, SAT preparation, how to apply to colleges, seeking financial aid, and much more. CollegeNet, ✑ *www.collegenet.com*, offers information on scholarship searches, financial aid, college fairs, college searches, and college preparation tips.

Colleges often have their own specific subject requirements. One college may require only one year of a foreign language, while another may require two years. Still other colleges may require particular math, history, science, or lab courses. If your child is set on a certain college, find out well in advance what subjects that college requires your child to take. Also determine if the college requires your home-educated student to meet any other special requirements in order to attend their school.

Transcripts and Documentation

During the high-school years, your child will want to collect and document the materials that are generally requested with the college applications package. Of course, you'll want to keep his high-school transcript up to date, along with his portfolio and daily learning log. Most colleges can provide you with a transcript form to fill out. Many make them available on their Web sites for downloading and printing, or you can contact the colleges that interest your child and ask for a blank transcript form.

Letters and Essays

He'll want to assemble letters of recommendation from mentors, teachers, or tutors, and people he has worked for or apprenticed with. He'll also want to write and polish his personal admissions essay to include with the package. This essay can include his reasons for selecting that college, as well as the career or field of study he's chosen, along with information on his interests, hobbies, abilities, and goals.

If a college requires that your child have a General Equivalency Diploma (GED), he may be able to take the exam upon completion of his high-school years. States have varying age restrictions. Check with your local school district to find out what age restrictions may apply in your state.

Read More about It

These books might help you and your child make decisions regarding a college education:

- *And What About College?* by Cafi Cohen.
- *Bear's Guide to Earning Degrees Nontraditionally,* by John and Mariah Bear.
- *Choosing the Right College,* by William J. Bennett.
- *College Credit without Classes,* by James L. Carroll.
- *Free (and Almost Free) Adventures for Teenagers,* by Gail Grand.
- *Teenager's Guide to School Outside the Box,* by Rebecca Greene.

Entrance Exams and Interviews

As noted in Chapter 18, your child will want to begin preparing for the SAT or ACT exams if he plans to apply to colleges that require the tests. Students usually take the SAT or ACT tests during the eleventh or twelfth grades, although there are no age restrictions. The exams are only given at certain times of the year, so your child will want to register ahead of time and be well prepared for them. To find the location of test sites and dates in your area, and how to register, contact your local school district or college. They may also be able to advise you on how to prepare for the test, the test fees, and related information.

ALERT!

Many colleges and universities do not use SAT or ACT scores for admission decisions. Be sure to check ahead to see what they require for your homeschooled child, though. To view a list of over 300 of these schools, visit the Fair Test Web site at *www.fairtest.org/univ/optional.htm.*

Getting College Credit

The College Level Examination Program (CLEP) provides college credit for students, based upon information they've learned and how well they perform on the test. The CLEP exams can be taken at various testing sites. Contact your local school district, community college, or university for more information.

College Admissions

A meeting with the college admissions officer is especially important for the homeschooled student, as they base much of their evaluation on the face-to-face interview. You'll want your child to prepare well for the interview.

Admissions officers are accustomed to meeting with thousands of students over the years. They can tell if your child is somewhat nervous during the interview, and they won't hold that against him. However, in preparation for interviews—not only with college officials, but also with potential employers—you can work with your child on improving his self-confidence, communication skills, pleasant personality, and positive attitude.

In addition to the interview with your child, admissions officers will consider the real-world experiences your child has had, volunteerism, internships, work opportunities, and community involvement.

Financial Aid

Scholarships are available for homeschooled students, but it can take some searching and perseverance in locating them. Check with your local reference librarian or school district to help guide you in the pursuit of scholarships and student loans. Scholarships are often awarded based upon SAT and ACT scores, so be sure to look into those exams before the junior or senior year. Check these Web sites for more information on homeschool scholarships and financial aid: *www.eho.org/ hsscholarships.htm*, *www.hsadvisor.com/scholarships.html*, *www.finaid.org*, and *www.fafsa.ed.gov*.

ALERT!

If your child expresses an interest in attending college, it could be beneficial for him to occasionally take a standardized test. This can help to familiarize him with test taking, determine his comfort level with tests, and monitor how well he performs on exams.

Online and Distance Learning

A large majority of well-known colleges and universities offer distance-learning courses. However, some may require on-campus time for a few weeks out of each year, or at some point during the enrollment period. If your child has done especially well with distance-learning courses or independent self-study programs during his homeschool years, distance-learning or online courses may be perfect for him.

CollegeDegree.com provides a list of colleges and universities that offer degrees through distance learning. Check their Web site at *www.collegedegree.com*. The Distance Education and Training Council, *www.detc.org*, maintains a list of accredited degree programs and certificates for specialized training.

Check these books for schools that offer college degrees via distance-learning or correspondence courses:

- *Barron's Guide to Distance Learning*, by Pat Criscito.
- *Campus-Free College Degrees*, by Marcie Thorson.

- *College Degrees by Mail & Internet,* by John and Mariah Bear.
- *Complete Book of Distance Learning Schools,* by Paul Jay Edelson and Jerry Ice.
- *Get Your Degree Online,* by Matthew Helm and April Leigh Helm.

Colleges may have preferences regarding the SAT and ACT. If your child has a particular college in mind, be sure to check well in advance to determine which admissions tests they accept, and if any special requirements apply to your child. Check current test preparation books at your local library, and have your child try some of the sample practice tests.

The Job Hunt

As your child prepares for college and life beyond, it's a good time to conduct a serious job search and attend job interviews. He may want to take a part-time summer job before he enters college to amass extra spending money before September rolls around. He may also want a part-time job that complements his college or career plans, providing real-life experiences and background for his future goals.

Special Interest Jobs

Help your teen search the weekly classifieds section of your newspaper or online job postings for your area. Focus on the type of work he most enjoys or that centers around his interests. For instance, if he enjoys writing and reporting and plans to major in journalism, then he'll want to focus on jobs relating to newspaper or magazine publishing, or perhaps television and radio stations. If he's interested in helping others and plans to work toward a social services degree, he might want to seek employment in a counseling or rehabilitation center. Even if he must start as a part-time clerk, he may have the opportunity to further his career goals in a field that he enjoys.

Resumes and Interview Preparations

To apply for job openings, your child will probably need assistance composing his first resume. Although he hasn't had a lot of work experience yet, he can still make his resume shine. Good books for helping to prepare first resumes are *101 Best Résumés for Grads*, by Jay Block and Michael Betrus; *Kick Off Your Career*, by Kate Wendleton; and *Résumés for First-Time Job Hunters*, by VGM Career Horizons. Books that help your child prepare for first job interviews include *How to Get Your First Job and Keep It*, by Deborah Perlmutter, and *Your First Interview*, by Ronald W. Fry.

Here are some tips to help your young adult make the best impression during the job interview:

- Practice proper social skills and manners daily so they are second nature.
- Role-play the job interview in a serious, professional manner.
- Dress in a professional manner, even if others on the job are casually attired.
- Take copies of the resume to the interview, along with letters of recommendation.
- Arrive ahead of time for the scheduled interview.
- Make eye contact, smile, shake hands, and exhibit positive body language.
- Listen carefully, answer questions honestly, and show interest in the company.
- Thank the interviewer for their time, and follow up with a thank-you note a few days after the interview.

Keeping a Positive Attitude

Even if your child doesn't get the job he applied for, a follow-up thank-you note makes a good impression on the interviewer. She will most likely remember that, and if the selected candidate doesn't work out, your child may just receive a phone call from the company to come in for a second interview.

If your child has difficulty finding a position during his job hunt, help him stay upbeat, and avoid putting pressure on him. He will find a job soon enough. In the meantime, he can continue to pursue his interests, make contacts with people in the fields relating to his interests, and volunteer his time, all of which will help to bolster his self-confidence and lead him in the direction of his ultimate goals. Ⓔ

Chapter 22

Adult Homeschoolers

Not every young adult wants to attend college. Many have spent years homeschooling or unschooling, and they are more interested in "homecollege" or "uncollege." In other words, they are eager to continue with their self-directed studies in the way that has served them well over the past several years. The world is their oyster, and they are ready to shine.

Life After Homeschool

The transition from homeschool to real life is generally pretty easy for the homeschooler. Homeschoolers are already in tune with the ebb and flow of their days, have an established routine that revolves around their daily lifestyle within the home, and have developed hobbies and activities that fill their days with interest. The homeschooled teen has been acclimating himself for the day when his high-school obligations no longer take top priority. He can now focus wholeheartedly on the interests he's developed over the years, the fields of study he wants to pursue further, and the adventures and projects he's ready to undertake. He may still intend to enroll in college at some point, after he's taken time to investigate his options, desires, and dreams. He may even want to travel before he makes a commitment to attending college in a particular city or state.

QUESTION?

How can I be sure my child will continue learning on his own?
Because this was the way he was raised and homeschooled. Through actions and experience, he's learned *how* to learn, year after year. Good habits become good lifestyles. This is the glorious legacy you have given him.

Rather than travel or pursue higher education, the homeschool graduate may be eager to put his skills to good use right away—going to work in a Web design firm, producing documentaries of local historic sites or events, painting murals for businesses and residences, reporting and writing articles for newspapers and magazines, tutoring school children, or working in the local teen shelter. Whatever he chooses to do, you can be sure that he will most likely continue to hone his skills, seek ways to further his knowledge and education, and strive to be the best he can be in the areas that fascinate him, today and in the future.

Options for Homeschooled Graduates

Homeschooled graduates can be anyone or anything they want to be. Most already know this from firsthand experience during their homeschool years. By this point in their lives, many have experienced a wide range of fulfilling ventures, from acting on the stage to helping injured animals to building boats to playing trumpet in the community band. Many will continue in this vein, going on to acting school and performing in the theater, becoming a veterinarian, a yacht designer and builder, a musician in the symphony orchestra.

Those who have the undying passion to draw, paint, sing, and make music have probably already found their niche in the art studio or concert hall. When sports is what drives their active bodies and competitive spirits, they have probably already joined the local ski club, swim team, or hockey club, and may be working toward a coaching position. If they're working on opening their own business in their area of fascination, they may immerse themselves in business and marketing courses.

When our youth know that they can be anything they want to be, life takes on deeper meaning for them. Each day has purpose; each day holds promise. They are not floating in midstream, with no direction to their lives. They've already tasted what life is about, and they're eager to get on with it and live it to the fullest.

Most homeschoolers have special interests that were never put down, never discouraged, or never set aside due to lack of time. They have, instead, pursued their interests heartily and woven them into the very fabric of their lives. They have goals and dreams to achieve, and they know how to go about achieving them. Life is a great adventure, and they are thrilled to play their part in it.

But what if your child has so many interests, he's undecided which to follow first now that school is over? Or, what if he knows what he wants to do, but is unsure of how to go about it? Here are some options he may want to consider.

Internships

Internships allow your child to work in areas that interest him before he has the actual experience to be hired as a full-time employee. He may work in an architectural firm, book publishing company, computer technology business, marine biology center, or health-care facility. Internships are most often offered during the summer or for a few weeks out of the year. The position may be paid or not, but the experience and contacts in the business are invaluable.

In many cases, the intern may be asked to come back again, and the temporary position can evolve into an actual paying job. The company may even offer to pay for training courses that keep skills up to date and help workers continue being an asset to the company. Help your teen make calls to businesses he is interested in to see if they offer an internship or on-the-job training program.

Travel

A simple change of scenery can help us view our daily lives in a different light and from a fresh perspective. Travel to another region of the country or to an entirely different country helps us to view all of life from a very different angle. Your homeschooled graduate may feel the pull of the oceans, the call of the mountains, and the undeniable desire to roam and explore this world before him. If he's determined to strike out on his travels, you can help him find the assistance he needs.

ALERT!

"The world is a book, and those who do not travel, read only a page," observed St. Augustine of Hippo. Before your child strikes out on his own, however, be sure he's mature enough, responsible, cautious, and prepared. Research youth travel programs thoroughly. Ask for references and speak with others who have had experience with the program. Contact homeschool organizations for information on educational programs they recommend.

He can contact organizations such as the American Youth Hostels, *www.hiayh.org;* Teen Tours of America, *www.teentoursof america.com;* and Volunteers for Peace, *www.vfp.org.* Adventure travel programs, such as Earth Watch, *www.earthwatch.org;* Outward Bound, *www.outwardbound.org;* Pacific Challenge, *www.pacificchallenge.org,* or Friends of the National Zoo, ✍ *www.fonz.org/getinv/travel.htm,* offer well-planned trips geared to young adults. Many of these have age and group size limits, so check any restrictions that may apply.

Learning Abroad

Once your teen has been bitten by the travel bug, he may decide to postpone that trip back home. He might not have been too keen on attending college at home, but the allure of studying at the American University of Paris is too enticing to pass up. Education in another country not only improves one's knowledge of geography and foreign language, but also of new cultures, life and business styles, social skills, history, art, literature, music. It can, indeed, open one's mind to a brand new world.

The Council on International Educational Exchange, ✍ *www.ciee.org,* provides additional information on exchange programs and study programs abroad. You can also search Peterson's list of programs at ✍ *www.petersons.com/stdyabrd/sasector.html* or Study Abroad's site at ✍ *www.studyabroad.com,* as well as contact the International Student Travel Confederation at ✍ *www.istc.org.*

FACT

All children, young or old, learn best when they follow the paths that interest and inspire them. As Marcel Proust said: "We do not receive wisdom, we must discover it for ourselves, after a journey through the wilderness, which no one else can make for us, which no one can spare us, for our wisdom is the point of view from which we come at last to regard the world."

Military Adventures

The military offers some of the greatest adventures for young people. The branches of the military provide the opportunity to travel, learn a lifelong career, and meet people in all corners of the world. To enter a military school, your child will need to take a military entrance exam. A high-school diploma from an umbrella or satellite school, or other distance-learning or private school, is also helpful. Without a diploma, the student will need to score higher on the entrance exams. If your homeschooler is interested in serving his country, contact your local recruiting office for details.

Online Learning

Your child may know exactly what he wants to do with his life, but has no intention of sitting in a classroom or doing lengthy assignments day after day. He wants to be an active participant in his life, rather than reading about life. He's ready to take off with his life and his life's work.

Yet, there may be just a few things he'd like to learn as quickly as possible, before he takes flight. He might need to learn C++ in the shortest amount of time, or how to create DLL pages for a computer program, or how to devise streaming video for a Web site. Short courses such as these are offered at many Web sites on the Internet, along with Microsoft Certification courses, Java Certification, HTML Certification, and similar courses.

Books on learning certain subjects and skills "in a day" or "over the weekend" are available at many libraries and bookstores. These bite-sized courses and nuggets of information may be all your child needs to set him on the track to a successful career or business venture.

Vocational Training

Book learning is all well and good, some may say, but give me down-to-earth, hands-on work to do, and I'll be more than happy. Tearing apart a car engine, rebuilding computer printers, wiring an alarm system, raising sheep, training seeing-eye dogs, building a house with their bare hands, or turning the earth on a farm, is what drives these hard-working young people. For them, the local vocational, trade, or technical school provides the additional knowledge they need in a fairly short amount of time. Many of these schools offer night classes, as well as full-day classes. The schools nearly always strive to match their skilled students with an internship program, or they assist students in finding jobs locally.

Alternative or Creative Careers

To learn more about careers available for those not wanting to spend four years in college, check out these books. They can provide ideas and food for thought as young adults consider their futures:

- *America's Top Jobs for People Without Four-Year College Degrees*, by J. Michael Farr.
- *But What If I Don't Want to Go to College?* by Harlow G. Unger.
- *Career Guide for Creative and Unconventional People*, by Carol Eikleberry.
- *Creating a Life Worth Living*, by Carol Lloyd.
- *Great Careers in Two Years*, by Paul Phifer.
- *Uncollege Alternative*, by Danielle Wood.
- *You're Certifiable*, by Lee and Joel Naftali.

Lifelong Learning

Homeschoolers tend to continue learning and teaching themselves well beyond the high-school years. Having taken responsibility for much of their learning through the years, it seems unnatural to *not* be learning. The real world has been their school; life has been their education. One can't be separated from the other. Life and learning are intricately and irrevocably interwoven.

FACT

Most homeschoolers retain their curiosity and "need to know," which they had as young children. It's this healthy curiosity that inspires them to keep pursuing new areas of interest, to attain higher knowledge, seek new ways, try new ideas, and teach themselves how to reach new heights and accomplish new goals.

This doesn't mean that you will see previously homeschooled children, who are now adults, sitting around with their noses buried in books, day in and day out. That's not how their school years were spent, and that's not how their life is spent today. If they need to consult books to learn something, they certainly will, as they have in the past. If they love to read, then they'll probably pick up a book to read nearly every day, as they always have in the past.

But their learning goes much further than that. It always has, and always will. They learned at an early age that education is a natural part of everyday life. They learned at an early age how to be lifelong learners—a skill that will benefit them all the years of their lives. You can be very proud of how you helped your children grow, learn, and live life to the fullest.

Homeschooled Parents Homeschooling Their Children

Now that they are parents themselves, your homeschooled young adult looks at home education in a different light. Always before, he had looked at it from his child's point of view, his student's point of view. Maybe there were times when he wished he'd been on the school's football team. Maybe there were times when your daughter wished she could go to the prom or the sweetheart dance. We *know* there were times when the traditionally schooled child wished he could stay home from school for days on end, or better yet, be taught at home.

Both sides, homeschooling and traditional schooling, have their trade-offs. One must weigh the pros and cons, and make the decision each feels is best for their children. But now that the previously homeschooled young adult has a child approaching school age, the missed prom and chance at the varsity football team no longer seem as important. The important question at this time in their lives is this: Do I send my five-year-old to school, or do I homeschool her myself?

"Now I Know Better"

"There's no way we'll send Brianna to school," Brandy agrees with her husband, Mike. "Sure, there were times when I thought I might be missing out on something by not going to public school. But I never let it bother me for longer than a day; then I had something more interesting to do, anyway. I didn't know any better back then. Now I know better. I wasn't hurt socially or academically by being homeschooled. I know our daughter won't be hurt, either."

"That's Just My Feelings"

Jason isn't married yet, but he's hoping his future wife shares his sentiments. "I was homeschooled—actually unschooled—all my life. I have lots of friends who went to regular school. Knowing what I know, about homeschooling and public school, I wouldn't want my kids to go to school. Kids can learn fine at home, grow up and get a great job. So, yes, I'd want my kids homeschooled. That's just my feelings. But I hope the mother of my kids will feel the same, when the time comes."

"I Homeschool My Girls"

"I homeschool my girls—they're five and seven," says Abigail. "My Mom homeschooled me, and I think I turned out fine! I went to school for a few years, then started homeschooling when I was eleven. The difference was night and day. In school, I was shy and awkward; I had no confidence in myself. At home, I became a different person, happy, confident, strong. That's why I'm homeschooling my daughters. Girls need to be happy, confident, and strong today."

ALERT!

"To parents I say, above all else, don't let your home become some terrible miniature copy of the school," warned John Holt, unschooling advocate. "Live together, as well as you can; enjoy life together, as much as you can. Ask questions to find out something about the world itself, not to find out whether or not someone knows it."

Comments from Homeschooled Adults

Although these adults don't yet have children, they have a multitude of memories and sentiments to share about their experiences, as they look back on their homeschool years.

"A Rewarding Life"

Jason, twenty-five, is a musician and runs his own recording studio. "School and I never got along," he explains. "It drove me crazy, sitting there all day long. So my parents started homeschooling me when I was twelve. At first, I didn't like it, and I pretty much resisted it. But I didn't like school, either. After a few months of friction at home, we had a 'family discussion,' which was the turning point for me. My parents told me if I would try to learn a few school things, which they had written down on a sheet of paper, then I could take the guitar lessons I'd been begging for.

"Well, that sounded like a deal to me! At first, I thought it was a bribe, but, hey, I got to learn guitar, and if I wanted to keep playing guitar, and drums, and bass guitar, then I had to keep doing the schoolwork. It made sense, and I even got to where I liked the schooling part. After we stumbled along for a year or so, things straightened out. Mom didn't push as hard, and I was less resistant. When I didn't resist it, the lessons were actually interesting.

"To make a long story short, I went on to college for a couple years and took some engineering courses. But music has always been the most important thing to me, and I kept coming back to it. Last year, I opened a small recording studio, and I give guitar lessons. It's a good life, a rewarding life. Plus, I have a lot more plans for it, which I'm really looking forward to!"

"I Was an Unschooler"

"I'm an assistant editor at a magazine publishing company," says Melissa, twenty-four. "But I homeschooled all my life, until I went to college. Basically, I was an unschooler, along with my younger brother and sister; we just didn't call it that at the time. We lived in a rural area, and I spent much of my time outdoors, visiting neighboring farms, helping with feeding the livestock, detassling corn, things like that.

"Mostly, I loved to read and write, and I spent several hours every day doing that—writing in my notebook in a tree, a haymow, by the stream. I knew when I was very young that I wanted to be a writer and be involved in publishing. By the time I reached my teen years, I felt I should go to college, so I decided, on my own, to find out what subjects I should take to prepare. My mom helped me find the resources I needed, and I talked to friends about getting into college.

"Looking back, it seems that my childhood was just that—a childhood—long, lazy days in a farming community, just living and learning about life, and having fun as a kid, as a family. When I hit the 'high school' years, I instinctively knew it was time to take some 'formal' lessons, to prepare for the next stage of my life. I had a goal and the desire, so doing schoolwork during my teen years was something I enjoyed. When a person has a special goal in life, they'll find out what it takes to reach that goal, and, if it means enough to them, they'll succeed."

"Afraid for Them"

John, twenty-five, a financial officer, laughs at a memory: "I remember watching the school bus go by when I was little and wondering where those kids were going. Mom finally drove me to the neighborhood school so I could see. It was one of those tall, brick schoolhouses, very plain, very unfriendly looking. I remember thinking that its windows looked like evil eyes.

"The kids were running around in circles inside a small, fenced-in concrete playground. Around and around in circles. It scared me, watching them do that. At home, I had a big backyard to run in every day, trees and rocks to climb. After that, I avoided looking at the school bus when it went past our house. I'm still not sure if it's because I was afraid *of it,* or if I was afraid that the kids on the bus would see that I was afraid *for them.*"

"I Didn't Miss Anything"

"I never went to public school," says Liz, nineteen, a muralist, "so I don't really have anything to compare it to. I don't feel like I missed anything by not going. My best friend was also homeschooled.

I did have two good friends who went to school. They sometimes talked about their teachers, boys at school, the outfit some girl was wearing that day, but since I didn't relate to that, I didn't pay much attention.

"As far as public school goes, it seems like it's a social gathering place. My friends rarely talked about lessons or what they actually *did* in school. I asked a couple times what they did in school, and they'd always say, 'Nothing.' Sometimes they'd complain about an assignment they had, but their homework wasn't anything like the homeschooling I did. So it's still all a mystery to me! Since I did fine homeschooling, I don't see the need to go someplace else just to learn."

"Would Do It All Over Again"

"It's been ten years since my homeschool days," says Crystal, twenty-seven, a registered nurse. "But they were some of the best years of my life. I went to school through eighth grade, then homeschooled the rest.

"My mom worked full time, but she always had time to spend with me and help me with lessons when I needed it. She encouraged me to study and learn anything I wanted. We had a lot of fun; it never seemed difficult at all. I graduated and went to college, just like my friends. I would do it all over again.

"I'm married now, and we plan to start a family soon. We're positioning ourselves so that I can stay at home, educate our kids, and maybe work a day or two a week, just to keep my hand in the nursing field. I want to give my kids the type of education and free learning style that I had. I wouldn't do it any other way."

ALERT!

"We need to recognize that educational achievement is ultimately up to the efforts of individual mothers, fathers, and families," said William J. Bennett, former U.S. Secretary of Education. "Homeschoolers are tangible proof that advanced education degrees and piles of money are not necessarily the key to educating children."

Life After the Nest Is Empty

Once you have homeschooled a child, truly educated that child, spent days and months and years of your life homeschooling, it's difficult to imagine life any other way. When you make the most important realization that homeschool is not "school at home," it becomes life itself. It's just life. There's really no other way to explain it.

Yet, life is continually changing, and the day comes when it's time for the young ones to spread their wings and leave the nest. Most parents with grown children can empathize with the feelings associated with the empty-nest syndrome. Many parents who also homeschooled their children feel it even more intensely. Not worse, mind you, but more intensely.

A house that was once full of homeschoolers, lesson plans, learning logs, dioramas, artwork displays, LEGO inventions, tumbling stacks of library books, fingerpaints, modeling clay, construction paper, math books, papier-mâché solar systems, chemistry sets, computers, musical instruments, and portfolios—now seems quite stark. And a bit sad.

On a Happier Note

You need only visit your child in his new apartment, and there you'll see the artwork on the hall wall, a fistful of modeling clay on the coffee table (fresh fingerprints pressed into its beige flesh), pieces of the LEGOs on the nightstand (in an odd, but abstract sort of sculpture), remnants of the chemistry set in the kitchen (is he drinking from the test tubes instead of the glasses you gave him?), and the papier-mâché solar system, which still swirls through time and space above his computer workstation. All is still intact and well in his world.

He calls you to the computer to show you the program he just created. Although he has the weekend off from his computer programming job, he's still doing what he enjoys the most—programming. Just like the old days.

As you drive home from your visit, you know you have made a profound impression upon your child's life. He has found his niche in life, he has found the work that most satisfies him, and he loves it—enough, even, to spend his weekends doing it, too. He is happy, he is successful, and he continues learning, even as he melds his past to his future.

True, your home may feel a little empty and stark, but his life, his successes, and his future more than fill that small void. True, you may not know what to do with yourself now, or all that time you now have on your hands. But you, like him, know how to keep learning, how to keep finding new interests, how to stay busy, and how to expand your mind and your spirit. After all, you're the one who helped to guide him to where he is today.

FACT

Mark Twain could have been speaking to us all when he said, "Twenty years from now you will be more disappointed by the things that you didn't do than by the ones you did do. So throw off the bowlines. Sail away from the safe harbor. Catch the trade winds in your sails. Explore. Dream. Discover."

Ideas for a Full and Happy Life

If you need a little prodding, here are some ideas to help you get started as you consider the many possibilities that yet await you:

- Set up and pursue your own self-directed educational program.
- Return to college and get a degree in education.
- Volunteer or substitute in schools or child-care facilities.
- Establish a day-care service for homeschooled children of working parents.
- Offer specialty classes or mentorships for homeschooled children.
- Start a tutoring service for children and adults.
- Teach in a private or charter school.
- Learn how to ski, skydive, surf, or sail.
- Travel to new and exotic lands.
- Become a state-certified, homeschool-friendly teacher who can work with homeschoolers, reviewing portfolios, administering exams, and inspiring other homeschool families.

The world is your oyster, just as it was and continues to be for your children. They are shining. They are sparkling. Now it's your turn. Get ready to shine!

Appendices

Appendix A

Resources

Appendix B

Curriculum Providers and Programs for Homeschoolers

Appendix C

National Homeschool Organizations

Appendix D

State Departments of Education

Resources

☑ Educational Materials

ACTS Textbooks	✍ www.actstextbooks.com
Back Pack	✍ www.thebackpack.com
Blue Spruce Biological Supply, Inc.	✍ www.bluebio.com
Bookmobile Online	✍ www.bookmobileonline.com
Cognitive Technologies	✍ www.cogtech.com
Delta Education	✍ www.delta-ed.com
Edmark	✍ www.riverdeep.net/edmark
Educational Innovations, Inc.	✍ www.teachersource.com
Educational Video Resources	✍ www.evrmath.com/instructors.html
Educational Videos	✍ www.ieducationalvideos.com
Educator's Exchange	✍ www.edexbooks.com
Home Training Tools	✍ www.hometrainingtools.com
Intelligent Tutor	✍ www.mathtutor.com
Kidware	✍ www.kidwaresoftware.com
Laurelwood Books	✍ www.laurelwoodbooks.com
Library Shelf	✍ www.libraryshelf.com
LibraryVideo	✍ www.libraryvideo.com
MathMedia	✍ www.mathmedia.com
MindPlay	✍ www.mindplay.com
MindWare	✍ www.mindwareonline.com
Newton's Quest	✍ www.education.com/newtonsquest1
Owl & Mouse	✍ www.yourchildlearns.com
School Express	✍ www.schoolexpress.com
School-Tech Inc.	✍ www.school-tech.com
Smart Kids Software	✍ www.smartkidssoftware.com
Special Interest Videos	✍ www.sivideo.com
SuperKids Educational Software	✍ www.superkids.com
Teacher's Video	✍ www.teachersvideo.com
Tobin's Lab	✍ www.tobinslab.com
Video Placement Worldwide	✍ www.vpw.com
Virtu-Software	✍ www.virtu-software.com

☑ Free Educational Materials

ABC Teach	✑ www.abcteach.com
Child Fun	✑ www.childfun.com
Ed Helper	✑ www.edhelper.com
Education for Kids	✑ www.edu4kids.com
Education Place	✑ www.eduplace.com/edugames.html
Enchanted Learning	✑ www.enchantedlearning.com
First-School	✑ www.first-school.ws
Free-Ed	✑ www.free-ed.net
FunBrain	✑ www.funbrain.com
Gamequarium.com	✑ www.gamequarium.com
Kids Games	✑ www.kidsgames.org
Kinder Start	✑ www.kinderstart.com
Learning Page	✑ www.learningpage.com
Perpetual Preschool	✑ www.perpetualpreschool.com
Preschool Rainbow	✑ www.preschoolrainbow.org
Puzzle Depot	✑ www.puzzledepot.com
School Express	✑ www.schoolexpress.com
Sites Alive	✑ www.sitesalive.com
Tampa Reads	✑ www.tampareads.com
Tot City	✑ www.totcity.com
Zero to Three	✑ www.zerotothree.org/ brainwonders/EarlyLiteracy

☑ Resources and Materials for Special-Needs Children

Another Path Hearing Impairments	✑ www.pacinfo.com/~handley
Autism List	✑ www.isn.net/~jypsy/home-aut.htm
Don Johnston	✑ www.donjohnston.com
Families for Early Autism Treatment (FEAT)	✑ www.feat.org
IntelliTools	✑ www.intellitools.com
National Association for Child Development, Inc.	✑ www.nacd.com
Parent Pals	✑ www.parentpals.com
Special Education Products	✑ www.iser.com/specialproducts.html
Teaching LD	✑ www.teachingld.org
✑ Yahoo! Groups' *Blindhomeschoolers*	✑ http://groups.yahoo.com/group/blindhomeschoolers
✑ Yahoo! Groups' *Deafhomeschool*	✑ http://groups.yahoo.com/group/deafhomeschool

☑ Resources and Materials for Gifted Children

Castle Heights Press	www.castleheightspress.com
Education Program for Gifted Youth (EPGY)	www-epgy.stanford.edu
Gifted Education Press	www.giftededpress.com
Gifted Psychology Press	www.giftedpsychologypress.com
Hoagies Gifted Education	www.hoagiesgifted.org/parents.htm
Prufrock Press	www.prufrock.com
Westbridge Academy	www.westbridgeacademy.com

☑ Faith-Based Supply Resources

A.R.E. Publishing Inc.	www.arepublish.com
Atco School Supply	www.atco1.com
Behrman House Publishers	www.behrmanhouse.com
Catholic Homeschool Resources	www.stgabriel.com/homeed.html
Christian Book Distributors	www.christianbook.com
Heritage Catholic Curricula	www.chcweb.com
Instructional Fair	www.instructionalfair.com
Torah Aura Productions	www.torahaura.com

☑ Free Lesson Plan Ideas

Ask Eric Lesson Plans	http://askeric.org/Virtual/Lessons
Awesome Library	www.awesomelibrary.org
Discovery School	www.school.discovery.com/lessonplans
Ed Helper	www.edhelper.com
Education World	www.educationworld.com/a_lesson
Hands-On Activities	www.homeschoolfun.com
Lesson Plan Search	www.lessonplansearch.com
Lesson Plans Page	www.lessonplanspage.com
LessonPlanZ.com	www.lessonplanz.com
PBS	www.pbs.org/teachersource/standards.htm
ProTeacher	www.proteacher.com
Teachers.net	www.teachers.net/lessons

☑ Correspondence and Online Schools

Abeka Academy	www.abekaacademy.org
Alger Learning Center	www.independent-learning.com
Alpha Omega	www.aop.com
American School	www.americanschoolofcorr.com
Angelicum Academy	www.angelicum.net
Babbage Net School Online	www.babbagenetschool.com
Brigham Young University ISP	http://ce.byu.edu/is
Calvert School	www.calvertschool.org
Cambridge Academy	www.cambridgeacademy.com
Christa McAuliffe Academy	www.cmacademy.org
Christian Light Education	www.clp.org
Chrysalis School	www.chrysalis-school.com
Citizen High School	www.citizenschool.com
Clonlara High School	www.clonlara.net and www.compuhigh.com
CompuHigh Online	www.compuhigh.com
Dennison Online Internet School	www.dennisononline.com
Distance Learning Resource Network	www.dlrn.org/virtual.html
Education Direct	www.educationdirect.com
Electronic High School	www.ehs.uen.org
Florida Virtual School	www.flvs.net
Francis Virtual School	www.francisvirtualschool.org
Home Study International	www.hsi.edu
Indiana University High School	http://scs.indiana.edu/hs/hsd.html
International High School Online	www.internationalhigh.org
InternetHomeSchool.com	www.internethomeschool.com
Keystone National High School	www.keystonehighschool.com
Kolbe Academy	www.kolbe.org
Laurel Springs School	www.laurelsprings.com
Malibu Cove Private School	www.seascapecenter.com
North Atlantic Regional Schools	www.narsdiploma.com
North Dakota Division of Independent Study	www.dis.dpi.state.nd.us
Oak Meadow School	www.oakmeadow.com
Seton School	www.setonhome.org
Summit Christian Online Academy	www.scahomeschool.com
Sycamore Academy Home School	www.sycamoretree.com

Texas Virtual School	www.texasvirtualschool.org
University of Missouri, IPS	http://cdis.missouri.edu/
University of Nebraska, ISHS	www.unl.edu/ishs
Willoway Cyber School	www.willoway.com

☑ College Resources

Christian College Search	www.christiancollegesearch.com
College Board	www.collegeboard.com
College Fairs	www.nacac.com/exhibit/fair.cfm
College Net	www.collegenet.com
College View	www.collegeview.com/college/niche/christian
Distance Learning Colleges	www.collegedegree.com
FairTest	www.fairtest.org/univ/optional.htm
Federal Student Aid	www.fafsa.ed.gov
Financial Aid	www.finaid.org
Homeschool Scholarships	www.eho.org/hsscholarships.htm
Online College Fair	www.onlinecollegefair.com
Scholarships for Homeschool Students	www.hsadvisor.com/scholarships.html

☑ Publications

Eclectic Homeschool	www.eho.org
Home Education Magazine	www.home-ed-magazine.com
Home School Digest	www.homeschooldigest.com
Homeschooling Today	www.homeschooltoday.com
Link Homeschool Newspaper	www.homeschoolnewslink.com
Old Schoolhouse	www.thehomeschoolmagazine.com
Practical Homeschooling	www.home-school.com
Teaching Home	www.teachinghome.com

☑ Driver Education

Driver Ed in a Box   ✎ www.driveredtraining.com

Keystone High School Driver's Ed   ✎ www.keystonehighschool.com

National Driver Training   ✎ www.nationaldrivertraining.com

☑ Virtual Field Trips and Museums

Discovery School   ✎ school.discovery.com/schooladventures/students

Exploratorium   ✎ www.exploratorium.edu

Questacon   ✎ www.questacon.edu.au/kids.html

Smithsonian Institution   ✎ www.si.edu

Virtual Dissections, Labs, and Field Trips   ✎ www.accessexcellence.org/RC/virtual.html

Virtual Field Trips   ✎ www.home-educate.com/fieldtrip.shtml

Virtual Field Trips and Guidelines   ✎ www.surfaquarium.com/virtual.htm

☑ Travel

American Youth Hostels   ✎ www.hiayh.org

Council on International Educational Exchange   ✎ www.ciee.org

Earth Watch   ✎ www.earthwatch.org

Friends of the National Zoo   ✎ www.fonz.org/getinv/travel.htm

International Student Travel Confederation   ✎ www.istc.org

Outward Bound   ✎ www.outwardbound.org

Pacific Challenge   ✎ www.pacificchallenge.org

Peterson's Study Abroad   ✎ www.petersons.com/stdyabrd/sasector.html

Study Abroad   ✎ www.studyabroad.com

Teen Tours of America   ✎ www.teentoursofamerica.com

Volunteers for Peace   ✎ www.vfp.org

Curriculum Providers and Programs for Homeschoolers

Abeka Books
P.O. Box 19100
Pensacola, FL 32523
(850) 478-8933
www.abeka.com

Alpha Omega
300 North McKemy Avenue
Chandler, AZ 85226
(800) 622-3070
www.aop.com

Bob Jones University Press
(800) 845-5731
www.bjup.com

Center for Talent Development/AP Courses
617 Dartmouth Place
Evanston, IL 60208
(847) 491-3782
www.ctd.nwu.edu

Charlotte Mason Supply Company
P.O. Box 758
Union, ME 04862
www.charlottemason.com

ChildU E-Knowledge
316 NE Fourth Street, Suite 200
Ft. Lauderdale, FL 33301
(877) 424-4538
www.childu.com

Christian Liberty Academy School System
502 West Euclid Avenue
Arlington Heights, IL 60004
(800) 348-0899
www.homeschools.org

Classes2You
300 North McKemy Avenue
Chandler, AZ 85226
(800) 622-3070
www.classes2you.com

Core Curriculum of America
14503 South Tamiami Trail
North Port, FL 34287
(888) 689-4626
www.core-curriculum.com

Covenant Home Curriculum
W23421 Main Street
Sussex, WI 53089
(800) 578-2421
www.covenanthome.com

Curriculum Services
26801 Pine Avenue
Bonita Springs, FL 34135
(877) 702-1419
www.curriculumservices.com

Design-A-Study
408 Victoria Avenue
Wilmington, DE 19804
www.designastudy.com

E-Tutor
1524 South Prospect Avenue
Park Ridge, IL 60068
(877) 687-7200
www.e-tutor.com

Excellence in Education
2640 South Myrtle Avenue, Suite A-7
Monrovia, CA 91016
(626) 821-0025
www.excellenceineducation.com

Explorer's Bible Study
P.O. Box 425
Dickson, TN 37056
(800) 657-2874
www.explorerbiblestudy.org

Five In A Row
P.O. Box 707
Grandview, MO 64030
(816) 331-5769
www.fiveinarow.com

Gateway to Educational Materials
621 Skytop Road, Suite 160
Syracuse, NY 13244
(800) 464-9107
www.thegateway.org

Heart of Wisdom
13503 Minion Street
Woodbridge, VA 22192
(800) 266-5564
www.homeschoolunitstudies.com

K12 Curriculum
8000 Westpark Drive, Suite 500
McLean, VA 22102
(888) 968-7512
www.k12.com

KONOS Curriculum
P.O. Box 250
Anna, TX 75409
(972) 924-2712
www.konos.com

Moore Foundation
Box 1
Camas, WA 98607
(360) 835-5500
www.moorefoundation.com

Robinson Curriculum
2251 Dick George Road
Cave Junction, OR 97523
www.robinsoncurriculum.com

Rod & Staff Publishers
P.O. Box 3
Crockett, KY 41413
(606) 522-4348

School of Tomorrow
P.O. Box 299000
Lewisville, TX 75029
(800) 925-7777
www.schooloftomorrow.com

Trisms Jr. & Sr. High Curriculum
1203 South Delaware Place
Tulsa, OK 74104
(918) 585-2778
www.trisms.com

Unit Study Guides
P.O. Box 1777
Dunlap, TN 27327
www.unitstudy.com

Waldorf Education
9022 Fair Oaks Boulevard
Fair Oaks, CA 95628
(916) 961-8727
www.steinercollege.org

National Homeschool Organizations

Alliance for Parental Involvement in Education
(AllPIE)
P.O. Box 59
East Chatham, NY 12060
(518) 392-6900
www.croton.com/allpie

American Homeschool Association
P.O. Box 3142
Palmer, Alaska 99645
(800) 236-3278
www.americanhomeschoolassociation.org

ArabesQ Islamic and Muslim Homeschoolers
(206) 374-2723
www.arabesq.com

Attention Deficit Disorder Association
1788 Second Street, Suite 200
Highland Park, IL 60035
www.add.org

Autism Society of America
7910 Woodmont Avenue, Suite 300
Bethesda, MD 20814
(301) 657-0881
www.autism-society.org

Catholic Homeschool Network of America
P.O. Box 2352
Warren, OH 44484
www.chsna.org

Children and Adults with Attention Deficit
Hyperactivity Disorder (CHADD)
8181 Professional Place, Suite 201
Landover, MD 20785
(301) 306-7070
www.chadd.org

Christian Home Educators Network (CHEN)
P.O. Box 2010
Ellicott City, MD 21043
(301) 474-9055
www.chenmd.org

Family Unschoolers Network
1688 Belhaven Woods Court
Pasadena, MD 21122
(410) 360-7330
www.unschooling.org

Harvest Home Educators
P.O. Box 1551
Clarkesville, GA 30523
(770) 455-0449
www.harvesthomeeducators.com

Home School Legal Defense Association (HSLDA)
P.O. Box 3000
Purcellville, VA 20134
(540) 338-5600
www.hslda.org

Jewish Home Educator's Network
2122 Houser
Holly, MI 48442
www.snj.com/jhen

Latter-Day Saint Home Educators Association
(LDS-HEA)
2475 South 1150 West
Syracuse, UT 84075
(801) 776-3555
www.ldshea.org

Learning Disabilities Association of America
4156 Library Road
Pittsburgh, PA 15234
(412) 341-1515
www.ldanatl.org

Moore Foundation
P.O. Box 1
Camas, WA 98607
(360) 835-5500
www.moorefoundation.com

Muslim Homeschool Network and Resources
P.O. Box 803
Attleboro, MA 02703
www.muslimhomeschool.com

National Association for Gifted Children
1707 L Street NW, Suite 550
Washington, DC 20036
(202) 785-4268
www.nagc.org

National Association for Mormon Home Educators
2770 South 1000 West
Perry, UT 84302

National Association of Catholic Home Educators
P.O. Box 2304
Elkton, MD 21921
www.nache.org

National Challenged Homeschoolers Association
(NATHHAN)
P.O. Box 39
Porthill, ID 83853
(208) 267-6246
www.nathhan.com

National Foundation for Gifted and Creative
Children
395 Diamond Hill Road
Warwick, RI 02886
www.nfgcc.org

National Home Education Network
P.O. Box 7844
Long Beach, CA 90807
www.nhen.org

National Organization of Parents of Blind Children
1800 Johnson Street
Baltimore, MD 21230
(410) 659-9314
www.nfb.org/nopbc.htm

Native American Home School Association
P.O. Box 979
Fries, VA 24330
www.expage.com/page/nahomeschool

Schwab Learning
1650 South Amphlett Boulevard, Suite 300
San Mateo, CA 94402
(650) 655-2410
www.schwablearning.org

State Departments of Education

To determine your state's homeschool regulations, curriculum guidelines, or homeschool organizations, contact the homeschool division of your state department of education.

Alabama Department of Education
50 N. Ripley St.
Montgomery, AL 36104
(334) 242-9700
www.alsde.edu

Alaska Department of Education
801 W. 10th St., Ste. 200
Juneau, AK 99801
(907) 465-2800
www.educ.state.ak.us

Arizona Department of Education
1535 W. Jefferson
Phoenix, AZ 85007
(602) 542-4361
www.ade.state.az.us

Arkansas Department of Education
4 Capitol Mall
Little Rock, AR 72201
(501)682-4475
http://arkedu.state.ar.us

California Department of Education
721 Capitol Mall
Sacramento, CA 95814
(916) 657-2451
www.cde.ca.gov

Colorado Department of Education
201 E. Colfax Ave.
Denver, CO 80203
(303) 866-6600
www.cde.state.co.us

Connecticut Department of Education
165 Capitol Ave.
Hartford, CT 06145
(860) 713-6548
www.state.ct.us/sde

Delaware Department of Education
401 Federal St.
Dover, DE 19903
(302) 739-4601
www.doe.state.de.us

Florida Department of Education
325 W. Gaines St.
Tallahassee, FL 32399
(850) 487-8428
www.firn.edu/doe

Georgia Department of Education
205 Jesse Hill Jr. Dr. SE
Atlanta, GA 30334
(404) 656-2454
www.doe.k12.ga.us

Hawaii Department of Education
P.O. Box 2360
Honolulu, HI 96804
(808) 586-3230
www.doe.k12.hi.us

Idaho Department of Education
650 W. State St.
Boise, ID 83720
(208) 332-6800
✍ www.sde.state.id.us

Illinois Department of Education
100 N. 1st St.
Springfield, IL 62777
(217) 782-4321
✍ www.isbe.state.il.us

Indiana Department of Education
200 W. Washington St., Room 229
Indianapolis, IN 46204
(317) 232-0808
✍ www.doe.state.in.us

Iowa Department of Education
400 E. 14th St.
Des Moines, IA 50319
(515) 281-5294
✍ www.state.ia.us/educate

Kansas Department of Education
120 SE 10th Ave.
Topeka, KS 66612
(785) 296-3201
✍ www.ksbe.state.ks.us

Kentucky Department of Education
500 Mero St.
Frankfurt, KY 40601
(800) 533-5372
✍ www.kde.state.ky.us

Louisiana Department of Education
626 N. 4th St.
Baton Rouge, LA 70804
(225) 342-3473
✍ www.doe.state.la.us

Maine Department of Education
23 State House Station
Augusta, ME 04333
(207) 624-6776
✍ www.state.me.us/education

Maryland Department of Education
200 W. Baltimore St.
Baltimore, MD 21201
(410) 767-0100
✍ www.msde.state.md.us

Massachusetts Department of Education
350 Main St.
Malden, MA 02148
(781) 338-3000
✍ www.doe.mass.edu

Michigan Department of Education
608 W. Allegan
Lansing, MI 48933
(517) 373-1262
✍ www.michigan.gov/mde

Minnesota Department of Education
1500 Highway 36 West
Roseville, MN 55113
(651) 582-8200
✍ www.educ.state.mn.us

Mississippi Department of Education
359 N. West St.
Jackson, MS 39205
(601) 359-3513
✍ www.mde.k12.ms.us

Missouri Department of Education
205 Jefferson St.
Jefferson City, MO 65101
(573) 751-4212
✍ http://services.dese.state.mo.us

Montana Department of Education
P.O. Box 202501
Helena, MT 59620
(406) 444-3095
www.opi.state.mt.us

Nebraska Department of Education
301 Centennial Mall South
Lincoln, NE 68509
(402) 471-2295
www.nde.state.ne.us

Nevada Department of Education
700 E. Fifth St.
Carson City, NV 89701
(775) 687-9200
www.nde.state.nv.us

New Hampshire Department of Education
101 Pleasant St.
Concord, NH 03301
(603) 271-3494
www.ed.state.nh.us

New Jersey Department of Education
225 E. State St.
Trenton, NJ 08625
(609) 292-5935
www.state.nj.us/education

New Mexico Department of Education
300 Don Gaspar
Santa Fe, NM 87501
(505) 827-5800
www.sde.state.nm.us

New York Department of Education
89 Washington Ave.
Albany, NY 12234
(518) 474-3852
www.nysed.gov

North Carolina Department of Education
301 N. Wilmington St.
Raleigh, NC 27601
(919) 807-3300
www.dpi.state.nc.us

North Dakota Department of Education
600 E. Boulevard Ave., Room 201
Bismarck, ND 58505
(701) 328-2260
www.dpi.state.nd.us

Ohio Department of Education
25 S. Front St.
Columbus, OH 43215
(877) 644-6338
www.ode.state.oh.us

Oklahoma Department of Education
2500 N. Lincoln Blvd.
Oklahoma City, OK 73105
(405) 521-3301
www.sde.state.ok.us

Oregon Department of Education
255 Capitol St. NE
Salem, OR 97310
(503) 378-3569
www.ode.state.or.us

Pennsylvania Department of Education
333 Market St.
Harrisburg, PA 17126
(717) 783-6788
www.pde.state.pa.us

Rhode Island Department of Education
255 Westminster St.
Providence, RI 02903
(401) 222-4600
www.ridoe.net

South Carolina Department of Education
1429 Senate St.
Columbia, SC 29201
(803) 734-8393
✑ www.sde.state.sc.us

South Dakota Department of Education
700 Governors Dr.
Pierre, SD 57501
(605) 773-4771
✑ www.state.sd.us/deca

Tennessee Department of Education
710 James Robertson Pkwy.
Nashville, TN 37243
(615) 741-2731
✑ www.state.tn.us/education

Texas Department of Education
1701 N. Congress Ave.
Austin, TX 78701
(512) 463-9734
✑ www.tea.state.tx.us

Utah Department of Education
250 E. 500 South
Salt Lake City, UT 84114
(801) 538-7500
✑ www.usoe.k12.ut.us

Vermont Department of Education
120 State St.
Montpelier, VT 05620
(802) 828-5406
✑ www.state.vt.us/educ

Virginia Department of Education
101 N. 14th St.
Richmond, VA 23219
(800) 292-3820
✑ www.pen.k12.va.us

Washington, DC, Department of Education
825 N. Capitol St. NE
Washington, DC 20002
(202) 724-4222
✑ www.k12.dc.us/dcps

Washington State Department of Education
P.O. Box 47200
Olympia, WA 98504
(360) 725-6000
✑ www.k12.wa.us

West Virginia Department of Education
1900 Kanawha Blvd. East
Charleston, WV 25305
(304) 558-2118
✑ http://wvde.state.wv.us

Wisconsin Department of Education
125 S. Webster St.
Madison, WI 53707
(800)441-4563
✑ www.dpi.state.wi.us

Wyoming Department of Education
2300 Capitol Ave.
Cheyenne, WY 82002
(307) 777-7675
✑ www.k12.wy.us

Index

101 Best Résumés for Grads, 265
365 Manners Kids Should Know, 215

A

ABC Teach Network, 98
ABC's of College Life, 259
Abeka, 46, 48, 220
Academic learning, 21
Accreditation, 56
Achievement awards, 150
Achievement tests, 16, 206, 263
Activities. *See also* Learning activities
  extracurricular activities, 82, 124,
    215–16
  interest-led activities, 68–70, 75–76,
    94, 108–9, 138, 247, 249
  for socializing, 81–85
  stimulating activities, 20, 59, 68–70,
    75–76, 239
  for unschooling, 68–70, 75–76, 94,
    109
Activity centers, 156–60, 189–90
ACTs, 226–27, 261–62, 263, 264
Adolescence, 213, 215, 218
Adult homeschoolers, 267–79
  comments from, 274–78
  lifelong learning, 267–68, 273–74
  options for, 268–73
Advanced subjects, teaching, 100–101,
  108, 218–19, 221–22
African-American Homeschoolers, 38
Alger Learning Center, 220
*Allison's Story: A Book about
  Homeschooling*, 159
Alpha Omega, 46, 48–49, 57, 220
*America's Top Jobs for People Without
  Four-Year College Degrees*, 273
American Adventure videos, 183
American Homeschool Association, 38
American School, 56, 220

American Youth Hostels, 270
And What About College?, 261
Another Path, 239
Apprenticeships, 225, 269–70
ArabesQ, 49
A.R.E. Publishing, Inc., 49
Art activities, 204
Ask Eric Lesson Plans, 96
Assessment methods, 96, 99, 147–48,
  205–6. *See also* Tests
Attendance records, 145, 146–47
Attention Deficit Disorder Association,
  237
Attention Deficit Disorder/Attention
  Deficit Hyperactivity Disorder
  (ADD/ADHD), 16, 29, 232, 233,
  235–37, 238, 283
Atypical days, 131–32
Audiotapes, 100–101
Auditory learners, 22, 23–24
Austen, Jane, 17
Autism, 237–38
Autism Society of America, 237–38
Awards, 150

B

Babbage Net School, 57
Babies, learning activities, 186
Back Pack, The, 47
Barron's Guide to Distance Learning,
  263
Barton, Clara, 95
Bear, John, 261, 264
Bear, Mariah, 261, 264
*Bear's Guide to Earning Degrees
  Nontraditionally*, 261
Behavioral problems, 16, 79
Behrman House Publishers, 49
Bennett, Amanda, 60
Bennett, William J., 57, 215, 261, 278

Benson, Peter, 223
Betrus, Michael, 265
Block, Jay, 265
BN.com, 211
Bnos Henya Project, 49
Bob Jones University Press, 46, 49
Bonding, 6–7, 79–80
Book choices, 211
Book loan programs, 14
Book of Virtues for Young People, 215
Book sales, 13
Book storage, 158, 159–60
BookMuse.com, 211
Borba, Michele, 215
Boredom, 62, 112, 130–32, 166, 243, 250,
  251
Boston Latin School, 2
Boyles, Nancy, 236
Brain, workings of, 20, 189
Brainerd, Lee Wherry, 240
Breaks. *See* Vacations
Bright Start, 188
Building Moral Intelligence, 215
Burnout, 241–53
  changes in curriculum, 246–48
  flexibility, 252
  free time, 246, 252
  goal-setting, 251–52
  joy of learning, 248, 249
  learning resistance, 249–51
  lesson plans, 244–45
  new ideas, 245–49
  preventing, 243
  record-keeping, 244–45
  relaxation, 252–53
  stress, 242–43
  unschooling, 246–48
BusinessTown, 176
*But What If I Don't Want to Go to
  College?*, 273

C

Cambridge Academy, 56
Campus-Free College Degrees, 263
Career couples. *See* Working parents
Career Guide for Creative and Unconventional People, 273
Careers
  for homeschoolers, 214, 216, 225–26, 264–66, 268–73
  interviews for, 265
  for parents, 168–70, 175–76
  résumés for, 265
Carroll, James, 240, 261
Carter, Stephen, 88
Castle Heights Press, 239
Catholic curriculum materials, 49
Catholic Home School Network of America, 49
Cerebral palsy, 238
Certificates, 150
Character education, 87–88, 215
Charter schools, 51
Child and Adolescent Health and Development (CAHD), 80
Child-care options, 172, 175
Child development, 78–81, 189
Children
  bonding with, 6–7
  guiding, 5
  input from, 99–100, 114, 125, 156, 248, 249–51
  listening to, 7–8, 71, 72, 166–67, 216, 219
  maturity of, 85–87
  number homeschooled, 3
  reconnecting with, 5–6
  returning to school, 39
  as teachers, 70–72, 131, 250, 252
  withdrawing from school, 38–39, 208–9
Children and Adults with Attention Deficit Hyperactivity Disorder (CHADD), 236
Choosing the Right College, 261
Christian College Search, 257
Christian curriculum materials, 48–49
Christian Liberty Academy, 49
Christian schools, 48
Chrysalis School, 56

Citizen High School, 56
Citizenship, 88, 137
Civility, 87, 88
Civility: Manners, Morals, and the Etiquette of Democracy, 88
Class rings, 84, 228
Classes2You.com, 49, 57
Clonlara School, 53, 56, 220
Cognitive Technologies Corporation, 221
Cohen, Cafi, 261
College
  admission package, 226, 260–61
  alternatives to, 268–74
  entrance exams, 226–27, 260–62, 263, 264
  essay for, 261
  financial aid for, 227, 260, 263
  interviews, 262–63
  for learning-challenged students, 233
  letters of recommendation, 261
  preparing for, 226–28, 258, 259–60
  resources for, 286
  scholarships for, 17, 227, 260, 263
  searching for, 256–57
  students in, 258–59
  study abroad, 271
  subject requirements, 220–22, 259–60
  success in, 248
  touring, 259
  transcripts for, 147, 149–50, 227–28, 260
  welcoming homeschoolers, 17, 256–58
College Board, 226, 260
College Credit without Classes, 261
College Degrees by Mail & Internet, 264
College Level Examination Program (CLEP), 262
College Success of Students from Three High School Settings, 16
College View, 257
CollegeDegree.com, 263
CollegeNet, 260
Comments from homeschoolers, 274–78
Communication, lines of, 166–67, 216, 219
Complete Book of Distance Learning Schools, 264
Comprehension skills, 209–12
CompuHigh, 57

Compulsory attendance laws, 2
Computer software, 190
Conferences, 36
Contadino, Darlene, 236
Cooperatives, 51–53, 171
Core Curriculum of America, 47
Correspondence schools
  advantages of, 53–54
  for college, 263–64
  cost of, 55
  enrolling in, 54–55
  for gifted children, 240
  for high school, 219–20
  schedules for, 104
  selection of, 56, 285–86
Council of International Educational Exchange, 271
Covey, Sean, 224
Creating a Life Worth Living, 273
Creative Home Schooling for Gifted Children, 240
Creativity, 69, 188–89, 204–5, 239
Credits for high school, 148–50, 219–21, 227–28
Criscito, Pat, 263
Curiosity, 63, 64, 239, 246, 273–74
Curriculum
  choosing, 89–102
  components of, 92–93
  cost of, 55, 91–92, 166
  courses on, 99
  creating, 42, 92–96
  faith-based materials, 47–50, 284
  guidelines for, 12, 90, 141, 143
  lesson plans for, 94–96, 284
  ordering, 140
  packaged materials, 56, 90–92, 140, 288–89
  from public schools, 43–44, 46
  record-keeping, 139–50
  resources for, 13–15, 96–99, 282–87
  scope-and-sequence method, 91
  secular materials, 46–47
  for special-needs children, 234–35
  supplementing, 57–58
  types of, 45–62, 69, 90–96
  writing plans for, 93–94
Curriculum fairs, 14–15

Curriculum providers, 56, 90–92, 140, 288–89
Curriculum Services, 47
Cyber schools, 56–57, 263–64, 272, 285–86

D

Dads homeschooling, 177–78
Daily log, 128–30, 133, 143–47, 219
Daily planners, 181
Decision-making skills, 223–24
Decompression time, 11–12, 104
Departments of education, 35–36, 43, 81, 292–95
Deschooling, 58–59, 69–70
Deschooling Society, 69
Diplomas, 150, 219–20, 228, 261
Discover Your Child's Learning Style, 26
DiscoverySchool.com, 96, 204
Discussions, importance of, 71, 72, 167, 187, 251
Distance Education and Training Council (DETC), 56, 263
Distance Learning Resource Network, 57
Distance-learning schools
    advantages of, 53–54
    for college, 263–64
    cost of, 55
    enrolling in, 54–55
    for gifted children, 240
    for high school, 219–20
    schedules for, 104
    selection of, 56, 285–86
Donahue, Michael, 256
DonJohnston.com, 236
Dougherty, Karla, 215
Down Syndrome, 238
Dramatic play, 201–2
Driver education, 222–23, 287
Dyslexia, 232, 233, 237, 238
Dyslexia.com, 237

E

E-Z Grader, 149
Early learning activities, 186–90
Earth Watch, 270
Eberly, Sheryl, 215
Eclectic schooling, 57–58, 75–76, 246

Edelson, Paul Jay, 264
EdHelper.com, 98
Education for Kids, 98
Education laws, 2. *See also* State laws
Education Place, 98
Education Program for Gifted Youth, 240
Education secretary, 4, 5, 57, 215, 261, 278
Education World, 96
Educational activities. *See* Learning activities
Educational excursions, 101–2, 183–84
Educational games, 98, 282–83
Educational goals, 41, 92–94, 140–41, 148, 234, 251–52
Educational materials. *See also* Curriculum
    cost of, 12–15, 96–99, 166
    ordering, 140
    resources for, 13–15, 96–99, 282–87
Educational objectives, 41–42, 92–94, 140–41, 234
Educational philosophies, 41, 92–93
Educational Resources Information Center (ERIC), 16, 86
Educational Review, 86
Educational theorists, 20–21
Educational Video Resources, 101
Educator's Exchange, The, 47
Eikleberry, Carol, 273
Electives, 220–21
Elementary students, 197–206
    art, 204
    history activities, 201–2
    math skills, 199–201
    music, 204–5
    reading, 198–99
    science activities, 202–4
    socialization, 206
    testing, 205–6
    time requirements, 8–9, 110–11, 182
Ellison, Emily, 199
Emily Post's Teen Etiquette, 223
Emotional ties, 79
Employment options. *See* Careers
Empty-nest syndrome, 279–80
Encyclopedias, 159
Enthusiasm, 245–46, 248

Etiquette, 87
Evaluations, 145–48, 167
Evening homeschooling, 167–68
Exchange programs, 271
Expectations, 124–25, 162–63, 242–43
Experimenting, 64, 97
Exploratorium, 204
Extracurricular activities, 82, 124, 215–16

F

Fabulous Fractions, 201
Fair Test, 262
Faith-based homeschooling, 47–50, 284
Families for Early Autism Treatment (FEAT), 238
Family ties, 79–80
Family values, 87, 88, 215, 223
Farr, J. Michael, 273
Field trips, 101–2, 183–84, 193
Filing tips, 152, 155–56
Financial aid, 227, 260, 263
Financial issues, 12–15
First-grade activities, 195
Flexibility
    and burnout, 252
    importance of, 107–8, 243
    in packaged curricula, 91
    in schedules, 9–10, 61, 104, 106–10, 124, 252
    in single-parent homes, 163, 164, 167–70
    with special-needs children, 232, 234–35
    in unschooling, 69
    in working-parent homes, 174, 176–77
Florida Parent-Educators Association (FPEA), 36
Florida Virtual School, 36, 57
Forced learning, 214
Foreign languages, 100, 222
Forms for record-keeping, 147
Francis Virtual School, 57
Franklin, Benjamin, 95
Free (ana Almost Free) Adventures for Teenagers, 261
Free-Ed.net, 98–99
Free resources, 13, 97–99, 194, 283, 284
Free time, 10, 106, 126, 246, 252

Free worksheets, 13, 98, 194, 283
Freed, Jeffrey, 236
Friends of the National Zoo, 271
Froehner, Melissa, 224
Fry, Ronald, 265
FunBrain, 98

G

Galloway, Rhonda, 16
Gamequarium.com, 98
Games online, 98, 282–83
Gardner, Howard, 21
General Equivalency Diploma (GED), 261
Get Ready for Standardized Tests, 206
Get Your Degree Online, 264
Gift of Good Manners, 215
Gifted children, 239–40, 284
Gifted Education Press, 239
Gifted Psychology Press, 239
Goal-setting, 113–14, 251–52
Grade books, 147, 148–49, 193, 219
Grades, calculating, 149
Grading papers, 149
Graduation
    ceremonies for, 84, 228
    life after, 268–74
    requirements for, 149–50, 219–20, 227–28
Grand, Gail, 261
Great Careers in Two Years, 273
Greene, Rebecca, 261
Griffith, Mary, 248
Guidelines, 12, 90, 141, 143

H

Hands-on learning, 24, 25, 97, 203
Hands-on manipulatives, 199–200, 209
Hands-On Math, 201
Hands-On Science Activities, 183
Hannaford, Carla, 16
Hayes, Lenore C., 236
Healthy eating, 29–30
Hearing impairments, 238–39
Heart of Wisdom, 60
Helm, April Leigh, 264
Helm, Matthew, 264
Helping Gifted Children Soar, 240

Helping Gifted Children Succeed at Home, 240
Hensley, Sharon, 236
Heritage Catholic Curricula, 49
High-school students, 217–28
    activities for, 220–26
    advanced subjects, 100–101, 108, 218–19, 221–22
    career opportunities, 225–26
    college preparations, 220–22, 226–28
    credits earned, 148–50, 219–21, 227–28
    diplomas for, 150, 219–20, 228, 261
    driver education, 222–23, 287
    electives, 220–21
    financial aid, 227
    programs for, 56–57
    reading skills, 210
    scholarships, 17, 227
    self-directed learning, 175, 219
    socialization, 223–24, 228
    teen behavior, 87, 218
    tests, 226–27, 260–62, 263, 264
    time requirements for, 8–9, 110–11, 182
    transcripts, 147, 149–50, 227–28, 260
    volunteerism, 224–25
Hirsch, E. D., 191
Hirsch, Gretchen, 240
History activities, 201–2
Hoagies Gifted Education, 240
Hodson, Victoria Kindle, 26
Holdren, John, 191
Holidays. *See* Vacations
Holt, John, 70, 275
Home businesses, 168, 169, 170, 176
Home School Legal Defense Association (HSLDA), 34–35, 36, 38
Home Study International, 53, 56
Homeschool conferences, 36
Homeschool dads, 177–78
Homeschool groups
    finding, 38
    purchasing supplies, 14–15, 221
    role of, 36–37, 83–84
    and single parents, 170–71
    state organizations, 37–38, 290–91
    and working parents, 184
Homeschool laws, 34–36, 143

Homeschool organizations, 37–38, 290–91
Homeschooling
    adjusting to, 11
    benefits of, x, 15–18
    cost of, 12–15, 55, 91–92, 96–99, 166
    definition of, 113, 186
    getting started, 33–44, 104
    history of, 2–3
    legal requirements for, 34–36, 39–40, 146, 164
    life after, 267–80
    reasons for, 3, 40–41, 118
    record-keeping, 128–30, 133, 139–50, 181, 219–21, 227–28, 244–45
    registering for, 39–40
    resources for, 13–15, 96–99, 282–87
    time requirements, 8–9, 110–11, 164–65, 182, 195–96, 208, 212
    tips for, 31, 115–16, 152–56
    types of, 45–62
    typical days, 127–38, 145
Homeschooling Children with Special Needs, 236
Homeschooling the Child with ADD, 236
Homeschooling Your Gifted Child, 240
Housework, 114–15, 180
How to Get Your First Job and Keep It, 265
How to Prepare Your Child for Kindergarten, 191
How to Start a Christian School, 48

I

Ice, Jerry, 264
Idea files, 155–56
Identity formation, 213
Illich, Ivan, 69
Illingworth, Mark, 201
Immunization records, 146
Independent study programs (ISPs)
    advantages of, 53–54
    for college, 263–64
    cost of, 55
    enrolling in, 54–55
    for gifted children, 240
    for high school, 219–20

schedules for, 104
selection of, 56, 285–86
Indiana University High School, 220
Indiana University-Purdue University (IUPUI), 256
Individualized education program (IEP), 234
Individualized instruction, 4–5, 182, 229
Inspiration, 245–46
Instruction. *See* Teaching
Intellect, 20–21
Intelligent Tutor, 221
IntelliTools, 236
Intent to homeschool, 38, 39, 40
Interest-led activities, 68–70, 75–76, 94, 108–9, 138, 247, 249
International Dyslexia Association, 237
International High School, 57
International Student Travel Confederation, 271
Internet
    education online, 56–57, 263–64, 272, 285–86
    resources online, 96–99, 282–87
Internships, 225, 269–70, 272
Intuitive learning, 21
Islamic curriculum needs, 49
Islamic School, 49

J

Jewish curriculum needs, 49
Jewish Home Educators Network, 49
Jobs. *See* Careers
Johnson, Samuel, 64
Journals, 109, 143, 145

K

K12 Homeschool, 57
Kandoo Kangaroo Hops into Homeschool, 159
Karnofsky, Florence, 191
Keystone National High School, 220, 222
Kick Off Your Career, 265
Kids Games, 98
Kindergarten
    activities for, 191–95
    resources for, 191, 192, 194, 282–84
    social skills, 190–91

time requirements, 8–9, 110–11, 182, 195–96
Kinesthetic learners, 22, 24–25
Knowledge
    mastery of, 96, 147–48
    retaining, 22, 31, 68, 109, 112, 116, 166–67
Knowles, Gary, 78
Kolbe Academy, 49

L

Lab equipment, 97, 157, 183
Labels, 230
Language disorders, 232
Latter-Day Saints Home Educators Association, 49–50
Laurel Springs School, 56, 220
Laurelwood Books, 47
LD Online, 234, 235
LDS Homeschooling Organization, 49
Learning activities. *See also* Activities
    for elementary students, 198–204
    hands-on learning, 24, 25, 97, 103
    for high-school students, 220–26
    for kindergarten, 191–95
    for middle-school students, 209–15
    for preschoolers, 186–90
    and record-keeping, 145–46
    for unschooling, 68–70, 75–76, 94, 109
Learning centers, 156–60, 189–90
Learning-challenged children, 229–40. *See also* Special-needs children
Learning Differences Sourcebook, 236
Learning Disabilities Association of America, 232
Learning environments, 20–21, 59, 189–90
Learning experiences, 20, 88
Learning, joy of, 88, 248, 249, 273–74
Learning logs, 128–30, 133, 143–47, 219, 244
Learning Page, 98
Learning patterns, 28–29
Learning processes, 20–21, 245–46
Learning rates, 94, 193, 208
Learning styles, 19–30
    courses on, 98–99

observing, 25–26, 110, 156
of special-needs children, 232, 234
types of, 22–25, 70
Learning through play, 10, 58–59, 125, 185, 188–89, 201–2
Learning together, 212
Legal requirements, 34–36, 39–40, 146, 164
Lesson Plan Search, 96
Lesson plans
    and burnout, 244–45
    children's ideas, 99–100
    creating, 94–96
    elements of, 95
    ideas for, 96–101, 142, 155–56
    plan book, 141–43, 145, 147, 244
    resources for, 96, 284
Lesson Plans Page, 96, 205
LessonPlanZ.com, 96
Libraries in-home, 158, 159–60
Library Video, 101, 183, 221
Life after homeschooling, 267–80
Life skills, 220–21
Life Strategies for Teens, 224
Lifelong learning, 267–68, 273–74
Light, Richard, 259
Lincoln, Abraham, 14
Listening skills, 7–8, 71, 72
Littlefield, Cynthia, 201
Living history, 201–2
Lloyd, Carol, 273
Long, Lynette, 201
Low-cost resources, 13–15, 96–99, 166

M

Magazine storage, 154–55
Magazines, 286
Making the Most of College, 259
Malibu Cove Private School, 220
Mandatory schooling, 2
Manners, 78, 81, 87, 137, 215, 223, 265
Massachusetts Bay Colony, 2
Math Builder, 98
Math Media, 221
Math skills, 199–201, 221
Math Tutor, 221
Math Wise, 201
Maturity levels, 85–87

McBroom, Frances, 201
McGraw, Jay, 224
Meighan, Roland, 86
Mentors, 101, 222
Meyerhoff, Michael, 188
Middle-school students, 207–16
    activities for, 209–15
    comprehension skills, 209–12
    reading, 209–12
    socialization, 215–16
    strengths and weaknesses, 208–9
    time requirements, 8–9, 110–11, 182,
        208, 212
Military programs, 271–72
Mini-vacations, 126
Monotony, 130–32
Montessori, Maria, 21
Montgomery, Linda, 86
Moore Academy, 56
Morals, 87, 88, 215
Motivation, 245–46, 249
Multiple children, teaching
    examples of, 120–24
    one-on-one interaction, 122–23
    routines, 122
    siblings, 122–23
Multiple intelligences, 21, 99
Museums, 97, 287
Music activities, 204–5
Muslim Homeschool, 49
My Reading List, 199
Myers, Bob, 218

N

Naftali, Joel, 273
Naftali, Lee, 273
National Assessment of Educational
    Progress (NAEP), 210
National Association for Child
    Development, Inc., 238
National Association for College Admission
    Counseling (NACAC), 256–57
National Association for Gifted Children,
    240
National Association of Catholic Home
    Educators, 49
National Association of Hispanic-
    American Homeschoolers, 38

National Challenged Homeschoolers
    Association Network (NATHHAN), 38,
    238
National Driver Training Institute, 222
National Foundation for Gifted and
    Creative Children, 240
National Home Education Research
    Institute (NHERI), 12, 16
National homeschool associations, 38
National Household Education Survey
    (NHES), 3, 43
National Organization of Parents of Blind
    Children, 238–39
Native American Homeschool
    Association, 38, 50
Natural learning. *See also* Unschooling
    activities for, 94, 109
    daily schedules, 107, 165
    examples of, 64–68
    importance of, 6
    trusting, 109–10, 138, 246–47, 249
Niches, 212–13, 269, 279
Nova Adventures in Science videos, 183
Nutrition, 29–30

O

Oak Meadow School, 56, 220
One-on-one interaction, 122–23, 166–67,
    175, 182, 186, 205, 229
Online College Fair, 256–57
Online education, 56–57, 263–64, 272,
    285–86
Online resources, 96–99, 282–87
Only children, teaching
    benefits for, 119–20
    examples of, 118–20
    socialization for, 118, 120
Organization, 151–60
    activity centers, 156–60, 189–90
    idea files, 155–56
    lab stations, 156, 157
    libraries, 158, 159–60
    storing supplies, 152–55
    tips for, 115, 152, 155–56, 160
Orientation to College Learning, 259
Otis, Don, 215
Outdoor schooling, 131–32
Outward Bound, 270

Overholt, James, 201
Overseas education, 271
Owl and Mouse, 98

P

Pacific Challenge, 270
Palmer, Pat, 224
Panzarine, Susan, 218
Parent Pals, 236
Parent's Guide to the Teen Years, 218
Parental influence, 78–79
Parental involvement, 80–81
Parental rights, 35
Parents
    empty-nest syndrome, 279–80
    keeping faith, 109–10, 138, 246–47, 249
    single parenting, 161–72
    strengths and weaknesses, 32
    as teachers, 3–5, 9, 30–32, 218–19, 242
    working parents, 173–84
Parsons, Laurie, 236
Patterns, and learning, 28–30
Paulsen, Gary, 111
Peer pressure, 78, 84–85, 88, 210
Perlmutter, Deborah, 265
Perry, Bruce Duncan, 189
Phifer, Paul, 273
Phonics, 198
Physical handicaps, 238
Piaget, Jean, 20–21, 98–99
Plan book, 141–43, 145, 147, 244
Planning ahead, 140–41, 181, 244–45
Play, learning through, 10, 58–59, 125,
    185, 188–89, 201–2
Playroom, 160, 189
Portfolios, 145–47, 219, 244
Positive attitudes, 31, 265–66
Post, Elizabeth, 223
Post, Peggy, 215
Power Home Biz, 176
Preschool, 185–90
    activities for, 186–90, 192
    resources for, 186, 188, 282–84
    social skills, 190–91
    time requirements, 8–9, 110–11
Preschool Play and Learn, 188
Priorities, setting, 162–63
Progress report, 148

Projects, recording, 145–46
Proust, Marcel, 271
Prufrock Press, 240
Public school
    confines of, 69, 81
    curriculum materials, 43–44, 46, 91
    definition of, 113
    history of, 2
    reinstating child in, 39
    support from, 42–44, 83
    withdrawing child from, 38–39, 208–9
Publications, 286
Puzzle Depot, 98

Q

Qualifications for teaching, 8
Questacon, 204
Quiet areas, 158–59

R

Raising Responsible Teenagers, 218
Ray, Brian, 16
Re-enactments, 201–2
Reading aloud, 198, 211
Reading corners, 158
Reading problems, 230–32, 233
Reading readiness, 192–93, 198
Reading skills, 198–199, 209–12
Real-Life Math Problem Solving, 201
Real Lives: Eleven Teenagers Who Don't Go to School, 159
Real world education, 69, 84, 262, 273–74. *See also* Unschooling
Real-World Math for Hands-On Fun, 201
Record-keeping, 139–50
    attendance records, 145, 146–47
    and burnout, 244
    credits, 148–50, 219–21, 227–28
    daily log, 128–30, 143–45, 147
    evaluations, 145–48
    forms for, 147
    grade books, 147, 148–49
    lesson plan books, 141–43, 145
    materials used, 144–45
    planning ahead, 140–41, 181, 244–45
    portfolios, 145–47
    progress report, 148
    of projects, 145–46

tips for, 115
transcripts, 147, 149–50
typical days, 128–30, 133, 145
    for unschooling, 109
    weekly log, 133
Registration requirements, 34–40, 146, 164
Reider, Jon, 256
Reinstating child in school, 39
Relatives, 171, 178–79
Relaxation, 116, 124, 126, 163, 252–53
Religion-based homeschooling, 47–50, 284
Report cards, 147, 148–49, 193, 219
Resistance to learning, 249–51, 276
Resources
    for curricula, 13–15, 96–99, 282–87
    free resources, 13, 97–99, 194, 283, 284
    low-cost resources, 13–15, 96–99, 166
    online resources, 96–99, 282–87
    for special-needs children, 235–39, 283
    for unschooling, 71
Respect, 87, 88, 137
Responsibilities
    of child, 88, 108, 114, 174, 218, 223–24
    for education, 106, 175, 219
    sharing, 174, 179–81
Résumés for First-Time Job Hunters, 265
Retaining information, 22, 31, 68, 109, 112, 116, 166–67
Retired professionals, 101
Rett Syndrome, 238
Rewards, 245
Right-Brained Children in a Left-Brained World, 236
Right to homeschool, 35
Riley, Richard W., 4, 5
Rivero, Lisa, 240
Role models, 79, 81, 86
Routines, 105, 108–9, 122, 123, 125
Rudner, Lawrence, 16
Rules to Be Cool, 215

S

Salemi, Vicki, 259
Saso, Patt, 218

Saso, Steve, 218
Satellite schools, 50–51
SATs, 226–27, 260–62, 263, 264
Saxon Math, 221
Schedules, 103–16
    establishing, 105–6
    examples of, 110–12
    flexibility in, 9–10, 61, 104, 106–10, 124, 252
    simplifying, 114–15, 125
    staying on track, 123–24
    strict schedules, 106–8
    time management, 112–16
    time off, 116, 124, 126
    for unschooling, 108–9
    year-round schooling, 60–62
Scholarships, 17, 227, 260, 263
School Express, 98
School, traditional. *See* Public school
Schoolroom, 160, 189
Schwab Learning, 233
Science experiments, 202–4
Science for Every Kid, 183
Science labs, 97, 157, 183
Scope-and-sequence method, 91
Scott, Sir Walter, 66
SeaScape Educational Center, 56, 220
Secular homeschooling, 46–47
Self-confidence, 214, 231
Self-directed learning. *See also* Unschooling
    activities for, 94, 109
    as adults, 267–68, 273–74
    in college, 267
    daily schedules, 107, 165
    examples of, 64–68
    for gifted children, 239
    at high-school level, 175, 219
    in large households, 124, 125
    at middle-school level, 214–15
    trusting, 109–10, 138, 246–49
Self-esteem, 79, 87, 120
Self-motivation, 214, 246, 249
Self-reliance, 214
Seneca, Lucius, 70
Senning, Cindy Post, 215
Sense of Self: Listening to Homeschooled Adolescent Girls, 159

Seton School, 49
Seven Habits of Highly Effective Teens, The, 224
Shyers, Larry, 79, 87
Shyness, 120, 190–91
Simplifying housework, 114–15
Simplifying routines, 125
Single parenting, 161–72
   budgeting costs, 166
   child-care options, 172
   flexibility for, 163, 164, 167–70
   options for, 161, 164–67
   quality time, 164–67
   setting priorities, 162–63
   support for, 162, 163–64, 170–72
   and time requirements, 164–65
   timesaving services, 164
   weekend homeschooling, 167–68
   work options, 168–70
Six Steps to an Emotionally Intelligent Teenager, 223
Skills
   building upon, 96
   mastery of, 96, 147–48
   quick courses, 272
Sleep patterns, 29
Small Business Administration (SBA), 169, 176
Social adjustment, 79–81, 86–87
Social skills, 78–81, 87, 137, 215, 223, 265
Socialization, 77–88
   daily events, 84–86
   for elementary students, 206
   for high-school students, 223–24, 228
   and maturity levels, 85–87
   for middle-school students, 215–16
   for only children, 118, 120
   opportunities for, 17–18, 81–85, 88
   parental influence, 78–81, 87–88
   with peers, 84–85
   for preschoolers, 190–91
   and social skills, 78–81
   with varied age groups, 82, 85
Software, 190
Special Education Products, 236
Special-education programs, 233
Special-needs children, 229–40
   nd college, 233

curriculum for, 234–35, 238
flexibility with, 232, 234–35
homeschool regulations, 233
IEP (individualized education program), 234
input from, 233
learning styles, 232, 234
professionals, 232–33, 234
resources for, 235–39, 283
structure for, 232, 234
support groups, 235
Speech disorders, 232
Sports, 43, 83
Standardized tests, 16, 206, 263
Stanford University, 240, 256
State departments of education, 35–36, 292–95
State laws, 34–36, 39–40, 146, 164
State organizations, 37–38, 290–91
Statistics, 3
Stay-at-home dads, 177–78
Stay Strong, 224
Stimulating activities, 20, 59, 68–70, 75–76, 239
Storage tips, 152–55
Stranger suspicion, 190–91
Strengths of child, 26–28, 147–49, 205, 208–9
Stress
   reducing, 15–16, 116, 124–25, 242–43
   results of, 16
   and single parenting, 162–64
   and special-needs children, 234
Strip, Carol, 240
Structure, 105, 232, 234, 243
Study Abroad, 271
Subjects to teach. *See* Guidelines
Success
   keys to, 4–5, 9, 107–8, 252–53
   and motivation, 245–46
   and parental involvement, 81, 108, 113
   and self-directed learning, 214
   of unschooling, 58–59, 76
Summer school, 62, 72, 141, 166
Supplies
   cost of, 12–15, 55, 91–92, 96–99, 166
   ordering, 140
   purchasing, 14–15

   storing, 152–55
Support groups. *See* Homeschool groups
Sutton, Joseph, 16
Synapses, 20

T
Tactile-kinesthetic learners, 22, 24–25
Talents, 213–14
Tampa Reads, 98
Taylor, John W., 79, 87
Teach-nology, 98
Teach Your Children Well: Helping Kids Make Moral Choices, 215
Teacher's Video, 101
Teachers
   challenges of, 5
   children as, 70–72, 131, 250, 252
   courses for, 98–99
   parents as, 3–5, 9, 30–32, 218–19, 242
   retired teachers, 101
Teachers.net, 96
Teaching
   advanced subjects, 100–101, 108, 218–19, 221–22
   guidelines for subjects, 12, 90, 141, 143
   qualifications for, 8
   tips for, 3–5, 31
Teaching LD, 237
Team sports, 43
Teen Esteem, 224
Teen Tours of America, 270
Teenage Liberation Handbook, The, 159
Teenager's Guide to School Outside the Box, 261
Teenagers. *See* High-school students
Telecommuting, 168, 169, 175
Tell Me Why videos, 183
Ten Best Gifts for Your Teen, 218
Tests. *See also* Assessment methods
   ACTs, 226–27, 261–62, 263, 264
   for assessment, 16, 96, 145, 147, 205–6, 263
   practice with, 263
   SATs, 226–27, 260–62, 263, 264
   scores of homeschoolers, 16
Texas Virtual School, 57
Textbook publishers, 47

Thematic studies, 59–60, 74–75. *See also* Unit studies
Therapists, 232–33, 234
Thinking skills, 69
Thorson, Marcie, 263
Time management, 112–16
Time requirements
  all age groups, 8–9, 110–11, 182
  kindergarten, 195–96
  middle-school students, 208, 212
  and single parenting, 164–65
  and working parents, 182
Toddlers, 185–90. *See also* Preschoolers
Torah Aura Productions, 49
Tourette Syndrome, 238
Transcripts, 147, 149–50, 227–28, 260
Travel, 270–71, 287
Trustworthiness, 88
Tutors, 101, 108, 222
Twain, Mark, 280
Two-career families. *See* Working parents
"Typical Course of Study", 12, 90, 141, 143, 192
Typical days, 127–38
  examples of, 128–30, 133–38
  explanation of, 128
  recording, 128–30, 133, 145
  for unschoolers, 64–68, 276–77

U
Umbrella schools, 50–51
Uncollege Alternative, 273
Unger, Harlow G., 273
Unit studies
  for burnout prevention, 246
  ideas for, 59–60, 73–74, 155
  introducing, 72–73
  length of, 59–60, 104
  planning for, 74–75
Universities. *See* College
Unschooling. *See also* Natural learning

  activities for, 68–70, 75–76, 94, 109
  boredom with, 251
  for burnout prevention, 246
  and curricula, 94
  evidence of, 94
  examples of, 64–68, 276–77
  record-keeping, 109
  schedules for, 108–9
  success of, 58–59, 76
  trusting, 109–10, 138, 246–47, 249
Unschooling Handbook, The, 248
U.S. Department of Education, 43, 81, 292–95
U.S. Secretary of Education, 4, 5, 57, 215, 261, 278

V
Vacations, 116, 124, 126, 163, 252
Values, 87, 88, 215, 223
Van Blerkom, Dianna, 259
Variety, 57–58, 75–76, 91, 112
Veteran homeschoolers, 241–53
Videotapes, 100–101, 183, 221
Virtual learning, 56–57, 101–2, 263–64, 272, 285–86, 287
Vision impairments, 238–39
Visual learners, 22, 23
Vocational training, 272
Volunteerism, 82, 95, 216, 224–25, 262
Volunteers for Peace, 270
Vouchers, 51

W
Warner, Penny, 188
Weaknesses of child, 26–28, 147–49, 205, 208–9
Weekend homeschooling, 167–68, 177, 183–84
Weekly log, 133, 146, 147
Weiss, Trudy, 191
Well-rounded education, 60, 132–33

Wendleton, Kate, 265
Westbridge Academy, 240
What Teens Need to Succeed, 223
What Your Kindergartner Needs to Know, 191
Wile, Jay W., 17
Williams, Terrie, 224
Willis, Mariaemma, 26
Windell, James, 223
Withdrawing child from school, 38–39, 208–9
Woman's Work, 168
Wood, Danielle, 273
Work options. *See* Careers
Working parents, 173–84
  balancing work and family, 174–76
  child-care options, 175
  flexibility for, 174, 176–77
  sharing responsibilities, 174, 179–81
  and time requirements, 182
  weekend homeschooling, 177, 183–84
Worksheets
  and creative play, 188–89
  free worksheets, 13, 98, 194, 283
  and record-keeping, 145
World Book, Inc., 12, 90, 141
World Health Organization (WHO), 80
Wrightslaw.com, 236
Writing centers, 158–59

Y
Year-round schooling, 60–62, 72, 165–66
Yearbooks, 84, 228
You're Certifiable, 273
Your First Interview, 265
Youth travel programs, 270–71

THE EVERYTHING GAMES BOOK

By Tracy Fitzsimmons and Pamela Liflander

*T*he *Everything® Games Book* has everything you'll need for hours of family entertainment, featuring a wide selection of the most popular games. Not only will you find new and exciting games to play, but you'll also have a complete source of easy-to-follow rules and regulations for hundreds of activities right at your fingertips. Whether you're planning a party or just spending a rainy afternoon at home, The Everything® Games Book provides challenging fun and friendly competition for all ages and every level of play.

Trade paperback,
$12.95 ($18.95 CAN)
1-55850-643-8, 304 pages

OTHER *EVERYTHING®* BOOKS BY ADAMS MEDIA CORPORATION

BUSINESS

Everything® **Business Planning Book**
Everything® **Coaching & Mentoring Book**
Everything® **Home-Based Business Book**
Everything® **Leadership Book**
Everything® **Managing People Book**
Everything® **Network Marketing Book**
Everything® **Online Business Book**
Everything® **Project Management Book**
Everything® **Selling Book**
Everything® **Start Your Own Business Book**
Everything® **Time Management Book**

COMPUTERS

Everything® **Build Your Own Home Page Book**
Everything® **Computer Book**

Everything® **Internet Book**
Everything® **Microsoft® Word 2000 Book**

COOKING

Everything® **Bartender's Book, $9.95**
Everything® **Barbecue Cookbook**
Everything® **Chocolate Cookbook**
Everything® **Cookbook**
Everything® **Dessert Cookbook**
Everything® **Diabetes Cookbook**
Everything® **Low-Carb Cookbook**
Everything® **Low-Fat High-Flavor Cookbook**
Everything® **Mediterranean Cookbook**
Everything® **One-Pot Cookbook**
Everything® **Pasta Book**
Everything® **Quick Meals Cookbook**
Everything® **Slow Cooker Cookbook**

Everything® **Soup Cookbook**
Everything® **Thai Cookbook**
Everything® **Vegetarian Cookbook**
Everything® **Wine Book**

HEALTH

Everything® **Anti-Aging Book**
Everything® **Dieting Book**
Everything® **Herbal Remedies Book**
Everything® **Hypnosis Book**
Everything® **Menopause Book**
Everything® **Stress Management Book**
Everything® **Vitamins, Minerals, and Nutritional Supplements Book**
Everything® **Nutrition Book**

HISTORY

Everything® **American History Book**

Everything® **Civil War Book**
Everything® **World War II Book**

HOBBIES

Everything® **Bridge Book**
Everything® **Candlemaking Book**
Everything® **Casino Gambling Book**
Everything® **Chess Basics Book**
Everything® **Collectibles Book**
Everything® **Crossword and Puzzle Book**
Everything® **Digital Photography Book**
Everything® **Drums Book (with CD),**
 $19.95, ($31.95 CAN)
Everything® **Family Tree Book**
Everything® **Games Book**
Everything® **Guitar Book**
Everything® **Knitting Book**
Everything® **Magic Book**
Everything® **Motorcycle Book**
Everything® **Online Genealogy Book**
Everything® **Playing Piano and**
 Keyboards Book
Everything® **Rock & Blues Guitar**
 Book (with CD), $19.95,
 ($31.95 CAN)
Everything® **Scrapbooking Book**

HOME IMPROVEMENT

Everything® **Feng Shui Book**
Everything® **Gardening Book**
Everything® **Home Decorating Book**
Everything® **Landscaping Book**
Everything® **Lawn Care Book**
Everything® **Organize Your Home Book**

KIDS' STORY BOOKS

Everything® **Bedtime Story Book**
Everything® **Bible Stories Book**
Everything® **Fairy Tales Book**
Everything® **Mother Goose Book**

NEW AGE

Everything® **Astrology Book**

Everything® **Divining the Future Book**
Everything® **Dreams Book**
Everything® **Ghost Book**
Everything® **Meditation Book**
Everything® **Numerology Book**
Everything® **Palmistry Book**
Everything® **Spells and Charms Book**
Everything® **Tarot Book**
Everything® **Wicca and Witchcraft Book**

PARENTING

Everything® **Baby Names Book**
Everything® **Baby Shower Book**
Everything® **Baby's First Food Book**
Everything® **Baby's First Year Book**
Everything® **Breastfeeding Book**
Everything® **Get Ready for Baby Book**
Everything® **Homeschooling Book**
Everything® **Potty Training Book,**
 $9.95, ($15.95 CAN)
Everything® **Pregnancy Book**
Everything® **Pregnancy Organizer,**
 $15.00, ($22.95 CAN)
Everything® **Toddler Book**
Everything® **Tween Book**

PERSONAL FINANCE

Everything® **Budgeting Book**
Everything® **Get Out of Debt Book**
Everything® **Get Rich Book**
Everything® **Investing Book**
Everything® **Homebuying Book, 2nd Ed.**
Everything® **Homeselling Book**
Everything® **Money Book**
Everything® **Mutual Funds Book**
Everything® **Online Investing Book**
Everything® **Personal Finance Book**

PETS

Everything® **Cat Book**
Everything® **Dog Book**
Everything® **Dog Training and Tricks**
Everything® **Horse Book**
Everything® **Puppy Book**
Everything® **Tropical Fish Book**

REFERENCE

Everything® **Astronomy Book**
Everything® **Car Care Book**
Everything® **Christmas Book, $15.00,**
 ($21.95 CAN)
Everything® **Classical Mythology Book**
Everything® **Divorce Book**
Everything® **Etiquette Book**
Everything® **Great Thinkers Book**
Everything® **Learning French Book**
Everything® **Learning German Book**
Everything® **Learning Italian Book**
Everything® **Learning Latin Book**
Everything® **Learning Spanish Book**
Everything® **Mafia Book**
Everything® **Philosophy Book**
Everything® **Shakespeare Book**
Everything® **Tall Tales, Legends, &**
 Other Outrageous Lies Book
Everything® **Toasts Book**
Everything® **Trivia Book**
Everything® **Weather Book**
Everything® **Wills & Estate Planning**
 Book

RELIGION

Everything® **Angels Book**
Everything® **Buddhism Book**
Everything® **Catholicism Book**
Everything® **Judaism Book**
Everything® **Saints Book**
Everything® **World's Religions Book**
Everything® **Understanding Islam Book**

SCHOOL & CAREERS

Everything® **After College Book**
Everything® **College Survival Book**
Everything® **Cover Letter Book**
Everything® **Get-a-Job Book**
Everything® **Hot Careers Book**
Everything® **Job Interview Book**
Everything® **Online Job Search Book**
Everything® **Resume Book, 2nd Ed.**
Everything® **Study Book**

All Everything® books are priced at $12.95 or $14.95, unless otherwise stated. Prices subject to change without notice.
Canadian prices range from $11.95–$22.95 and are subject to change without notice.

WE HAVE EVERYTHING . . . .

SPORTS/FITNESS

Everything® **Bicycle Book**
Everything® **Fishing Book**
Everything® **Fly-Fishing Book**
Everything® **Golf Book**
Everything® **Golf Instruction Book**
Everything® **Pilates Book**
Everything® **Running Book**
Everything® **Sailing Book, 2nd Ed.**
Everything® **T'ai Chi and QiGong Book**
Everything® **Total Fitness Book**
Everything® **Weight Training Book**
Everything® **Yoga Book**

TRAVEL

Everything® **Guide to Las Vegas**
Everything® **Guide to New England**
Everything® **Guide to New York City**
Everything® **Guide to Washington D.C.**

Everything® **Travel Guide to The Disneyland Resort®, California Adventure®, Universal Studios®, and the Anaheim Area**
Everything® **Travel Guide to the Walt Disney World® Resort, Universal Studios®, and Greater Orlando, 3rd Ed.**

WEDDINGS & ROMANCE

Everything® **Creative Wedding Ideas Book**
Everything® **Dating Book**
Everything® **Jewish Wedding Book**
Everything® **Romance Book**
Everything® **Wedding Book, 2nd Ed.**
Everything® **Wedding Organizer, $15.00** ($22.95 CAN)

Everything® **Wedding Checklist, $7.95** ($11.95 CAN)
Everything® **Wedding Etiquette Book, $7.95** ($11.95 CAN)
Everything® **Wedding Shower Book, $7.95** ($12.95 CAN)
Everything® **Wedding Vows Book, $7.95** ($11.95 CAN)
Everything® **Weddings on a Budget Book, $9.95** ($15.95 CAN)

WRITING

Everything® **Creative Writing Book**
Everything® **Get Published Book**
Everything® **Grammar and Style Book**
Everything® **Grant Writing Book**
Everything® **Guide to Writing Children's Books**
Everything® **Writing Well Book**

ALSO AVAILABLE:
THE EVERYTHING® KIDS' SERIES!

Each book is 8" x 9¼", 144 pages, and two-color throughout.

Everything® **Kids' Baseball Book, 2nd Edition, $6.9**
Everything® **Kids' Bugs Book,**
Everything® **Kids' Cookbook,**
Everything® **Kids' Joke Book,**
Everything® **Kids' Math Puzzle**
Everything® **Kids' Mazes Book**
Everything® **Kids' Money Book**

Everything® **Kids' Monsters Book, $6.95** ($10.95 CAN)
Everything® **Kids' Nature Book, $6.95** ($11.95 CAN)
Everything® **Kids' Puzzle Book $6.95,** ($10.95 CAN)
Everything® **Kids' Science Experiments Book, $6.95** ($10.95 CAN)
Everything® **Kids' Soccer Book, $6.95** ($10.95 CAN)
Everything® **Kids' Travel Activity Book, $6.95** ($10.95 CAN)

Available wherever books are sold!
To order, call 800 us at everything.com

Everything® Media Corporation.